SECOND EDITION

CONSTRUCTING
SOCIAL RESEARCH

Sociology for a New Century Series

SOCIOLOGY FOR A NEW CENTURY

SECOND EDITION

CONSTRUCTING SOCIAL RESEARCH

The Unity and Diversity of Method

◆

CHARLES C. RAGIN
University of Arizona

LISA M. AMOROSO
Dominican University

Los Angeles | London | New Delhi
Singapore | Washington DC

For information:

Pine Forge Press
An Imprint of
  SAGE Publications, Inc.
2455 Teller Road
Thousand Oaks,
  California 91320
E-mail: order@sagepub.com

SAGE Publications India Pvt. Ltd.
B 1/I 1 Mohan Cooperative
  Industrial Area
Mathura Road, New Delhi 110 044
India

SAGE Publications Ltd.
1 Oliver's Yard
55 City Road
London EC1Y 1SP
United Kingdom

SAGE Publications Asia-Pacific Pte. Ltd.
33 Pekin Street #02-01
Far East Square
Singapore 048763

Printed in the United States of America

Library of Congress Cataloging-in-Publication Data

Ragin, Charles C.
Constructing social research: the unity and diversity of method / Charles C. Ragin and Lisa M. Amoroso.—2nd ed.
  p. cm.—(Sociology for a new century series)
Includes bibliographical references and index.
ISBN 978-1-4129-6018-2 (pbk. : acid-free paper)
  1. Social sciences—Research. I. Ragin, Charles C. II. Title.

H62.R23 2011
300.72—dc22   2010006544

This book is printed on acid-free paper.

12 · 13 14 10 9 8 7 6 5 4 3 2

Acquisitions Editor:	David Repetto
Editorial Assistant:	Maggie Stanley
Production Editor:	Libby Larson
Copy Editor:	Teresa Herlinger
Typesetter:	C&M Digitals (P) Ltd.
Proofreader:	Theresa Kay
Cover Designer:	Candice Harman
Marketing Manager:	Helen Salmon

Contents

Preface

M ost books on social research either do too much or they do too little. Those that do too much present exhaustive inventories of all the things that social researchers do, especially their different ways of collecting data and analyzing evidence. This orientation leaves the impression that social research is a hodgepodge of unconnected activities—that it lacks coherence. Books that do too little tend to present social research in a one-dimensional manner. Typically, social research is presented either as something that is much like research in natural sciences such as physics, or as something that is radically different from research in the natural sciences and more humanistic in its orientation. Neither portrayal of social research is accurate.

This book does not offer an exhaustive inventory of all the different techniques of data collection and analysis that social researchers use. Books that inventory methods often leave students disoriented. In the end, students can recognize a lot of different "trees," but they are lost in the forest of social research. As an alternative, this text offers a broad, integrative overview of social research, an invitation to social research that interprets the state of the art. It answers the question, "What is social research?" with diverse examples that illustrate current thinking about broad issues in social science methodology and the logic of analysis.

The book works best as a starting point for a course in methods of social research or as a capstone to a rigorous or advanced course introducing a social scientific discipline. In courses on methods of social research, it can be used to counterbalance books that present social research in a one-dimensional manner (for example, as an attempt either to approximate or to repudiate research practices in the natural sciences) or to supplement an omnibus text that attempts to present the great variety of methods that social researchers use.

The primary goal of this book is to show unity within the diversity of activities that are called social research—to make sense of social research in a way that brings it all together. In truth, social research *is* diverse. Some social researchers study census data on hundreds of thousands of people; some study one person at a time in an in-depth manner. Some monitor what is happening in the streets today; some try to reconstruct what life was like centuries ago. But there *is* unity in this diversity. This unity comes from special features of social research as a way of representing social life. In almost every article, every book, every report that social scientists write, they construct representations of social life. They do so by engaging in a dialogue of ideas ("theory") and evidence ("data"). In contrast to many other ways of constructing representations of social life, social research almost always involves a systematic collection and examination of large bodies of evidence.

This book's emphasis is very different from the typical portrayal of social science as having opposing "quantitative" and "qualitative" wings. The usual idea that follows from this portrayal is that quantitative researchers deal with numbers (such as frequencies and percentages), while qualitative researchers deal with experience and meaning (things that can be represented or described best with words, not numbers). But all social researchers must deal with both words and quantities in some way. The difference between quantitative and qualitative research is not numbers versus words, but the simple fact that quantitative researchers typically focus on the links among a smaller number of attributes across many cases when they construct representations of social life, while qualitative researchers focus on the links among a larger number of attributes across relatively few cases in their representations. While very different in orientation, the two kinds of research are similar in that both involve a systematic interplay between ideas and evidence.

In this second edition of *Constructing Social Research,* the new chapter on ethics recognizes the simple fact that social research involves interaction with individuals and society. The researcher's presence, even when that presence comes in the form of a survey, often has a direct influence on individuals, and difficult dilemmas may arise from that interaction. For example, at what point is it unethical to involve oneself in the lives of others to gain a better understanding of how a particular social group works? Participating in a group as a regular member is viewed as acceptable to many social scientists, but what if this participation involves having an intimate relationship with another group member or participating in the illegal activities of that group, or simply discussing illegal activities with group members? Even research that doesn't involve living individuals can still pose ethical dilemmas and still has an influence on individuals and society. Does the researcher have an obligation to the descendants of those being studied? The researcher's work also has an influence on the larger community, where his or her ideas may be used to shape policy or inform organizational decisions affecting people who were not part of the study. Again, ethical issues come to the fore. Is it a researcher's responsibility to worry about how his or her social representations may be received and used (or misused)? Ethical guidelines have been developed for social researchers, but these guidelines don't address the blurry boundary between ethical and unethical decisions. In keeping with the spirit of the book, this new chapter works best as a starting point for discussion and debate.

Part II of this book examines the strategies of qualitative and quantitative research in depth as well as a third kind of social research, the comparative approach. In many respects, this third approach is halfway between the two main types. Presenting the comparative approach is important because it helps to break down the apparent barrier between qualitative and quantitative strategies. In other words, it is easier to grasp the unity of social research when a third path, intermediate between the two most common types, qualitative and quantitative, is offered. Like qualitative research, comparative research pays close attention to individual cases; like quantitative research, comparative research focuses directly on differences across cases and attempts to make sense of them.

It is important to recognize that research can span these three types. We are presenting a framework—not an ironclad rule—for understanding the practice of social research. An individual might not be able to pinpoint a study as "qualitative" or "comparative" because the research sits at the boundary of these approaches. While these three strategies—qualitative, quantitative, and comparative—are clearly distinct from one another, they are best understood as different ways of conducting a social scientific dialogue of ideas and evidence. In each approach, clear ideas are essential to the process of constructing representations because they help researchers organize and make sense of the large bodies of evidence involved in every social scientific investigation.

Acknowledgments

My view of social research has developed gradually, over many years, with lots of help from people too numerous to name individually. Special thanks go to the good people who read this book in draft form and offered great advice about how to turn a very rough draft into something more coherent— Howie Becker, Mary Driscoll, Larry Griffin, Scott Long, Philip Morgan, Art Stinchcombe, and Peggy Thoits. I am indeed fortunate to have such gifted people offer their suggestions. Steve Rutter, Victoria Nelson, and my then series co-editors, Larry Griffin and Wendy Griswold, were generous with their support and encouragement during the writing of the first edition of this book.

My wife, Mary Driscoll, has been wonderfully supportive and incisively critical, investing her best energies in comments on drafts. When the pressure of time for the first edition grew to be too great, she became a coauthor and rescued the book's Afterword. I hope that I repay my debt to her in our life together and enrich her thinking and writing as much as she enriches mine.

—Charles C. Ragin

I cannot thank Charles Ragin enough for giving me the opportunity to collaborate with him on this edition of *Constructing Social Research*. I am deeply appreciative of his ongoing confidence and support. Since my first day in Charles' graduate statistics sequence at Northwestern, I have felt fortunate to be one of his students. My ideas have been shaped by Charles as well as many other colleagues and friends during my graduate school years. In particular, I am grateful to Brian Donovan, Kathy Hull, Terri Kurtzberg, Rodney Lacey, Peter Levin, Denise Lewin Loyd, Ann Orloff, Marc Ventresca, and Jim Witte for many cherished conversations centered squarely on methodology as well as those that were not on topic at all.

I am also indebted to Amy Amoroso, Laney Amoroso, Josetta McLaughlin, Nichole Swafford, Martha Thompson, and Phil Tracy for their advice, suggestions, and patience throughout this process. My love to Phil Tracy for sharing equally in the work involved in our daily lives, taking on quite a bit more of that work as deadlines drew near and reminding me to have fun occasionally.

—Lisa M. Amoroso

We were fortunate to have had an incredibly conscientious and thoughtful group of reviewers for this edition:

Michael K. Abel, Brigham Young University–Idaho

Greg Andranovich, California State University, Los Angeles

Melissa A. Barfield-Works, McKendree College

Lisa D. Brush, University of Pittsburgh

Jason Crockett, University of Arizona

Jill Doerner, University of Rhode Island

Robert Dunkley, Chapman University

Janet Enke, Metropolitan State University

Gregory Hooks, Washington State University

Douglas Lee Lauen, University of North Carolina, Chapel Hill

Kathryn D. Linnenberg, Beloit College

Salvador Jimenez Murguia, California State University, San Bernardino

Nancy Riley, Bowdoin College

Wade Roberts, Colorado College

Andrew Schrank, University of New Mexico

Richard Tardanico, Florida International University

Michael Timberlake, University of Utah

Rebecca Utz, University of Utah

The many suggestions and ideas of the reviewers not only informed our decisions for this edition, but will influence subsequent revisions. This edition also benefited from series editor Joya Misra's valuable guidance. We are grateful to Pine Forge Press acquisitions editor Dave Repetto for his ongoing support. Finally, our incredibly capable production team improved the book every step of the way. Special thanks go to Teresa Herlinger, Theresa Kay, and production editor Libby Larson. This group was a pleasure to work with and hopefully we will be lucky enough to work with them again.

PART I

Elements of Social Research

Too often, we take for granted the things that require the most explanation. After all, it is easier to assume we know what something means than it is to explain or define it.

So it is with the term *social research*. We seem to know what social research is because we are exposed to so much of it. There are frequent reports in the media about unemployment, homelessness, marriage and divorce rates, immigration, teenage suicide, school reform, world poverty, democratization, and other varied topics. These reports draw on the work and ideas of social researchers.

But can social research be clearly distinguished from other kinds of information gathering and presenting? If so, how? What are the differences between a report of the insights of a streetwise person and those of a social researcher who spends a lot of time studying social life on the same streets? Like many terms, the scope and meaning of social research can be contested.

Part I of *Constructing Social Research* offers several answers to this basic question—What is social research?—and uses this issue to introduce core features of social science. Some accounts of these core features emphasize the distinctive subject matter of social research, for example, the idea that social researchers study society as a whole and not the psyches of individuals, as psychologists do. Other accounts emphasize its distinctive methods, especially the idea that social researchers use analytic techniques that condense information on many observations. This book offers a more encompassing portrait.

Simply stated, social research is one among many ways of constructing "representations" of social life. A novel, for example, is a representation of social life; so is a documentary film. Many different ways of representing social life qualify as social research; many do not. By defining social research as one of many ways of constructing representations of social life, it becomes clear that social research has a lot in common with many other kinds of work, for example, the work of writers, journalists, and documentary film producers. While the representations constructed by social researchers may be similar to those produced by others, they also have important distinctive features, which should not be overlooked.

Chapter 1 critically evaluates several common answers to the question of how social research differs from other ways of representing social life. These include (1) the proposition that social research has a distinctive subject matter—that it offers a special way of understanding society, (2) the argument that social researchers use a special language to tell about society, and (3) the idea that social research is distinguished from other ways of telling about society by its use of the scientific method. The chapter goes on to compare social research with several other ways of constructing representations of social life. Sometimes it is difficult to tell different kinds of representations apart. For example, when news reporters study issues such as homelessness or poverty in a city, their reports focus on much the same factors that social researchers working on the same topic might study. While the similarities between social research and other ways of representing are striking, several important features distinguish social research. These features reflect the goals of social research and the impact of these goals on the construction of social scientific representations.

Chapter 2 examines the diverse goals of social research, with a special focus on the tensions among different goals. Too often, social research is portrayed simply as a process of testing general ideas or theories and producing broad statements or generalizations. That is, social research is portrayed as a natural science like physics or chemistry, with the main difference of focus on a distinctive and difficult subject matter—social life. However, many social researchers pursue goals that are at odds with those of testing theory or producing generalizations. For example, some researchers offer new interpretations of historical events, others seek to "give voice" to marginal groups in society, and still others try to pinpoint the cultural significance of new trends. The current diversity of goals should be both acknowledged and examined because different research goals often lead to very different strategies of social research.

Chapter 3 addresses general features of the process of social research—how social researchers construct representations of social life. Social research, like almost all research, is organized and systematic, and social researchers generally follow a plan that helps them make sense of the phenomena they study. For example, social researchers typically collect a lot of evidence when they conduct their studies. However, every person, every situation, every event potentially offers an infinite amount of information. Which bits of information should the researcher pay attention to? How is this to be decided? Imagine being interviewed by a social researcher about everything you did yesterday. The interview could take weeks to complete.

The more explicit a researcher's initial ideas (or "analytic frame"), the clearer the guidance they offer about what should be studied and what can safely be ignored in the infinity of information that every case and every situation presents. While this guidance is helpful, it also can be limiting and thus restrict the researcher's view. Sometimes, therefore, initial ideas are intentionally underdeveloped, so that the researcher can be more open to new insights. The interplay of ideas and evidence is common to all strategies of social research; however, the nature of this interplay can differ substantially from one strategy to the next.

Chapter 4 explores some of the ethical dilemmas arising in the course of studying social phenomena and constructing representations of social life. The history of ethical travesties (such as the Tuskegee Syphilis Trials) in the name of scientific discovery has played a significant role in shaping the current practices and systems of oversight for research involving human subjects. Ironically, the ethical standards governing such research frequently fail to provide adequate or useful guidance to social researchers. The strategies of social research are typically quite different from those strategies used for biomedical research and, therefore, pose a unique set of dilemmas. These dilemmas do not have simple answers. The boundary between ethical and unethical decisions is often blurry. For example, is it ethical to write a book or article about a group whose actions and ideas the researcher sees as reprehensible when that exposure has the potential to benefit the group? Is it ethical for a researcher to become emotionally or physically intimate with the people in the community he or she is studying? What about observing crimes without reporting them to the police? Or even more extreme, what about *participating* in the criminal activity? Just as individuals in the course of their daily lives disagree about what is ethical, social scientists, too, disagree about what is the right or wrong course of action. This chapter tackles some of the dilemmas at the center of these disagreements—most likely raising more questions than offering answers.

1

What Is (and Is Not) Social Research?

Introduction

There are many ways to study and tell about social life. Sometimes it is hard to tell which of these are social research and which are not. Consider a few examples.

Pierrette Hondagneu-Sotelo wrote a book, *Doméstica: Immigrant Workers Cleaning and Caring in the Shadows of Affluence* (2001), in which she describes the recent expansion of domestic jobs in the United States. Her work focused particularly on Latina immigrants in Los Angeles. Hondagneu-Sotelo spoke at length with nannies, housekeepers, and housecleaners about their experiences in entering and exiting paid domestic work, as well as the quality of their relationships with their employers. In addition, she spent a lot of time talking to employers, attorneys dealing in this area, and owners of domestic employment agencies. She also analyzed the results of a survey of over 150 domestic workers. One of her findings was that many Latina immigrants want to be viewed as individuals by their employers and to develop personal relationships with their employers, while many employers want to keep these workers at arm's length. By maintaining distance, the employers do not need to spend time or emotional energy on these employees, nor do they develop any sense of personal obligation to the worker. In addition, by maintaining this distance, the employers have more flexibility in controlling the employee or terminating the relationship.

Hondagneu-Sotelo wrote about the experiences of Latina immigrants doing paid domestic work in order to bring to light some of the problems with this growing sector of the economy. She was motivated by her belief that this type of research will build understanding and appreciation, which may ultimately result in an "upgrading" of this form of employment.

Charles Clotfelter was interested in the process of school desegregation during the 50 years after Supreme Court Justice Earl Warren wrote the landmark *Brown v. Board of Education of Topeka, Kansas* decision in 1954. In his book, *After Brown: The Rise and Retreat of School Desegregation* (2004), he considers the degree to which interracial contact has changed within and across school districts due to desegregation efforts. Unlike Hondagneu-Sotelo, Clotfelter does not interview people who were attending schools between 1954 and 2004; instead, his research relies on statistical analyses of school enrollment data. He concludes that desegregation efforts fell short for four reasons: "apparent white aversion to interracial contact, the multiplicity of means by which whites could sidestep the effects of the policy, the willingness of state and local governments to accommodate white resistance, and the faltering resolve of the prime movers of the policy" (p. 8). This lack of progress is due in part to the 1974 Supreme Court decision, *Milliken v. Bradley*, that ruled against cross-district busing as a required step in desegregation efforts. This ruling amounted to higher levels of segregation in the Midwest and the Northeast where school districts are smaller than in other parts of the country, so whites could easily circumvent integration efforts by moving short distances. Thus, racial inequality decreased within public school districts but actually grew larger across districts. In the Northeast, in fact, segregation rose steadily from 1960 to 2000. School districts in the Northeast remain the most segregated districts in the nation.

In his book *Votes and Violence: Electoral Competition and Ethnic Riots in India,* Steven Wilkinson (2004) examines why violence erupts in one town but not in other similar towns. He also considers the political incentives shaping the ways in which politicians in control of the police and army use these forces to quell or fuel Hindu–Muslim riots. Since the data needed to test possible explanations for these riots were not available, he and another researcher developed a database of 2,000 riots in India from 1950–1995. Along with his quantitative analysis of these riots, Wilkinson also compares three instances of communal violence in depth to better understand the institutional and political process influencing the occurrence or avoidance of violence. He found that politicians in local-level elections select and frame issues such that the chances of ethnic violence are increased. His findings on state-level elections challenge the prevailing idea that political instability and violence are the inevitable result of ethnic heterogeneity; increased levels of state-level competition among Hindu parties for votes increases the value of minority votes, thus giving state governments a political incentive to prevent anti-minority violence. Wilkinson asserts that his evidence demonstrates that violence is not "an inevitable by-product of electoral competition in plural societies" (p. 236). He is optimistic about the ability of democratic values and ethnically heterogeneous countries to coexist peacefully.

These books address important issues: What is the nature of work when the workplace is someone else's home? What are the factors that are fueling the expansion of paid domestic work? What are the consequences of this expansion on the lives of immigrant women? In what ways has the U.S. school system succeeded in racial desegregation? In what ways has it failed, and why? What is the impact of democracy on ethnic conflict? To what degree do political campaigns influence ethnic violence? These questions and the studies that address them are as relevant to the everyday concerns of the informed public as they are to government officials responsible for formulating public policies. The conclusions of any of these three authors could be reported on a television news or magazine show such as *Nightline*, *60 Minutes*, or the *The NewsHour With Jim Lehrer*. The nature of the nanny–employer relationship could even be the basis for a talk show.

At first glance, it might appear that these three books were written by journalists or freelance writers. Yet all three were written by social researchers trying to make sense of different aspects of social life. What distinguishes these works as social research? More generally, what distinguishes social research from other ways of gathering and presenting evidence about social life? All those who write about society construct **representations** of social life—descriptions that incorporate relevant ideas and evidence about social phenomena. Are the representations constructed by social researchers distinctive in any way from those constructed by non–social scientists, and, if so, how?

At the most general level, **social research** includes everything involved in the efforts of social scientists to "tell about society" (Becker 2007). Both aspects of social research—that it involves a *social scientific way* of *telling about society*—are important. Telling about society has special features and some special problems. These problems affect the work of all those who tell about society, from social researchers to novelists to documentary filmmakers, and separate those who tell about society and social life from those who tell about other things. Social researchers, like others who tell about society, are members of society. They study members of society, and they present the

---

Note: **Boldface** terms in the text are defined in the glossary/index.

results of their work to members of society. Thus, at a very general level, social researchers overlap with those whom they study and with the audiences for their work, and those they study—other members of society—also overlap with their audiences.

Among those who consider themselves scientists, this three-way mixing of researcher, subject, and audience exists only in the social and behavioral sciences (anthropology, sociology, political science, and so on) and has an important impact on the nature and conduct of research. For example, it is very difficult to conduct social research without also addressing questions that are fundamentally interpretive or historical in nature—who we are and how we came to be who we are. It is very difficult to neutralize social science in some way and see studying people the same as studying molecules or ants.

The importance of the other part of the definition—that there is a specifically social scientific way of telling—stems from the fact already noted, that there are lots of people who tell about society. Journalists, for example, do most of the things that social scientists do. They try to collect accurate information (data), they try to organize and analyze the information they gather so that it all makes sense, and they report their conclusions in writing to an audience (typically, the general public). Do journalists conduct social research? Yes, they often do, but they are not considered social scientists. It is important to contrast social research with a variety of other activities so that the special features of the social scientific way of representing social life are clear.

Social Research Defined

Social research is one among many ways of constructing representations of social life—of telling about society. It is the product of the efforts of an individual (or group of individuals) that addresses socially significant phenomena, engages directly or indirectly with ideas or social theory, incorporates large amounts of appropriate evidence that has been purposefully collected, and results from systematic analysis of this evidence.

The main concern of this chapter is what is and what is not social research. We first examine conventional answers to the question of the distinctiveness of social research. Most of these conventional answers are too restrictive—too many social researchers are excluded by these answers. Next, we compare social research to some other ways of telling about society to illustrate important similarities and differences. Too often, social researchers are portrayed as ivory tower academics poring over their facts and figures. In fact, social researchers are quite diverse. Some have a lot in common with freelance writers; others are more like laboratory scientists. Finally, we argue that it is important to focus on how social researchers construct their representations of social life for their audiences, especially for other social scientists. By examining the nature of the representations that social researchers construct, it is possible to see the distinctive features of social research—the social scientific way of representing social life.

Some Conventional Views of Social Research

There are three conventional answers to the question, "Does social research constitute a distinctive way of telling about society?" The first argues that social scientists have a special way of defining *society,* and this makes social research distinctive. The second asserts that social research relies heavily on the *language of variables* and *relationships among variables* and that this special language sets social scientists apart. The third emphasizes the use of the *scientific method* and the consequent similarities between the social sciences and natural sciences like physics and chemistry. All three conventional answers offer interesting insights into how social scientists construct social research, yet none of these answers sets social research apart from other ways of telling about society.

Do Social Researchers
Have a Special Way of Defining Society?

One reason social research has so many close relatives, such as journalism and documentary filmmaking, is that many different kinds of work involve telling about society. Can we distinguish social researchers from others who tell about social life and social events by giving the term *society* a special meaning for social researchers? Or can we do so by showing that social scientists all use the term *society* in a special way?

Society could be used to refer to all inhabitants of a nation (for example, all people living in Peru). Social research would then involve making statements about whole countries. For example, a social researcher might show that Peruvians are more acquisitive or more tolerant than people in other countries. Another might show that the occupational rewards for educational achievement are better in Germany than in most other advanced countries. To understand social research in this way is to see countries as the fundamental unit of social scientific knowledge.

The problem with this way of restricting the definition of social research is that very few of the people who call themselves social researchers make statements that are so broad. Some social researchers study the social relations of a single individual. For example, in *Working Knowledge,* Douglas Harper (1987) examined the social world of a single rural handyman (see also Shaw 1930). Some social researchers use their lives as the basis for their analysis of social relationships, such as Betsy Lucal (1999) in her work on the implications of gender misattribution during social interactions. Even those who examine whole countries readily admit that in every country there is great social diversity—that many different "social worlds" exist side by side, entwined and overlapping.

Social researchers also acknowledge that they don't have a good working definition of the term *society.* When U.S. citizens visit Canada for an extended period, are they no longer members of "U.S." society? Is there a separate Canadian society or only a single American society, embracing both Canada and the United States? What about Native Americans or the Amish? And what about Mexico or Quebec? While it is tempting to equate nation-states and societies—and many social scientists routinely do this—it is a hazardous practice. Most of the entities that might be called societies transcend national boundaries.

Alternatively, society might be restricted to *formal properties* of human organization and interaction. A **formal property** is a generic feature or pattern that can exist in many different settings. When only two people interact, they form a dyad; when three people interact, they form a triad; and so on. As the sociologist Georg Simmel (1950) noted a long time ago, dyads and other basic forms of association have special features, regardless of where they are found. This is what makes them "formal" or "generic" properties.

For example, forming a business partnership with another person, a dyad, has a lot of the same qualities as getting married, another dyad. The relationship is both intense and fragile and typically involves many mutual obligations and rights. Thus, group size is a formal property. Interaction patterns are different in small and large groups, regardless of setting. Degree of hierarchy is also a formal property of human organization. *Hierarchy*—the regulation, management, or domination of many by a few—is another key feature of human social life (Michels 1959). Organizations and groups that are more hierarchical differ systematically from those that are "flatter"—again, regardless of setting.

While formal properties are important, and almost no one other than social researchers studies them in depth, the investigation of formal properties today constitutes only a relatively small portion of all social research.

Many of the things that interest social researchers and their audiences are important, not because of their generic features such as their size or their degree of hierarchy, but because of their historical or cultural significance.

It is of special importance to Americans, for example, that some hierarchies overlap with racial differences. One overlap is in education: Schools with a larger percentage of nonwhite students have significantly fewer resources, ranging from larger class sizes to less qualified teachers to fewer college preparatory courses (such as calculus), than schools with predominantly white students. Such overlapping hierarchies are historically rooted, and they are the focus of frequent and intense political debate. These and many other topics of great importance to social researchers and their audiences cannot be addressed as generic features of human social organization. It is difficult to neutralize their social and political significance, to sanitize them, and treat them as abstract, formal properties. If one did succeed in this type of exercise in abstraction, important information would be lost in the process.

What Is Society?

Society is best understood as *social life,* which, in turn, can be understood in simple and conventional terms as *people doing things together* (Becker 2007). Telling about society basically involves studying how and why people do things together. They make and unmake families and firms; they join and leave neighborhoods and religious congregations; they resist authority; they form political parties and factions within them; they go on strike; they organize revolutions; they make peace, they have fun, and they rob gas stations. Historical events and trends (for example, the Islamic revolutions in West Africa or declining rates of childbearing in 19th-century France) are examples of people doing things together. The list is endless. People doing things together is sometimes history making; more often, it is ordinary, everyday, unrecorded social life. Social scientists study all kinds of social activity. Some prefer to study the ordinary; others prefer to study the momentous.

While it may seem contradictory, the category "people doing things together" also includes people *refusing* to do things together (see Scott 1990). For example, when someone decides not to vote in an election because she dislikes all the candidates or is disillusioned with the whole electoral process, a non-action (that is, not voting) has a social character. Not voting, in this light, is intentional and thus can be viewed as an accomplishment. It has a clear and interpretable basis and meaning in everyday social life.

Many refusals are clear acts of defiance (Scott 1976, 1990). The prison inmate who starves himself to protest inhuman conditions may seem contradictory or self-destructive, but his body may be his only possible arena for self-assertion in a setting that imposes such severe restrictions. An apolitical act of suicide, which at first glance seems very personal and individual, is the ultimate refusal to do things together and thus falls well within the purview of social research. Émile Durkheim (1951), an early French sociologist, was one of the very first social scientists to argue that such refusals are inherently social. They have social causes, social consequences, and social meaning.

The category "people doing things together" and its companion category "refusals" encompass a broad range of phenomena. This breadth is necessary because a close examination of the work of social researchers shows that their topics are diverse and almost unbounded. This working definition of society does little, however, to distinguish social research from other ways of telling about society.

Do Social Researchers Use a Special Language?

Alternatively, it might be possible to distinguish social research from other ways of telling about society by the *language* that social researchers use when they tell about society (Lazarsfeld and Rosenberg 1955). Some social researchers argue that when they tell about society they use the language of variables and relationships among variables to describe patterns, and that this language distinguishes social research from other ways of telling about society. (This general approach is discussed in detail in Chapter 7.)

For example, a social researcher might argue that the most racially segregated cities in the United States have the worst public schools (or, conversely, that the least racially segregated cities have the best public schools). This statement expresses a **relationship** between two variables, degree of racial segregation and quality of public schools.

More generally, a **variable** is some general feature or aspect (such as degree of racial segregation) that differs from one case to the next within a particular set (such as cities in the United States). Variables link abstract *concepts* with specific *measures*. In the example, the researcher might believe that the key to having good public schools in racially mixed cities is a high level of *interracial interaction*. The **concept** of interracial interaction, like most concepts, is very general and can be applied in a variety of ways to very different settings (for example, countries, cities, shopping malls, bus stops, high schools, and so on). One way to apply this concept to racially mixed cities is through the variable *racial segregation* (the degree to which different races live in their own, separate neighborhoods).

A **measure** is a specific way a variable is quantified (or measured). Most variables can be measured in a variety of ways. For example, "percentage of a city's population living in racially homogeneous neighborhoods" is one possible measure of racial segregation. The higher this percentage is, the greater the segregation. Another possible measure of segregation is the **index of qualitative variation (IQV)**. IQV is a measure that captures the dispersion of cases across categorical variables (such as race and ethnicity) ranging from complete homogeneity to maximal diversity. IQV is 1.0 when there is the maximum amount of diversity possible (so if there are five possible categories, then 20% of the cases fall into each category). At the other extreme, IQV is 0.0 when there is no diversity (100% of the cases fall into just one category). There are many other, more sophisticated measures of racial segregation (see Massey and Denton 1993). Quantitative researchers have to select from among the available measures or develop new ones; they also may have to justify the specific measures they use for each variable.

To see if it is true that the most racially segregated cities have the worst public schools, it would be necessary to measure both variables, the degree of racial segregation and the quality of the public schools, in each city. The quality of public schools might be measured by average scores on standardized tests, graduation rates, or some other measure. Once the two variables are measured, it would be possible to assess the link between them—these two attributes of cities in the United States. Is there a correspondence? Is it true that the cities that are more racially integrated have better public schools? Is it true that the worst public schools are in the most racially segregated cities? In other words, do these two features of cities vary together, or "covary"? Social researchers use the term **covariation** to describe a general pattern of correspondence.

Examining the covariation between two features across a set of **cases** (racial segregation and quality of public schools across U.S. cities) is the most common way of assessing the relationship between two variables. When we say that two variables are related, we are asserting that there is some pattern of covariation. If we found the expected pattern of covariation across U.S. cities (high levels of racial segregation paired with poor public schools and low levels of racial segregation paired with good public schools), then we could say that these two variables covary and we would use quantitative methods (see Chapter 7) to assess the strength of their correspondence. Social researchers calculate *correlations* in order to assess the *strength* of a pattern of covariation.

Just because two variables covary across a set of cases does not *necessarily* mean that one is the **cause** of the other. However, a pattern of systematic covariation can be offered as evidence in support of the idea or proposition that there is some sort of causal connection between them. The language of variables and relationships among variables provides a powerful shorthand for describing general patterns of correspondence. In this example, evidence on many cities can be condensed into a single number, a **correlation**, describing the strength of the covariation between two measures (see Chapter 7).

It is true that the language of variables and relationships among variables peppers the discourse of most social research. However, there are many who do not use this language. For example, a researcher might chart the history of a declining public school system and include consideration of the impact of racial segregation and other racial factors without resorting directly to the language of variables and relationships. This examination would focus on the unfolding of events—who did what, and when, why, and how.

Similarly, systematic observation (that is, fieldwork) in a single, failing school might be the focus of another social researcher's investigation. This work, like the historical study, might not entail explicit use of the language of variables and relationships. Instead, it might center on an effort to uncover and represent "what it's like" to be a student or a teacher at this school. This understanding, in turn, might help determine whether there is a link between racial segregation and the quality of public schools.

Some social researchers try to avoid using the language of variables and relationships among variables altogether. They believe that this language interferes with their attempts to make sense of social life, especially when the goal of the research is to understand how something came to be the way it is (that is, conduct research on historical origins) or to understand something as an experience (that is, conduct research on how people view their lives and their social worlds).

While some social scientists avoid using the language of variables, many *non*–social scientists use it regularly. Social researchers do not have a monopoly on the understanding of social life through variables and their relations. Many journalists use this language, for example, when they discuss differences from one situation to the next or when they talk about social trends and problems. For instance, a journalist discussing a recent outbreak of violence in a major city might note that cities with more serious drug problems also have higher rates of violent crime. Policymakers and others who routinely consume the writing of social scientists also use this language. Even politicians and ministers use it, especially when they warn of dark days ahead or the current trends that are ushering in unwanted or dangerous changes.

In addition, the language of variables and relationships among variables is not a special language. This way of describing social life crops up often in everyday life. For example, we may say that we learn more in smaller classes, or that we enjoy athletic events more when the game is close, or that families living in rural areas are more closely knit, or that local politicians address real issues while national politicians address made-for-TV issues. In each example, two variables are related. The first, for instance, argues that how much students learn (a variable that can be quantified with standardized tests) is influenced by another measurable variable, class size. This way of describing and understanding social life is in no way the special province of social scientists or social research.

Does the Scientific Method Make Social Research Distinctive?

The third conventional answer to the question of what makes social research distinctive is the idea that social researchers follow the "scientific method," while most of the others who tell about society, like journalists, do not. This answer makes social research seem a lot more like research in the natural sciences such as physics. Progress in these fields is driven primarily by **experiments,** often conducted in laboratories. If social research can claim to follow the same general scientific plan as these natural sciences, then it gains some of their legitimacy as purveyors of scientific truths. At least, this is the thinking of those who argue that the use of the scientific method distinguishes social research from other ways of telling about society.

The core of the scientific method concerns the formulation and **testing of hypotheses.** A **hypothesis** is best understood as an educated guess about what the investigator expects to find in a particular set of evidence. It is an "educated" guess in the sense that it is based on the investigator's knowledge of the phenomenon he or she is studying and on his or her understanding of relevant ideas or *social theories* (see discussion of social theory below). Social researchers often develop hypotheses by studying the writings and research of other social scientists. These writings include not only research on a given topic but also relevant theoretical works. Social scientists use these writings in combination with whatever they know or can learn about their research subject to formulate hypotheses. These hypotheses are most often formulated as propositions about the expected relationship between two or more variables across a particular set or **category** of cases.

Generally, a hypothesis involves the **deduction** of a specific proposition or expectation from a general theoretical argument or perspective. It is a mental act, based on existing knowledge. For example, a researcher might be interested in the impact of occupation on voting behavior, especially the political differences between industrial workers who interact only with machines compared to those who must interact with other workers to coordinate production. In addition to the many studies of voting behavior, the researcher might also consult Karl Marx's (1867/1976) ideas about work and class consciousness presented in his three-volume work, *Das Kapital;* Max Weber's (1922/1978) ideas about social class in *Economy and Society;* and the ideas of contemporary scholars such as Seymour Lipset (1982), Erik Wright (1985), and Michèle Lamont (2002). After consulting all the relevant studies and theoretical writings, the researcher might derive a specific hypothesis: that industrial workers who interact more with machines vote less often than industrial workers who interact with other workers on the job, but when they do vote, they vote more consistently for the Democratic Party.

After formulating a hypothesis, social researchers collect relevant data and then use them to test the hypothesis. The test usually involves an examination of patterns in the data to see if they match up well with the patterns predicted by the hypothesis. Analysis of the data may refute or support the hypothesis. Typically, analysis of the data also suggests revisions of the hypothesis that could be explored in a future study.

Information to test the hypothesis just described could be collected in a variety of ways (for example, via telephone interviews, mailed questionnaires, and so on). Once collected, the researcher could use statistical methods to test the hypothesis. The researcher would compare the two categories of industrial workers with respect to their different voting histories—how often they voted and who they voted for—to see if there are substantial differences between the two groups in the ways predicted by the hypothesis.

The examination of the data has important implications for the ideas used to generate the hypothesis. On the basis of the newly collected evidence, for example, the researcher might conclude that these ideas need serious adjustment. The use of evidence to formulate or reformulate general ideas is called **induction.** Induction is a process whereby the implications of evidence, especially new evidence combined with existing evidence, for general ideas are assessed.

In the **scientific method,** deduction and induction work together. The hypothesis is derived from theory and from existing knowledge about the research subject. Data relevant to the hypothesis are assembled or collected, and the correctness of the hypothesis is assessed. The new knowledge that is generated through these efforts can then be used, through the process of induction, to extend, refine, or reformulate existing ideas. In short, deduction starts with general ideas and applies them to evidence; induction starts with evidence and assesses their implication for general ideas.

Figure 1.1 shows the specific steps dictated by the scientific method. At the end of a research project, when the data analysis is complete, the data support or refute the hypothesis. Then the cycle begins again. The scientific method works best when different theories can be used to deduce competing hypotheses. When diametrically opposed hypotheses are deduced from two or more theories, the analysis of relevant data provides a decisive, or "critical," test of opposing arguments. Both theories can't be supported by the same data if they make opposite predictions.

For example, if one theory predicts that national economies subject to *more* government regulation (rules and restrictions on what businesses can do) should have higher economic growth rates when world trade slumps,

Figure 1.1   The Scientific Method

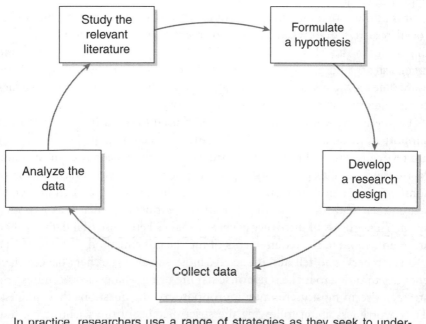

The **scientific method** is a set of research steps intended to further the acquisition of knowledge such that researchers can avoid making subjective conclusions based on biased evidence. The specific steps are represented in the diagram below.

Study the relevant literature

Formulate a hypothesis

Analyze the data

Develop a research design

Collect data

In practice, researchers use a range of strategies as they seek to understand a social phenomenon. An alternative model of the process of social research, called the *Interpretive model,* is presented in Chapter 3.

and a second theory predicts that national economies subject to *less* government regulation should fare better under these conditions, then examination of relevant data on national economies should permit a decisive test of these competing arguments.

While there are many social researchers who use the scientific method as described here, there are also many who do not. For example, some social scientists (see, for example, Smith 1987) believe that the most important thing a social scientist can do is to give *voice* to **marginalized groups**—to tell the stories of those who have been shoved aside by the rest of society (see Chapter 2).

For example, Leila Rupp and Verta Taylor (2003) got to know the drag queens from a club in Key West, the 801 Cabaret, over the course of 3 years by talking with them, attending their performances, and even participating in the shows themselves. The greater the role of pre-existing theories and ideas in a project of this sort, the more the voices of the research subjects are blocked by the trappings of natural science imposed on an elusive social phenomenon. The voices of the subjects are lost as the loudspeaker of social science theory drowns out all competitors. This reasoning is inconsistent with the logic of the scientific method, which emphasizes the testing of hypotheses.

It is also worth noting that it is not easy to follow the scientific method in social research, even when the goal of the researcher is strict adherence to this framework. Most social scientific theories are abstract, vague, and inconsistent, and it is difficult to deduce clear hypotheses from them. Sometimes a theory is so vaguely formulated that it is possible to deduce contradictory arguments from the same theory.

Furthermore, when analyses of the data used to test a hypothesis do not support it, most researchers are reluctant to conclude that the theory they are testing is wrong. Instead, they usually point to inadequacies in the data, to the impossibility of measuring social phenomena with precision, or to some other practical problem. Finally, social researchers are often known to search their data for interesting patterns, regardless of what was hypothesized. This process of discovery generally makes better use of a data set than strict adherence to the requirements of the scientific method (Diesing 1971).

Like others who tell about society, most social researchers devote their energies to trying to make sense of social life using whatever procedures and strategies seem most useful and appropriate for the questions they address. They worry less about following the strict dictates of the scientific method in their efforts to construct well-grounded representations of social life. Thus, there is no single "method" used by social scientists. In Chapter 3, we discuss an alternative to the scientific method called the *interpretive model*.

This alternative model encompasses a much broader range of the types of activity researchers engage in when conducting social research.

To summarize the discussion of conventional views of the distinctiveness of social research, social researchers don't have one special way of defining society that they all agree on, nor do they have one special way of telling about it. While many social researchers respect the scientific method, not all follow its prescribed steps strictly, and some ignore its steps altogether. It *is* true that social researchers have tried harder than others to define society and social life, they *do* tend to use the language of variables and relationships among variables more than anyone else, and many of them *do* test hypotheses according to systematic rules. But these are not *defining features* of social research; they are better seen as *tendencies* of social research.

Social Research and Other Ways of Representing Social Life

Novelists and other writers, journalists, documentary photographers and filmmakers, and a host of others, in addition to social researchers, construct representations that "tell about society." They all address the subtleties of social life—people doing or refusing to do things together. Is it possible to distinguish social researchers from these other people who also tell about society?

Consider documentary filmmakers first. In some ways, the makers of documentaries seem more concerned than social researchers with constructing valid representations of social life. When social researchers represent society, they often use tables and charts that condense and simplify the vast amount of evidence they have collected. When a researcher states, for example, that people with more education tend to be more politically tolerant, the conclusion may summarize information on thousands of people canvassed in a survey. Or social researchers may select a quote or two to illustrate a conclusion based on an analysis of hundreds of hours of taped, face-to-face interviews. In almost all social scientific representations of social life, the social researcher explains in detail his or her *interpretation* of the evidence used in the representation.

Documentary filmmakers, by contrast, try to present much of their evidence up front, often without commenting directly on its meaning or significance. While it is true that filmmakers select which clips to show and then arrange them in sequence, the representation itself is made up of actual recordings. Also, many documentary filmmakers avoid injecting verbal or written interpretations of the evidence that is presented. Thus, while documentary films, like all representations of social life, are constructed in ways that reflect the goals and intentions of their makers, these representations often have less interpretation of the evidence, and in most instances they display a higher proportion of all the primary evidence collected than representations produced by social researchers. Viewers of documentary films are sometimes left to draw their own conclusions from the representation. Social researchers, by contrast, usually state their conclusions openly, and they carefully organize their representations around these clearly stated conclusions.

At the other extreme, consider the work of novelists. Some novelists strive to write stories that are as realistic as possible. They create fiction, but their fictions are believable representations of social life, representations that often strike at the core of what it means to live in a complex social world. Imagine a novelist concerned about race in the South. She bases her novel on her experience of race relations as a child growing up in the Deep South in the 1950s. She wants to capture, as much as possible, the essence of what it was like. Much of the book might be based on actual experiences—true events—but much of it might be pure fiction as well—events fabricated by the author. Yet this fictional account might do a much better job of capturing the essence of what it was actually like to live in the South during this period than a careful recounting of true events. In short, by creating fiction, the novelist might do a better job of capturing the reality, the true character of race during this period, than she might if she were to present a straight history of relevant childhood events.

At one extreme, a documentary film is a representation based on recorded slices of social life. At the other extreme is the novel, the creation of insightful fiction. Both ways of representing social life have important strengths that are only rarely found in social research. In some ways, social research may seem ineffective when compared to these other, more dramatic approaches.

But we really don't expect to find these qualities in social research. We don't expect social researchers to present mounds of data. In fact, the social researcher who simply presents mounds of data is considered a failure because the work is not complete. Likewise, we do not want social researchers to create deliberate fictions to enhance the points they want to make. The social researcher who knowingly presents fiction as truth is considered dishonest and, if discovered, will be charged with violating professional ethics (see Chapter 4).

From the perspective of most social researchers, the representation of social life offered in a novel is overprocessed compared to social science because the representation goes far beyond the evidence. The representations constructed by social researchers are more processed and condensed than those offered in documentary films and less processed than those created in novels. At least, this is the happy medium that most social researchers strive for—to go beyond raw data and provide a clear interpretation of the evidence, but stop well short of fiction.

In this respect, social research is a lot like journalism. Journalists process and condense information about social life, but they also try to avoid manufacturing fiction. Among the many ways of telling about society that could be compared to social research, journalism offers the closest and most fruitful comparison.

Journalism and Social Research: The Similarities

Journalists write about what's going on in society; they represent social life. Most often they report on current events, but they also write stories that offer historical perspectives and in-depth interpretations. Journalists also address major trends and social problems, not just the news of the day, and sometimes these reports are very similar to the research reports of social scientists. Also like social researchers, journalists develop special topic areas: Some focus on political events, economic trends, or women's issues; some report on everyday life; some analyze major international events and issues; and so on. Virtually all aspects of social life fall within the purview of journalism. If people will read about a topic, journalists will report on it.

Regardless of topic, journalists all face the same problem regarding "evidence" or "facts." This problem parallels that of social researchers facing "data." Like social researchers, journalists collect an enormous amount of information that, potentially at least, might become evidence for a report. They have to decide which of this information is relevant as evidence and then identify the most pertinent bits. This process of gathering and selecting evidence goes hand-in-hand with developing the focus of the investigation and the report. As the report becomes more of a finished product—as it coalesces in the mind of the journalist as a story—the collection of evidence becomes more focused and more selective. Initial ideas become leads, some leads bear fruit and are pursued vigorously, and the story takes shape. In the process, much potential evidence and many potential stories are left behind.

The same holds true for social research. Social scientists must select from the vast amount of information that social life offers and construct their representations from carefully selected bits and slices. Data collection (that is, the process of gathering evidence) is necessarily selective, and becomes much more so as an investigation progresses. The researcher may start with a few ideas (for example, sensitizing concepts; see Chapter 5) and maybe a working hypothesis or two. These ideas determine the initial data collection efforts.

As more is learned about the subject, either through data collection or data analysis, the research becomes more focused and fewer avenues are kept open. As the results take shape in the mind of the investigator, much of what was initially thought to be important is cast aside as irrelevant.

Both social researchers and journalists find that, in the end, much of the evidence they collected at the start of the investigation was based on false leads, and that they could have been much more efficient in their collection of evidence if only they had known at the start what they learned toward the end of the investigation. The collection of evidence is necessarily selective because potentially there is an infinite quantity of evidence. However, both journalists and social researchers find that in the end they cannot use all the evidence they have collected.

There is great danger in both journalism and social research that follows from this need for **selective gathering of evidence.** Sometimes what may be a false lead is not recognized as such, and it may become the focus or at least an important part of the investigation. False leads pose serious problems in both journalism and social research because they may be biased by accepted knowledge; stereotypes; and common, everyday understandings of social life. For example, there are two common images of the African American male—the dangerous, inner-city ghetto teenager and the upwardly mobile young professional. As Mitchell Duneier points out in *Slim's Table* (1992), both of these images are media creations and have little to do with the lives of most African American men. Research or journalism that uses these images as starting points will fail to arrive at valid representations of the experiences of African American males.

Another problem is the simple fact that people questioned or studied by a journalist or a social researcher may unconsciously or deliberately seek to deceive those who study them. Both social researchers and journalists strive to get valid evidence. For journalists, this effort is often described as reporting "just the facts" or at least trying to balance different views of the same facts. Journalists check different sources against each other and maintain constant vigilance in their efforts to detect deception. After all, interested parties may have a lot to gain if their version of "the facts" is accepted by a journalist and then reported as the one true version.

While social researchers are less often the target of outright deception, like journalists they must deal with bias, distortion, faulty memories, and cover-up. For example, while it might seem a simple matter to determine the percentage of gay men among adult men in the United States, social researchers have come up with a range of answers, from 2% to about 10%. (These estimates are discussed in greater detail in Chapter 7.) There are various reasons for this wide range; one of them is people's reluctance to discuss their sexual behavior openly.

"Social facts" can be as elusive as bias-free journalism. Thus, the two fields have comparable obsessions with "truth," or **validity** as it is known to social researchers. For journalism, this concern is expressed in a concern for reporting only verifiable information. Thus, journalists are very concerned with "fact checking" and with the authority of their sources of information.

Social researchers' concern for validity is seen in their efforts to verify that their data collection and measurement procedures work the way they claim. Researchers attempting to determine the percentage of adult gay men in the United States, to follow the example above, would have to contend with a variety of threats to the validity of their measurement procedures. People with more varied sex lives, for example, are generally more likely to agree to talk about their sex lives or to fill out questionnaires on their sexual behavior. This **bias** would surely increase the size of the estimate of the percentage of adult gay men based on survey data. Thus, researchers would have to find some way to address this threat to the validity of their measurement procedures and their estimate of the percentage of adult gay men.

Another similarity between journalists and social researchers is that they must analyze and arrange evidence before they can offer their representations of social life for wider consumption (for example, as news or research reports). As evidence is gathered and selected, the investigator tries to make sense of it. Ongoing analysis of the evidence simplifies the task of what to collect next. Once the gathering and selecting of evidence is complete, the *analysis* of evidence intensifies. A thorough analysis of evidence, in both journalism and social research, is an important preliminary step to arranging it for presentation in a report.

When social life is represented, both social researchers and journalists make connections in their data. When a journalist reconstructs the story of a political scandal, for example, connections and timing are crucially important to the representation of the scandal. It matters who said or did what and when. The goal of analysis is to make these connections. In social research, connections are often *causal* in nature. An analysis of a decaying section of a city, for example, might focus on the long-term economic and social forces responsible for the decline.

Journalists analyze their evidence to make sure that the proper connections are made; then they arrange the evidence for presentation in a report. Readers want to know the big picture—the journalist's final synthesis of the evidence, and not all the bits of evidence that the journalist collected along the way before arriving at a synthesis. It is the same with social research. It isn't possible to include all the evidence the social researcher collected when reporting conclusions. The evidence that is represented in a research report is a select subset of the evidence collected, which of course is a select subset of the vast volume of potential evidence.

The similarities between the work of journalists and the work of social researchers are striking. Of necessity, they both selectively gather evidence relevant to specific questions, analyze it, and then select a subset of the evidence they have gathered for reporting. The report itself is an attempt to construct for the reader the investigator's conclusions regarding the evidence. Evidence is arranged and condensed in a way that illustrates the investigator's conclusions. In effect, the reader is presented with the investigator's arrangement of a fraction of the evidence the investigator collected, a small fraction of the potential evidence. Thus, in both social research and journalism, representations of social life (the end products of efforts to tell about society) are condensed descriptions structured according to the investigator's ideas. These representations emerge from a systematic dialogue between the investigator's ideas and evidence.

How Social Research Differs

Journalists write for wide audiences, usually for the literate public as a whole. They hope to reach as many people as possible. The primary audience for social researchers, by contrast, is social scientists and other professionals. Many social researchers hope to reach, eventually, the literate public with their findings and their ideas. Some social researchers, including policy researchers, engage in research to have a direct impact on society. They seek to influence and inform contemporary public debates and seek a broader audience for their work. For example, policy researchers are primarily concerned with factors that can be manipulated by public policy and therefore are more likely to be of interest to policymakers. These researchers frame their work so it directly addresses policy alternatives and makes recommendations about policy interventions, revisions, or removals. But most social researchers expect to reach these general audiences indirectly—through the work of others such as journalists and freelance writers who use the work and the ideas of social researchers.

The importance of this difference can be seen clearly in the work of social scientists who write for several different target audiences. When their primary audience is social scientists and other professionals, they emphasize, among other things, technical aspects of their research and its place in a specific research literature—that is, its relation to the work of others who have researched the same or similar topics. When these same researchers write for the general public, however, they usually skip over technical aspects of the research and the discussion of the work of others (research literatures), focusing instead on the relevance of their own research findings to the concerns of the general public.

The point is not that the nature of the target audience shapes the nature of the representation, although this is certainly an important consideration. Rather, it is pinpointing the distinctiveness of the social scientific way of representing social life. The *distinctiveness* of the social scientific way of telling about society is most apparent when representations of social life produced *by* social scientists *for* social scientists are examined, especially given the fact that social scientists consider it their professional responsibility to monitor and evaluate the quality of each other's representations. It is important, therefore, to address how social researchers construct these representations.

What makes a representation of social life especially relevant to a social scientist? Briefly, social scientific audiences expect social scientific representations to

- Address phenomena that are socially significant in some way;
- Be relevant to social theory, either directly or indirectly;
- Be based on or incorporate large amounts of appropriate evidence, purposefully collected; and
- Result from some form of systematic analysis of this evidence.

While *some* of these features are found in *many* journalistic representations of social life, *all four* features are commonly found together in most social scientific representations. Because social scientific representations of social life have these four features, they tend to be better grounded in *ideas* and *evidence* than other kinds of representations. Ultimately, it is their strong grounding in ideas and evidence that makes these representations especially relevant to social scientists.

Social Researchers Address Phenomena That Are Socially Significant

Many of the things that social researchers address are socially significant simply because they are general. Social scientists address all kinds of rates and percentages, for example, used to characterize large numbers of people (the homicide rate, the percentage of voters, and so on), and they study variations in these rates (for example, why some groups murder more than others, why some groups vote more than others, and so on). Sometimes rates and percentages are compared across whole countries (for example, rates of infant mortality in Asian versus Latin American countries). While a single murder might be relevant to theory in some way, common acts are more often studied across large populations, as rates and percentages.

However, it is not simply generality and the possibility of studying rates that make phenomena socially significant. Some phenomena are significant not because they are common, but because they are rare, unusual, or extreme in some way. A researcher might study a business, for example, that attempts to maintain a completely egalitarian structure, with no one giving orders to anyone else. How do they get things done? Or a researcher might study a country with great ethnic and cultural diversity but little ethnic conflict. Why is ethnic competition absent? Another researcher might study a poor immigrant group that assimilated quickly and overcame extreme prejudice while achieving breathtaking economic gains. How did they do it when so many other groups have struggled and failed? Finally, another researcher might study women who dress and pass as men. What do they gain? What do they lose?

These phenomena are worth studying because they are uncommon. However, they are studied not simply because of their interest value, but because they are relevant to how social researchers think about what is more common and thus challenge their basic assumptions about social life.

Social phenomena may also be selected for study because of their historical significance. An understanding of slavery, for example, is vitally important to the understanding and interpretation of race in the United States today. Similarly, an understanding of the relations between the United States and its Latin American neighbors, Mexico and Puerto Rico especially, is central to an understanding of Hispanic Americans. One key to understanding post–World War II U.S. society is the "A-bomb" and other nuclear weapons and the collective perception of their destructive potential. Our thinking about the military and military life in general is strongly influenced by the experience of the Vietnam War; the First Gulf War; and, more recently, the wars in Iraq and Afghanistan. In short, many different aspects of our history have an impact on who we are today. It is difficult to know and understand American society without exploring the impact of its history.

Social Researchers Connect Their Work to Social Theory

Social scientific representations of social life almost always address social theory in some way: A study of homicide rates is relevant to theories of social conflict. A study of women who dress and pass as men is relevant to theories that address gender differences and power. But what is social theory?

Most social scientists participate, in one way or another, in a set of loosely connected, ongoing conversations about abstract ideas with other social scientists and social thinkers. These conversations address basic features and processes of social life and seek to answer enduring questions. Such conversations started before any of today's social scientists were born and more than likely will continue long after they have all died. While they often focus on abstract social concepts that have been around a long time (such as the concept of equality, for instance, or the concept of society), they also shift over time, sometimes taking up new topics (gender and power, for example), sometimes returning to old topics (for example, the degree to which a group's culture can change in the absence of significant changes in material conditions such as level of technology).

These long-term, ongoing conversations provide a background for the development of specific social theories that are spelled out in the research process. A **social theory** is an attempt to specify as clearly as possible a set of ideas that pertain to a particular phenomenon or set of phenomena. Clarity is important because social theory guides research. Sometimes the ideas that make up a theory are expressed clearly at the start of a research project in the form of specific assumptions, concepts, and relationships. Research that seeks to follow the plan of the scientific method needs such clarity from the start. The researcher uses theory as a basis for formulating a specific hypothesis that is then tested with data especially collected for the test.

Sometimes, however, ideas are clarified in the course of the research. This approach is common in research that seeks to use evidence to formulate new ideas. Consider the social researcher who studies something a journalist might study, a new religious cult. More than likely, the researcher will compare this cult to a variety of other cults and in this way show the relevance of the cult to theories of religion. By contrast, a journalist might simply focus on the bizarre or unusual practices that set this cult apart from the rest of society.

The social researcher might also question the label "religious cult." Suppose the cult was also very successful at marketing a particular product, something produced by its members (see Zablocki 1980). Is it a cult, or is it a new type of business enterprise? Which set of social theories, those addressing religious cults or those addressing economic organizations, is more useful when trying to understand this group? What are the implications of this group for either set of theories? In most social research, there is a clear *dialogue* with social theory that is an essential part of the research process (see Chapter 3).

Social Researchers Use Large
Amounts of Purposefully Collected Evidence

Most social researchers summarize mountains of evidence in the representations they construct. Social researchers tend to incorporate a lot of in-depth information about a limited number of cases (as in much **qualitative research**) or a limited amount of information about a large number of cases (as in most **quantitative research**) in their representations. Either way, they collect a lot of data. When social researchers construct representations, they try to incorporate as much of this evidence as possible, either by condensing and summarizing it or by highlighting the essential features of the cases they study.

The audiences for social research expect representations to summarize large amounts of evidence. In journalism, investigation is often focused on fact checking—making sure that each piece of a story is correct. Social researchers, by contrast, usually focus on the "weight" of the evidence. For example, in survey research, the investigator expects some respondents to make mistakes when they try to recall how they voted in the last election. Such mistakes are not fatal because the investigator is interested primarily in broad tendencies in the data—in the average voter or in the tendencies of broad categories of voters, such as, "Do richer respondents tend to vote more often for Republican candidates?" Social researchers *do* strive for precision—they try to get the facts right, but when they construct representations, their primary concern is to present a synthesis of the facts that both makes sense and is true to the evidence.

While large amounts of evidence are incorporated into most social scientific representations, it is important to recognize that the evidence used is *purposefully collected*. In much social research, investigators put together a specific **research design.** A research design is a plan for collecting and analyzing evidence that will make it possible for the investigator to answer whatever questions he or she has posed. The design of an investigation touches almost all aspects of the research. The important ones to consider here are those that pertain to social scientists' use of large amounts of purposefully collected evidence. These include the following:

1. **Data collection technique.** Social researchers use a variety of different techniques: observation, interviewing, participating in activities, use of telephone and other types of surveys, collection of official statistics or historical archives, use of census materials and other evidence collected by governments, records of historical events, and so on. The choice of data

collection technique is in large part shaped by the nature of the research question. All these techniques can yield enormous amounts of evidence.

2. **Sampling.** In most research situations, investigators confront a staggering surplus of data, and they often need to devise strategies for sampling the available data. The survey researcher who wants to study racial differences in voting does not need to know every voter's preference, just enough to make an accurate assessment of tendencies. A **random sample** of 1,000 voters might be sufficient. A researcher who wants to study how protest demonstrations have changed over the last 20 years based on an in-depth investigation of 50 such demonstrations must develop a strategy for selecting which 50 to study.

3. **Sample selection bias.** Whenever researchers use only a subset of the potential evidence, as when they sample, they have to worry about the **representativeness** of the subset they use. A study of poor people that uses telephone interviews is not likely to result in a representative sample because many, many poor people (including thousands of homeless people) cannot afford phones. Likewise, the researcher who selects 50 protest demonstrations to see how these demonstrations have changed over the last 20 years must make sure that each one selected is sufficiently representative of the period from which it was selected.

4. **Data collection design.** Sometimes researchers collect a lot of evidence but then realize that they don't have the right *kinds* of evidence for the questions that concern them most. For example, a researcher interested in the differences between upper-income whites and upper-income blacks may discover too late that a random sample of a large population typically will not yield enough cases in these two categories, especially upper-income blacks, to permit a thorough comparison. Most issues in data collection design concern the *appropriateness* of the data collected for the questions asked. A study of the impact of a new job training program that provides workers with new skills, for example, should follow these workers for several years, not just several weeks or months. The *timing* of data collection (or "observation") is an important issue in almost all studies. More generally, social researchers recognize that the nature of their evidence constrains the questions that they can ask of it (see especially Lieberson 1985).

Systematic collection of evidence is important even in research that is more open-ended and less structured from the start of the investigation (as in most qualitative research; see Chapter 5). Often in research of this type, issues of sampling and selection bias are addressed in the course of the research, as the investigator's representation takes shape. A researcher who discovers some new aspect of a group in the course of informal observation will develop a data collection strategy that allows assessment of the generality of the phenomenon (Glaser and Strauss 1967; Strauss 1987).

Social Researchers Analyze Evidence Systematically

The power of the analytic tools social researchers apply to their evidence is sometimes staggering. Powerful computers, for example, are needed to examine the relationship between household income and number of children across the hundreds of thousands of households included in census data banks. Do families with larger incomes have more or fewer children? It's very difficult to answer this question without a computer and sophisticated statistical software. Most social scientific representations result from the application of some systematic technique of data analysis to a large body of evidence. Different procedures for analyzing evidence are used for different kinds of evidence.

Consider the researcher interested in why some women choose not to have children. First, it is clear that to answer this question, it would be necessary to interview a substantial number of women who are childless by choice (excluding women with children and those whose decisions may be conflated with fertility-related issues). Some effort should be made to talk to women from as many different walks of life as possible. Perhaps women from different ethnic or class backgrounds make this choice for different reasons. Alternatively, a researcher could explicitly limit the scope of the study to a particular type of woman (see, for example, Morell 1994). Because it is a personal topic, and rapport between these women and the researcher is important, these interviews would need to be in depth, perhaps stretching 2 to 4 hours each. It might be necessary to interview 30 to 60 women. Assume 50 women are interviewed for 3 hours each. The researcher then would have a total of 150 hours of taped interviews. How can this large body of evidence be shaped into a representation of the social significance and meaning of intentional childlessness for these women?

Social scientists have devised a variety of techniques for systematically analyzing this kind of evidence. Most focus on clarifying the concepts and categories that help make sense of this mass of evidence (see Chapter 5). The issue here is not the specific techniques, but the fact that most audiences for social research expect the representation of this kind of evidence to be based on systematic analysis of the entire body of evidence. A journalistic representation, by contrast, might simply tell the stories of a handful of the most interesting cases.

More generally, techniques for the systematic analysis of data are a central part of research design. As noted, the term *research design* embraces all aspects of the collection and analysis of data. Just as most researchers develop a systematic plan for the collection of data—to make sure their evidence is relevant to the questions they ask—they also develop a plan for *analyzing* their data. In the study of intentional childlessness, the plan would involve how to make best use of the hundreds of hours of taped interviews. How does one go about identifying commonalities in the things these women said and how they said them? In a very different type of study, say a survey addressing the relationship between social class and attitudes about abortion, the analysis plan would focus on the measurement of the main variables (social class and attitudes about abortion) and different ways of relating them statistically (see Chapter 7).

Conclusion

Social researchers, like many others, construct representations of social life. A study showing that single men are less satisfied with their lives than married men, single women, or married women is a *representation* of one aspect of society—the complex relations among gender, marital status, and personal satisfaction.

Social researchers construct representations of society and then publish them, usually in scientific journals (for example, *American Sociological Review, American Political Science Review, American Anthropologist,* and *Journal of Social History*); in scholarly books, reports, and monographs; in textbooks and other teaching material; and sometimes in magazines, newspapers, and trade books—when they want to reach nonacademic audiences. While social scientific representations usually appear in print, they are not limited to these media. They may also be oral (for example, public lectures). They may include tape recordings, photographs, videotapes, documentary films, and even dramatic productions. Thus, social research has a lot in common with other ways of representing social life, but it is also a distinctive way of representing. It is a lot like journalism, but most social research differs in important ways from journalism.

Social research is not for everyone. Many would rather not participate in age-old conversations about fundamental social questions. It's often easier to ignore what other researchers and social thinkers have said. Many consider it tedious to collect large quantities of evidence. It all seems repetitious and painstaking. Many don't want to bother learning how to conduct systematic analysis of large bodies of evidence. After all, it's much easier to find a few easy cases that are interesting and focus on them. Who wants to learn statistics or how to code evidence from hundreds of hours of taped interviews?

It's also true that the evidence itself may seem too constraining. Both journalists and social researchers have trouble with pesky evidence—data that don't give the exact message the investigator would like to present. The social "truths" that can be manufactured through novels, plays, and other forms of fiction may be much more appealing. Finally, some people want their cases to "speak for themselves" as much as possible. They may prefer to present exact recordings like videotapes and let their audiences choose their own messages in these representations.

While social research is difficult and limiting, it also offers special rewards for those willing to make the investments. People who like to read and write about social issues are drawn to social research. Often they have strong political commitments (for example, to fairness in the economic and political arenas). They hope to translate their concerns into publications— representations of social life—that influence social policy. Publications can influence policy directly by bringing issues to the attention of public officials, or indirectly by altering the social consciousness of the informed public. Like the three researchers mentioned in the introduction to this chapter, thousands of other social researchers have constructed representations of social life reflecting their concerns. Many have had a direct or indirect impact on social issues.

The beauty of social research is that it tempers and clarifies the concerns and interests of those who practice the craft. Social research has this impact on people who address social issues in several ways: Social researchers must engage the long-standing debates about society and social life when they conduct research. They must base their representations on systematic examination of large quantities of systematically collected evidence. Social researchers as a community pass judgment on the representations of social life produced by other social researchers (Kuhn 1962; Merton 1973). In effect, they inspect and evaluate each other's work.

Thus, of all ways of representing social life, those that emanate from social research have a very strong grounding in ideas and evidence and a great potential for influencing social policy. As a community of scholars, social researchers work together to construct representations of social life that fulfill the many and varied goals of social research, from documenting broad patterns and testing social theories to giving voice to marginal groups in society.

2

The Goals of Social Research

Introduction

Social life is infinitely complex. Every situation, every story, is unique. Yet people make their way through this world of complexity. Most situations seem familiar enough, and people can usually figure out how to avoid the unfamiliar. Also, there is order in complexity, even if people are not always conscious of the order. Some of this order-in-complexity is easy to describe (as in what sports fans do to mark certain events in a game). (For example, hockey fans will toss hats out onto the ice when a player scores a "hat trick"—three goals in a single game.) Other examples of order-in-complexity are difficult to explain, much less describe (such as the interplay of pagan and Christian symbols in the development of some religious rituals).

Social researchers seek to identify order and regularity in the complexity of social life; they try to make sense of it. This is a fundamental goal. When they tell about society—how people do or refuse to do things together—they describe whatever order they have found. There is even a describable order to what may appear to be social chaos, such as a mass political demonstration that gets out of hand and leads to a violent attack on nearby symbols of authority. Another fundamental goal exists for many social scientists: to generate knowledge with the potential to transform society. These social scientists conduct research with the hopes that their findings will lead directly to social change. They hope their work will have a broader impact on society—by affecting public policy or influencing the direction of social change. Leading sociologists, particularly Michael Burawoy (2005), have pushed in the last 10 years for more **public sociology**—that is, sociological research that is conducted and written specifically to reach people outside of academe, including policymakers, the media, and marginalized social groups. Along with being directed at a broader audience, public sociology defines, promotes, and informs public debate about topics ranging from social inequalities to state-sanctioned torture. Thus, there is an explicit activist element, though not specifically conservative or liberal in political bent. While the merits of public sociology have been debated recently, this tradition extends back to the work of Jane Addams, Harriet Martineau, and other feminist researchers. In addition, the research of W. E. B. Du Bois, centering on racism in the 20th century, is clearly in line with what is now being called public sociology.

While the above two fundamental goals (understanding the complexity of social life and generating knowledge with the potential to transform society) are present within a broad range of research projects, there are many other more specific goals that contribute to these larger ones. They are quite diverse. For example, the goal of testing theories about social life contributes to the larger goal of identifying order in complexity; so does the goal of collecting in-depth information on the diverse social groups that make up society. The goal of giving voice to a marginalized group contributes to the larger goal of generating transformative knowledge; so does the goal of making predictions about which policy alternatives will result in the desired outcomes. One factor that contributes to the diversity of the goals of social research is the simple fact that social research reflects society, and society itself is diverse, multifaceted, and composed of many antagonistic groups. It follows that the goals of social research are multiple and sometimes contradictory. Today, no single goal dominates social research.

Several of the main goals of social research resemble those of research in the natural sciences such as physics and chemistry. These goals include, for example, the identification of general patterns and relationships. When we show that people with more education tend to vote more often and that this link exists in many democratic countries, we have documented a general relationship for individuals living in democracies. Similarly, when we observe that countries with greater income inequality tend to be more politically unstable, we have identified a pattern that holds across entire nation-states. Knowledge of general patterns and relationships is valuable because it is a good starting point for understanding many specific situations and for making predictions about the future. Also, general patterns in society are directly relevant to the testing of social science theory—the body of ideas that social scientists often draw upon in their efforts to make sense of and tell about society.

Some of the other goals of social research, however, are not modeled on the natural sciences. These other goals follow more directly from the fact that social researchers are members of the social worlds they study (see Chapter 1). For example, some social researchers try to "give voice" to their research subjects—providing their subjects the opportunity to have their stories told, their worlds represented. If not for the interest or concern of social researchers, these groups might have little opportunity to relate their lives, in their own words, to the literate public. For example, the experiences of recent immigrants struggling for survival in the noise and confusion of our largest and most congested cities are rarely represented in the media. The goal of giving voice clearly does not follow from the model of the natural sciences. A physicist is not concerned about giving voice to the lives and subjective experiences of specific particles. The goal of giving voice may come into direct conflict with the goal mentioned above of identifying general patterns because it is difficult to both privilege certain cases by giving them voice and at the same time chart general patterns across many cases. When the goal is to identify general patterns, no specific case, no specific voice, should dominate.

Altogether, seven main goals of social research are examined in this chapter (see "Main Goals" box). Generally, the first three goals follow the lead of the natural sciences. The fourth and sixth goals, by contrast, follow from the social nature of social science—the fact that social researchers study phenomena that are relevant in some special way to the social world of the researcher. The fifth and seventh goals straddle these two domains. In some ways, they link up with natural science models; in other ways, they reflect the socially grounded nature of social research.

Main Goals of Social Research

1. Identifying general patterns and relationships

2. Testing and refining theories

3. Making predictions

4. Interpreting culturally or historically significant phenomena

5. Exploring diversity

6. Giving voice

7. Advancing new theories

The list of goals discussed in this chapter is not exhaustive; several others could be added. For example, **evaluation research,** which is a type of social research, seeks to measure the success of specific programs or policies, especially in education and the delivery of social services. Did the clients of an agency benefit when its record-keeping procedures were simplified and streamlined? Or did the resulting sacrifice of detailed information following the effort to streamline harm specific categories of clients? Which ones? While evaluation research usually has very specific goals tied to particular programs, such research is also relevant to general patterns, one of the key concerns of social research. Thus, most social research involves at least one and usually several of the seven goals discussed in this chapter.

Because social research has multiple and competing goals, a variety of different research strategies has evolved to accommodate those goals. A **research strategy** is best understood as the pairing of a primary research objective and a specific research method. The last part of this chapter introduces three common research strategies, among the many different strategies that social researchers use. The three research strategies discussed in this chapter and examined in detail in Part II of this book are

1. Qualitative research on the commonalities that exist across a relatively small number of cases

2. Comparative research on the diversity that exists across a moderate number of cases

3. Quantitative research on the correspondence between two or more attributes across a large number of cases

Seven Main Goals

1. Identifying General Patterns and Relationships

Recall that one of the key characteristics of social scientific representations discussed in Chapter 1 was the focus on social phenomena that are socially significant in some way. Phenomena may be significant because they are common, or general; they affect many people, either directly or indirectly. This quality of generality makes knowledge of such phenomena valuable. For example, suppose it can be shown that in countries where more public funds are spent on the prevention of illness (for example, by improving nutrition, restricting the consumption of alcohol and tobacco, providing children free immunization, and so on), health care costs less in the long run. Knowledge of this general pattern is valuable because it concerns almost everyone.

One of the main goals of social research is to identify general patterns and relationships. In some quarters, this objective is considered the primary goal because social research that is directed toward this end resembles research in the natural sciences. For some people, this resemblance gives social research more legitimacy, making it seem more like social physics and less like social philosophy or political ideology.

For most of its history, social research has tried to follow the lead of the natural sciences in the development of its basic research strategies and practices. These approaches to research are especially well suited for examining general patterns, and knowledge of general patterns is a highly valued form of knowledge. For example, if we know the general causes of ethnic antagonism (such as the concentration of members of an ethnic minority in lower social classes), we can work to remove these conditions from our society or at least counteract their impact and perhaps purge ourselves of serious ethnic antagonism. As more and more is learned about general patterns, the general stock of social scientific knowledge increases, and it becomes possible for social scientists to *systematize* knowledge and make connections that might otherwise not be made. For example, general knowledge about the causes of ethnic antagonism within societies might help to further understanding of nationalism and the international conflicts spawned by nationalistic sentiments.

Knowledge of general patterns is often preferred to knowledge of specific situations because every situation is unique in some way. Understanding a single situation thoroughly might be pointless if this understanding does not offer *generalizable* knowledge—if it doesn't lead to some insight relevant to other situations. From this perspective, knowing one situation thoroughly might even be considered counterproductive because we could be deceived into thinking an atypical situation offers useful general knowledge when it does not, especially if we are ignorant of *how* this situation is atypical.

Because of the general underdeveloped state of social scientific knowledge, we are not always sure which situations are typical and which are not. Furthermore, because every situation is unique in some way, it also could be argued that *every* situation is atypical and therefore untrustworthy as a guide to general knowledge. In short, when the goal is knowledge of general patterns, social researchers tend to distrust what can be learned from one or a small number of cases.

According to this reasoning, knowledge of general patterns is best achieved through examination of many comparable situations or cases, the more the better. The examination of many cases provides a way to neutral-ize each case's uniqueness in the attempt to grasp as many as possible. If a broad pattern holds across many cases, then it may reflect the operation of an underlying cause, which can be inferred from the broad pattern. (On issues of plausible inference, see Polya 1968.)

For example, while it may be possible to identify both "kind and benev-olent" dictators and democratic governments that terrorize their own citi-zens, the broad pattern across many countries is that the more democratic governments tend to brutalize their own citizens less. This correspondence between undemocratic rule and brutality, in turn, may reflect the operation of an underlying cause—the effect that the concentration of power has on the incidence of brutality. While not directly observed, this cause might be inferred from the observed correspondence between undemocratic rule and brutality. It is obvious that both brutality and benevolence exist in all coun-tries. Still, across many cases the pattern is clear, and exceptions should not blind us to the existence of patterns.

2. Testing and Refining Theories

General patterns matter not only because they affect many people but also because they are especially relevant to social theory. As described in Chapter 1, social theories come out of a huge, ongoing conversation among social scientists and other social thinkers. This conversation is an ever-changing pool of ideas, a resource to draw on and to replenish with fresh thinking.

It is also important to note that there is a virtually limitless potential for new ideas to emerge from within this pool because existing ideas can be com-bined with each other to produce new ones, and new implications can be drawn from these new combinations. Also, social theory is forever borrow-ing ideas from other pools of thinking, including philosophy, psychology, biology, and even physics, chemistry, and astronomy. The cross-fertilization of ideas is never ending.

For example, ideas about the relationship between workers and own-ers in industrial countries, especially the idea that workers are exploited, have been applied to the relations between countries. Some analyses of work emphasize the degree to which profits are based on keeping the wages of workers low, especially those with the fewest skills. From this perspective, there is natural conflict between the owners of firms and the workers: If wages are kept low, then profits will be higher; if wages are too high, profits will suffer.

This thinking has been transferred to the international arena by some theorists who assert that rich countries benefit from the poverty of poor countries (see, for example, Baran 1957; Frank 1967, 1969; Wallerstein 1974, 1979). Some theorists argue that "labor-intensive" production, which uses simpler technologies and tends to offer only very low wages, has been shifted to poor countries, while the rich countries have retained capital-intensive production, which uses advanced technology. Workers in rich countries benefit from the greater availability of high-wage jobs and from the cheap prices of the labor-intensive goods imported from low-wage countries. In this way, all the residents of rich countries—owners, managers, and workers—exploit the cheap labor of poor countries. Furthermore, 10 to 30% of the highly educated workforce in developing countries leave to reside permanently in developed countries—these outflows are commonly referred to as "brain drain" (Lowell 2001).

This argument, which is an example of the cross-fertilization of ideas, can be tested with economic data on countries. In this way, a new perspective—and a new source for testable hypotheses—is derived from existing ideas.

One of the primary goals of social research is to improve and expand the pool of ideas known as social theory by testing their implications, as in the example just presented, and to refine their power to explain. Typically, this testing is done according to the general plan of the scientific method, as described in Chapter 1. Hypotheses are derived from theories and their implications and then tested with data that bear directly on the hypothesis. Often the data are collected specifically for testing a particular hypothesis, but sometimes already existing data can be used (e.g., census and other official statistics published by government agencies).

By testing hypotheses, it is possible to improve the overall quality of the pool of ideas. Ideas that fail to receive support gradually lose their appeal, while those that are supported more consistently gain greater stature in the pool. While a single unsuccessful hypothesis rarely kills a theory, over time, unsupported ideas fade from current thinking. It is important to identify the most fertile and powerful ways of thinking and to assess different ideas, comparing them as explanations of general patterns and features of social life. Testing theories can also serve to refine them. By working through the implications of a theory and then testing this refinement, it is possible to progressively improve and elaborate a set of ideas.

It is possible to conduct social research without paying much direct attention to this pool of ideas. There are many aspects of social life and many different social worlds that attract the attention of social researchers, independent of the relevance of these phenomena to social theory. After all, social researchers, like most social beings, are curious about social life. However, improving the quality of social theory is an important goal because this pool of ideas structures much thinking and much telling about society, by social scientists and others.

3. Making Predictions

While social researchers use theories to derive "predictions" (hypotheses) about what they expect to find in a set of data (for example, a survey), they also use accumulated social scientific knowledge to make predictions about the future and other novel situations. It is this second meaning of the word **prediction** that is intended when we say that "making predictions" is one of the main goals of social research.

Consider an example of this second kind of prediction: Research indicates that ethnic conflict tends to increase when the supply of economic rewards and resources (jobs and promotions, for instance) decreases. Thus, a social scientist would predict increased ethnic tensions in an ethnically diverse country that has just experienced a serious economic downturn. Prediction is often considered the highest goal of science: We accumulate knowledge so that we can anticipate things to come. We make predictions based on what we know. Two kinds of knowledge help us make predictions: knowledge of history (past successes and failures) and knowledge of general patterns.

Knowledge of history helps us to avoid repeating mistakes. Understanding of the stock market crash of 1929 and the ensuing Great Depression, for example, has motivated our economic and political elites to attempt to moderate the violent swings of market-oriented economic life. The 1929 crash provides clear lessons about the need that arises for a balance between the free play of markets (for example, stock markets) and regulations imposed through hierarchies (for example, the Securities Exchange Commission). The prediction here is that unregulated markets will fluctuate widely and may even self-destruct.

The second kind of knowledge, understanding of general patterns, is useful for making projections about likely future events. For example, we know that certain types of crime (drug dealing, for instance) increase when legitimate economic opportunities decrease. We can use this knowledge, combined with assumptions about other causal factors, to extrapolate future crime rates given different employment conditions. If current trends toward higher production levels with fewer workers continue, it would seem reasonable to anticipate increases in certain types of crimes. Projections of this type are quite common and sometimes can be surprisingly accurate. It is much easier to predict a rate (the rate of homelessness, the rate of drug-related crimes, the rate of teenage pregnancy, and so on) than it is to predict what any single individual might do. For example, it is relatively easy to formulate a reasonable estimate of the number of people who will be murdered in Los Angeles next year, but it is far more difficult, if not impossible, to predict very much about which ones, among the millions, will be the perpetrators or the victims.

While making predictions is one of the most important goals of social research, it's not always the case that prediction and understanding go hand-in-hand. Sometimes our predictions are quite accurate, but our understanding of the actual underlying processes that produce outcomes is incomplete or simply erroneous. For example, the causes of drug addiction are quite complex, as is the process of becoming an addict. However, it is a relatively simple matter to forecast levels of drug addiction in major U.S. cities based on knowledge of the social conditions that tend to favor high levels of addiction.

Here is a simpler example: It might be possible to predict with fair precision how many murders will be committed next year based on the number of automobiles stolen this year. However, that doesn't mean that some fixed percentage of the people who steal cars one year graduate to homicide the next. More than likely, the two rates respond to the same causal conditions (such as unemployment or the formation of street gangs), but at different speeds.

Predicting rates is much easier than predicting specific events. The kinds of things many social scientists would like to be able to predict—namely, the occurrence of specific events at specific points in time in the future—are simply beyond the scope of any science. For example, many social scientists chastised themselves for being unable to predict the fall of communism in the countries of Eastern Europe in 1989. Their failure to predict these dramatic events made them feel inadequate. However, no science, social or otherwise, could possibly achieve this kind of prediction—the timing of specific future social or natural events. The key to understanding this is the simple fact that it is very difficult to predict specific future events.

Consider the natural science of meteorology. At best, this science can predict the probability of rain over the next several days. But what if we want to know when it will start, when it will stop, and how much it will rain? It should be possible to predict these things. After all, no human intervention, interpretation, or subjectivity is involved, only measurable, physical qualities such as temperature, wind direction and velocity, moisture, and so on. But the natural science of meteorology cannot offer this precision; it simply cannot predict specific events. Likewise, meteorology cannot predict which day or even which year a hurricane will again sweep across Louisiana. Even when there is a hurricane in the middle of the Gulf of Mexico, it's very difficult to tell which, if any, coastal area it will demolish.

In a similar manner, no social scientists could predict, say in 1980, that communism would fall in Eastern Europe in 1989. For many years, some social scientists claimed that communism was likely to fall in the near future. Even in 1980, a few would have been willing to attach specific probabilities to specific years, say a 40% chance of falling by the year 2000. In addition, social scientists have debated for many decades, and continue to debate, the possibility of Korean reunification and its economic and social consequences. Some argue that the process of reunification has already begun, but at a snail's pace—South Korea recognizes that its economy would not be able to handle a rapid reunification process such as that seen in Germany. Another example is the Communist Party of China that currently dominates the Chinese government. Will it retain its hold on power with the growth of capitalist markets? If not, how and when will a shake-up of this magnitude occur? Social science cannot provide a definitive answer. Social science is not inadequate but appears so because of the specificity of the predictions we desire.

Will a new religious movement, emphasizing conservative values, the sanctity of marriage and the family, self-reliance, and the rejection of white culture and its materialism sweep inner-city neighborhoods next year? Sometime in the next 10 years? Will wild spasms of nihilistic self-destructiveness sweep through teenage populations in the predominantly white suburbs of major U.S. cities in the year 2022? It would certainly be impressive to be able to predict events such as these, but it is outside the scope of any science to offer this degree of specificity. At best, social researchers can make broad projections of possibilities using their knowledge of general patterns.

4. Interpreting Culturally or Historically Significant Phenomena

Knowledge of general patterns is not the only kind of valuable knowledge, however, especially when it comes to understanding social life. In the social sciences, knowledge of specific situations and events, even if they are atypical (and usually *because* they are atypical; see Dumont 1970), is also highly valued. The significance of most historical phenomena derives from their atypicality—the fact that they are dramatically nonroutine—and from their impact on who we are today.

For example, many social researchers address important historical events such as the Fall of the Roman Empire or the U.S. Civil War. We care about these events and their interpretation because of their relevance for understanding our current situation—how we got to where we are. We are fascinated by the U.S. Civil War not because we expect it to be repeated, but because of its powerful impact on current race relations and the structure of power (who dominates whom and how they do it) in the United States today.

Other phenomena are studied not because of their *historical* relevance to current society but because of their *cultural* relevance. The bits and pieces of African cultures that slaves brought with them, for example, have had a powerful impact on the course and development of American culture. Other phenomena may be culturally significant because of what they may portend. The heavy metal rock culture of the late 20th century, for example, could signal future directions of American culture.

Often there is competition among social researchers to establish the "accepted" interpretation of significant historical or cultural phenomena. For example, social researchers have examined the events that led to the fall of the communist regimes (that is, of the power cliques that controlled the centrally planned economies of Eastern Europe). These events have been addressed because they are historically and culturally relevant and significant, and different researchers have different ideas about how and why these regimes fell. The interpretation of these events that prevails, especially the interpretation of the fall of the communist regime in the former Soviet Union, has important implications for how social scientists, policymakers, and the public think about "communism" and the possibility of centralized control of national economies. It is not always the case that a single interpretation prevails, not even in the very long run. The struggle to have an interpretation accepted as "correct" can extend over generations of scholarship and stretch over centuries of debate.

Social researchers who study general phenomena usually do not address specific events or their interpretation. They would rather know about a general pattern (for example, the covariation across countries between the extent to which democratic procedures are practiced, on the one hand, and the level of political repression, on the other) than about a specific set of events (for example, the detention of U.S. citizens deemed "enemy combatants" by the U.S. government following al-Qaeda's coordinated attacks on the United States on September 11, 2001). It is difficult, however, to address many of the things that interest social researchers and their audiences with research focusing only on that which is general.

For instance, social researchers sometimes address the subjectivity or consciousness of their subjects. There are many possible interpretations for any set of events: Did the Nazis intend to exterminate the Jews all along, or did they adopt this policy in response to the conditions of World War II? Was it necessary for Stalin to terrorize Soviet citizens in order to forge state socialism? Was he insecure and paranoid, or was terrorism simply an effective way of maintaining his personal power? In both episodes of massive inhumanity, it is not enough to know that millions of people died or how they died. We want to know *why*. However, the study of general patterns typically does not shed light on issues related to the consciousness of their research subjects.

5. Exploring Diversity

Another main goal of social research is to explore and comprehend the social diversity that surrounds us. While this goal may seem similar to the goal of identifying general patterns, and does complement it in some respects, it is quite different. For example, one general pattern is that educational and economic development tend to go together; countries with better schools and higher literacy rates tend to be richer. However, the fact that a general pattern exists doesn't mean that there aren't important and interesting exceptions. Some poor countries have well-developed educational systems and very high literacy rates—for example, Sri Lanka has a literacy rate of over 90% (United Nations Educational Scientific and Cultural Organization [UNESCO] 2010). Meanwhile, some rich countries have poorly developed schools and surprisingly low levels of literacy—for example, Saudi Arabia with a literacy rate of 85% (UNESCO 2010).

Exploring diversity often means that the researcher ignores dominant patterns and focuses on the variety of circumstances that exist. How is living in a poor country with a high level of literacy different from living in other poor countries? What happens when a low level of educational development or literacy is combined with wealth? In short, the study of diversity avoids an exclusive focus on what is most common.

More generally, exploring diversity furthers an understanding and appreciation of **sociodiversity,** a concept that parallels the ecological notion of biodiversity. We protect biological species close to extinction because we are concerned about biodiversity. The human species dominates all others, so much so that many species are threatened with extinction. Many environmentalists see declining biodiversity as an indicator of the degree to which human societies have threatened the self-regulating natural order of the biosphere we call Earth.

People tend to be less concerned about sociodiversity. Anthropologists have documented dramatic declines in sociodiversity. They have studied societies in all corners of the world over much of the last century. As the reach of global economic and political forces has expanded, these forces have more deeply penetrated many parts of the world. Small-scale societies that were once more or less external to the international system have been incorporated into it. One direct consequence of this incorporation is the disappearance of many cultural forms and practices and the transmutation of countless others.

Sociodiversity at the level of whole societies has declined dramatically. More and more, there is a single, dominant global culture.

A simple example of this change is the decline in arranged marriages and the increasing importance of romantic involvement in determining one's spouse in many cultures. For example, the percentage of arranged marriages in Japan fell from 63% to 7% between 1955 and 1998 (Retherford, Ogawa, and Matsukura 2001). From the perspective of the contemporary United States, this shift seems natural and inevitable, and arranged marriages seem quaint. But in fact, arranged marriages have been an important source of social order and stability in many societies, joining different families together in ways that undercut social conflict.

It is important to understand societies that differ from our own because they show alternative ways of addressing common social issues and questions. For example, societies cope with scarcity in different ways. In some societies, great feasts involving entire communities are a routine part of social life. These feasts not only provide protection against starvation, especially during lean years, but they also increase the strength of the social bonds joining members of communities. There has also been remarkable diversity among human societies in how basic arrangements such as the family, kinship, the gender division of labor, and sexuality have been structured or accomplished.

Of course, great social diversity exists today, despite the impact of that giant steamroller, the world capitalist economy, on sociodiversity worldwide. There are many social worlds (and social worlds within social worlds—see Chapter 1) in all parts of all countries. There is great diversity even in the most advanced countries—those most closely joined by the world economy. Often, much diversity is simply unacknowledged or ignored. Sometimes assumptions are made about sameness (for example, that people living in inner-city tenements think or act in certain ways) that turn out to be false when the diversity within a social category is examined closely. Also, people often respond to sameness and uniformity by crafting new ways of differentiating themselves from others. Sometimes these efforts lead only to new fads; other times they culminate in entirely new social formations (as when a religious cult withdraws from mainstream society).

At times social researchers start out not knowing if studying a new case or situation will offer useful knowledge of diversity. They study it in order to make this assessment. For example, some immigrant groups are very successful economically. It is important to find out how and why they achieve economic success in order to determine if this knowledge is relevant to other groups (or, more generally, to U.S. immigration policy). It may be that their success is due to circumstances that cannot be duplicated elsewhere, but there is no way to know this without studying the specific causes of their success. Here is another example: Catholic nuns tend to live longer and healthier lives than most other groups, religious or secular. We may not have to live like nuns to match their longevity, but we won't know this unless we study them and find out why they live longer, healthier lives (see Snowdon 2001). Whether or not the study of diverse groups offers knowledge that is useful, research on diverse groups contributes to social scientists' understanding of social life in general.

6. Giving Voice

Sometimes the goal of exploring diversity is taken one step further, and the researcher studies a group not simply to learn more about it but also to contribute to its having an expressed voice in society. In research of this type, the objective is twofold: to increase the stock of knowledge about different types, forms, and processes of social life, and to tell the story of a specific group, usually in a way that enhances its visibility in society.

Very often the groups studied in this way are marginal groups, outside the social mainstream (for example, the homeless, the poor, minority groups, immigrant groups, people labeled mentally ill, and so on). This approach to social research asserts that every group in society has a "story to tell." Some groups (for example, professionals, middle-class white families, and so on) are presented in the mainstream beliefs and values of society as the way life is and should be. Many social researchers believe it is their responsibility to identify excluded groups and tell their stories. By giving them voice, researchers often are able to show that groups considered deviant or different in some way do not deviate as much as most people think. For example, a common finding is that even people in the most dire and difficult circumstances strive for dignity.

While social researchers who do this kind of research often focus on marginal or deviant groups, this emphasis is neither necessary nor universal. Mary Blair-Loy (2003), for example, studied highly privileged women who were devoted to either their high-powered careers or their family life. She documented the balance between the level of commitment to work life expected of executives (work devotion schema) and the level of commitment to home life expected of mothers (family devotion schema). In both schemas, the expected level of commitment is so high that other obligations are to be considered secondary, never equal.

In research of this type, social theories may help the researcher identify groups without voice and may help explain why these groups lack voice, but theory is not considered a source of hypotheses to be tested. When the goal of a project is to give voice to research subjects, it is important for the researcher to try to see the world through their eyes, to understand their social world as they do. Thus, researchers may have to relinquish or "unlearn" a lot of what they know in order to construct valid representations of their research subjects—representations that embody their subjects' voice.

To achieve this level of in-depth understanding, researchers must gain access to the everyday world of the group. It might be necessary, for example, to live with the members of a marginalized group for extended periods of time and gradually win their confidence (see, for example, Pattillo 2008). When the researcher feels he or she knows enough to tell their stories, one goal of the telling might be to try to minimize, as much as possible, the voice of the researcher. *Minimizing the voice of the researcher* is viewed as an ethical imperative by some social researchers. The privileging of a researcher's voice over the research subjects' voices is seen as another source of marginalization for the individuals or groups being researched (see Chapter 4 for additional discussion).

Some researchers, for example, use photographs of the social group of interest. The researchers may even hand the camera over directly to the subject (a method known as auto-photography or self-directed photography, and pioneered by social psychologist Robert Ziller [1990]). The degree to which the research subjects' voices are filtered in the process of constructing the final representation varies greatly among researchers. In-depth interviews may be conducted, the subjects may be asked to interpret what they see in the photo images, or may be asked to actually write the captions for the pictures (for photography examples, see Harper 2001; Heath and Cleaver 2004; for a video example, see Holliday 2004). A variety of systematic techniques have been developed by social researchers to facilitate this type of in-depth knowledge and understanding (see Banks 2001; Emmison and Smith 2000; Knowles and Sweetman 2004).

Some social researchers consider research that seeks to give voice as activist or advocacy research and therefore doubt its objectivity. How can research that seeks to enhance the visibility of a marginal group be conducted in a neutral way? Isn't it inevitable that researchers will favor the positive aspects of marginal groups in their representations of these groups? In reality, most social researchers are committed to objectivity and neutrality in much the same way that most journalists are. However, some common cautions are as follows:

- Don't whitewash.
- Present the good and the bad.

- Be wary of how people rationalize what they do.
- Maintain skepticism.
- Examine the same events from several points of view.

Giving voice does not necessarily entail advocacy. Still, social researchers who seek to give voice must be vigilant in their efforts to represent their groups appropriately. Most social worlds, marginal or mainstream, are quite complex, and advocacy typically oversimplifies. Generally, it is not difficult to spot a one-sided representation or to recognize research that merely advocates for a group.

Those who argue that giving voice is not a valid research objective should acknowledge that almost *all* research gives voice in the sense that it enhances the visibility of the thing studied and represents the viewpoint of some group or groups, even implicitly. Even a study of the general social conditions that favor stable democracy across many countries enhances the importance and visibility of stable democracy as a desirable condition simply by studying it. Research that seeks to give voice is clear in its objectives.

7. Advancing New Theories

Many different kinds of social research advance social theory, even research that seeks to interpret historical or cultural significance. The testing of theories (goal 2) also advances theory in the limited sense that these tests indicate which theoretical ideas have more support as explanations of social life. The goal of advancing theory as it is used here, however, involves more than assessing and refining existing ideas. When theory is advanced, ideas are elaborated in some new way. To advance theory, it is not necessary to come up with a complete model of society or even some part of it. The development of new ideas and new concepts is the most that research seeking to advance theory usually accomplishes.

Theory testing is primarily deductive. Hypotheses about social life are derived from theories and then tested with relevant data. The researcher then draws the implications of the results of these tests for theory (see Chapter 1). Research that *advances* theory, by contrast, is usually described as having an inductive quality. On the basis of new evidence, the researcher develops a new theoretical concept or new relationship, or advances understanding of existing ones.

Not only does the researcher use data to illustrate the new concept, but he or she may also elucidate the relation of the new concept to existing concepts. Two researchers, for example, developed the concept of "interactional vandalism" to describe the violations of conversational norms that male street vendors, scavengers, or panhandlers commit when they "cat-call" women walking by their locations (Duneier and Molotch 1999). When developing a new concept, it is necessary to distinguish it from related concepts and to explain its logical and causal connections to others. The concept of the "sticky floor" was developed because of the great deal of attention given to the idea that women employees hit a glass ceiling. Catherine Berheide (1992) did not see women "maxing out" when she looked at low-wage government employees; rather, she saw very little job mobility of any kind.

Many theoretical advances come from detailed, in-depth examination of cases. Exploring diversity, for example, may lead to the discovery of new social arrangements and practices. The study of behavior of the groupies who surround certain kinds of rock bands, for example, might lead to new insights about the importance of rituals in contemporary social life. The mere existence of novel phenomena also may challenge conventional thinking. Existing theories may argue that certain ways of doing things or certain behaviors are incompatible, that it has to be either one or the other. The discovery that "incompatible" elements can coexist calls such theories into question and may force researchers to theorize about how such logically incompatible things can exist simultaneously.

Research that gives voice also may lead to theoretical advances because such research often leaves existing theories behind in its attempt to see social worlds through the eyes of their members. This openness to the viewpoints of low-status and low-visibility people may expose the inadequacies of existing theoretical perspectives. Finally, work that seeks to interpret cultural or historical significance may also advance theory because it, too, is based on detailed analyses of cases. For example, in-depth research on the Iranian Revolution of 1979 could lead to new insights on the importance of the interplay of religious ideology and political organization in the large-scale political changes occurring internationally.

Research that seeks to identify general patterns across many cases is usually associated with the goal of testing theory (via hypotheses), and less often with the goal of advancing theory, even though, as already noted, testing theory does refine it. However, the analysis of broad patterns can lead to theoretical advances (see, for example, Esping-Andersen 1990; Evans 1995; Rueschemeyer, Stephens, and Stephens 1992; Tilly 1984; Walby 2008). Sometimes hypotheses fail or are only partially supported, and researchers generally want to know why. They may study additional patterns in their data to find out why the theory they are testing does not fit the data well.

For example, using a generally accepted theory as a starting point, a researcher might test the hypothesis that richer countries tend to have a more equal distribution of income (that is, within their own borders) than poorer countries. Analysis of relevant data might show that while this pattern holds for most countries, among the richest 15 or so it does not—they might all have roughly the same degree of equality. This finding might lead the researcher to speculate about the newly discovered pattern: Why is it that greater wealth does not lead to greater equality once a certain level of economic development is reached? A variety of factors might be examined in the effort to account for this pattern. This search might lead to the identification of causal factors that suggest fundamental revision of the theory used to generate the initial hypothesis about patterns of income inequality.

While the deduction-versus-induction distinction is a simple and appealing way to differentiate types of social research, most research includes elements of both (see Stinchcombe 1968). For this reason, we argue that all research involves **retroduction**—a term developed by philosophers of science to describe the interplay of induction and deduction (Hanson 1958). It is impossible to do research without some initial ideas, even if the goal is to give voice to research subjects. Thus, almost all research has at least an element of deduction. Similarly, almost all research can be used to advance theory in some way. After all, social theories are vague and imprecise. Every test of a theory refines it, whether or not the test is supportive. Social research involves retroduction because there is typically a dialogue of ideas and evidence. The interaction of ideas and evidence culminates in theoretically based descriptions of social life (that is, social scientific representations) and in evidence-based elaborations of social theory.

The Link Between Goals and Strategies

It is clear that no researcher can tackle all seven goals at once, at least not in the same study. A classic view of science says that it is a violation of the scientific method to try to advance theory (goal 7) and test theory (goal 2) in the same study. Data used to generate a new theory should not also be used to test it. Most of the tensions between goals, however, revolve around practical issues.

It is difficult, for example, to examine many cases so that a general pattern can be identified (goal 1) and also study one case in depth so that its specific character can be understood (goal 6). Even when it is possible to do both, they don't always mix well. What if the findings from the in-depth study of one or a small number of cases contradict the results of the analysis of broad patterns across many cases? Which finding should the social researcher trust? However, both kinds of research are important because both help social researchers find order in complexity, order that they can represent in their reports. The first type of research helps social researchers identify what is general across many cases—to discern the underlying order that exists amid great variation; the other helps them comprehend the complexity of specific situations directly.

Many different strategies of social research have emerged to accommodate its multiple and competing goals. As already noted, a research strategy is best understood as a pairing of a general research objective and a specific research method. Each strategy constitutes a way of linking ideas and evidence to produce a representation of some aspect of social life. Research strategies structure how social researchers collect data and make sense of what they collect. Even though some strategies are clearly more popular than others, there is no single "correct" way of conducting social research.

While there are many different strategies of social research, three very broad approaches are emphasized here:

- The use of qualitative methods to study commonalities
- The use of comparative methods to study diversity
- The use of quantitative methods to study relationships among variables

These three strategies are discussed in detail in Part II of this book because they represent three common but different ways of carrying on a dialogue between ideas and evidence. The selection of these three strategies does not imply that other strategies are not important or do not exist. Indeed, there are plenty of qualitative researchers who study diversity, and there are many researchers who use comparative methods to study commonalities. The pairings emphasized here (qualitative methods with commonalities, comparative methods with diversity, and quantitative methods with relationships among variables) have been selected because they offer the best illustration of the core features of different methods. They also provide a strong testament to the unity and diversity of social research.

Qualitative researchers interested in commonalities examine many aspects or features of a relatively small number of cases in depth. A study of how women without partners decide to become mothers is an example of a qualitative study (Hertz 2006).

Comparative researchers interested in diversity study a moderate number of cases in a comprehensive manner, though not in as much detail as in most qualitative research. A study of the effects of decentralization on the redistribution of political power of regional and local governments in Latin America is an example of a comparative study (Falleti 2005).

Quantitative researchers interested in how variables covary across cases typically examine a relatively small number of features (that is, variables) across many, many cases. A study of the rate of invalid or missing ballot votes cast by different racial groups is an example of a quantitative study (Herron and Sekhon 2003).

These three strategies can be plotted in two dimensions showing the relation between the number of cases studied and the number of aspects of cases studied (see Figure 2.1). The figure illustrates the trade-off between studying cases and studying aspects of cases, or variables. Because the energies and capacities of researchers are limited, they often must choose between focusing on cases as wholes (qualitative research on commonalities), focusing on variables (quantitative research on relationships among variables), or balancing the two in some way (comparative research on diversity). It is possible to gain a detailed, in-depth knowledge of a small number of cases, to learn a moderate amount about an intermediate number of cases, or to focus on limited information from a large number of cases.

Figure 2.1   Cases, Aspects of Cases, and Research Strategies*

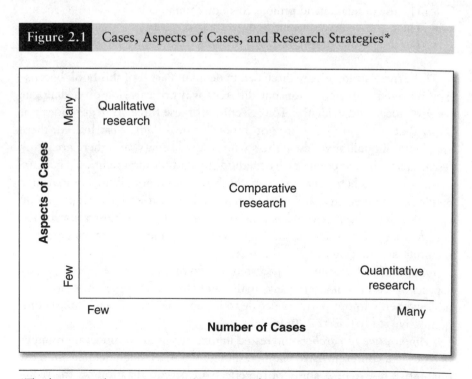

---

*The three research strategies are qualitative research on commonalities, comparative research on diversity, and quantitative research on relationships between variables.

The trade-off between number of cases and number of features does not concern how much information social researchers can collect. After all, social researchers can collect volumes of information on each of thousands and thousands of cases. The Bureau of Labor Statistics collects detailed information on millions of companies and individuals every year. Rather, the trade-off does concern how much information social researchers—or anyone else, for that matter—can study, how the information is studied (for example, is each case examined individually?), and the relevance of the information to a particular research question.

Imagine trying to grasp the nature of informal, interpersonal networks in each of the top 500 U.S. corporations. It might take years to unravel the informal networks of a single corporation. A social researcher can gain this kind of intimate knowledge about only a relatively small number of cases.

However, it might be possible to survey these same 500 corporations and find out basic information such as total assets, profitability, number of employees, and even the degree to which the board members of these corporations have intertwined social and professional networks. The information from this survey would not add up to intimate knowledge of each of the 500 corporations, but it could be used to examine relations among variables characterizing them. For example, does large corporate size pose an obstacle to profitability? Does the social network of board members shape CEO compensation? Answering these questions does not require in-depth knowledge of the workings of any of the 500 corporations. Of course, such in-depth knowledge would improve the analysis of the evidence on size and profitability or networks and compensation, as well as the representation of the results, but it is not essential to the study of the general relationship among these sets of variables.

It is important to note that Figure 2.1 represents the *tendencies* of these three strategies and does not establish absolute boundaries around the strategies in any way. Some quantitative researchers, for example, collect hundreds of variables on thousands of cases when they conduct research, and they try to squeeze as much of this information as possible into the representations they construct. Of course, these representations are still "big picture" representations of broad patterns of covariation across cases. Likewise, there are some qualitative researchers who work in teams to increase the number of cases they study. Thus, Figure 2.1 should be viewed as an attempt to depict the nature of the typical representations that result from these three common strategies.

Table 2.1 maps the relation between these three strategies and the seven goals of social research discussed in this chapter. The column headings of the

| Table 2.1 | The Goals and Strategies of Social Research* | | |

	Qualitative Research	Comparative Research	Quantitative Research
1. Identifying broad patterns		secondary	primary
2. Testing/refining theory	secondary	secondary	primary
3. Making predictions		secondary	primary
4. Interpreting significance	primary	primary	
5. Exploring diversity	secondary	primary	secondary
6. Giving voice	primary		
7. Advancing new theories	primary	primary	secondary

*The three research strategies are qualitative research on commonalities, comparative research on diversity, and quantitative research on relationships between variables. *Primary* indicates that the strategy is a very common way of achieving a goal; *secondary* indicates that the strategy is sometimes used to achieve a goal.

table are the three general strategies; the rows are the seven goals. The table shows the fit between goals and strategies, focusing on the three strategies emphasized here.

The three different strategies range from intensive (qualitative study of commonalities) to comprehensive (comparative study of diversity) to extensive (quantitative study of the relationships among variables) in their approach to cases. An intensive approach is best suited for goals that involve close attention to specific cases; a comprehensive approach is best suited for goals that involve examination of patterns of similarities and differences across a moderate number of cases; and an extensive approach is best suited for goals that involve knowledge of broad patterns across many cases. It is important to remember, however, that the strategies examined here and in Part II are three among many different strategies of social research.

The goal of identifying general patterns (Goal 1), for example, is best served by the quantitative approach, but it is also served by the comparative approach, though maybe not quite as well. (Thus, the primary strategy for identifying general patterns is the quantitative approach; a secondary strategy is the comparative approach.) A pattern is not general if it does not embrace many cases. Also, most statements about general patterns involve variables. Both of these features of general patterns point to the quantitative approach as the primary strategy. The goal of testing theory (goal 2) is also served by quantitative and comparative strategies. Most theories, however, are composed of abstract concepts that are linked to each other and thus concern general relationships that can be viewed across many cases or across a range of cases. Sometimes a single case will offer a critical test of a theory, but this use of individual cases is relatively rare (Eckstein 1992). Moreover, from the perspective of most theories, single cases are unique and therefore relatively unreliable as raw material for testing theories. Likewise, the most appropriate strategy for making predictions is the quantitative approach. Most predictions involve extrapolations based on many cases—the more the better, as long as they are appropriate and relevant to the substance of the prediction.

The goals of interpreting significance and giving voice, by contrast, are best served by strategies that examine a small number of cases (often a single historical episode or a single group) in depth—the qualitative approach. Similarly, the best raw material for advancing theory is often provided by strategies that focus on cases, which is the special forte of qualitative research and one of the strong points of comparative research. However, all research, including quantitative research, can advance theory. Finally, the goal of exploring diversity is best served by the comparative approach. However, because qualitative and quantitative research contributes to knowledge of diverse groups, they, too, serve this goal.

The Social Nature of Social Research

Imagine a chart comparable to Table 2.1 constructed for a natural science such as chemistry or physics. Goals 4 and 6 would not exist—at least, they would not be considered main goals—and Goal 5 would concern only a handful of researchers. The remaining four goals (1, 2, 3, and 7) are all well served by the quantitative approach—a strategy that addresses general relations between measurable aspects of the things social scientists study. Goals 4, 5, and 6 reflect the social nature of social research. It is also these goals that sometimes make social scientists seem "unscientific," especially to scientists, social or otherwise, strongly committed to the other goals.

Consider again the goal of giving voice. Why should any particular voice be privileged by social research? Why should a social researcher try to enhance a particular group's visibility in society? Who cares whether people who are not marginal can understand those who are? Consider the goal of interpreting cultural or historical significance. How do we know that the social researcher is not trying to whitewash horrific events, or perhaps make the members of a truly destructive group look like victims of oppression? Finally, consider the goal of exploring diversity. By highlighting diversity, a social researcher may glorify it. Or it may be that too much focus on differences in society is detrimental. Might it be better to emphasize the things that we have in common, what most members of society share?

These aspects of social research make it an easy target of criticism. However, it is important to understand that no social research exists in a vacuum. Research on general patterns, for example, may simply privilege what is normative. All social research gives voice in one way or another to some aspect of society. Similarly, research that tests theories has implications for how we think about human nature, social organization, and the different kinds of social worlds that are possible to construct. In fact, because of its social nature, all social research has implications for the interpretation and understanding of anything that people do or refuse to do together. Social research is inescapably social in its implications. For this reason, social researchers cannot escape bias, regardless of which goals motivate research.

3

The Process of Social Research

Ideas and Evidence

Introduction

Social research, in simplest terms, involves a dialogue between ideas and evidence. **Ideas** help social researchers make sense of evidence, and researchers use **evidence** to extend, revise, and test ideas. The end result of this dialogue is a representation of social life—evidence that has been shaped and reshaped by ideas, presented along with the thinking that guided the construction of the representation. This chapter focuses on how the dialogue of ideas and evidence is structured and how it is conducted—how ideas shape the understanding of evidence and how evidence affects ideas.

A major part in the dialogue between ideas and evidence is devoted to the analysis of the phenomena the researcher is studying. The term *phenomena* simply refers to facts or events. **Analysis** means breaking phenomena into their constituent parts and viewing them in relation to the whole they form. A researcher conducting an analysis of a revolutionary movement, for example, might try to dissect it in a way that illuminates all the different forces that combined to make the movement (see Jenkins 1994). This analysis would examine not only the social groups that joined the movement (for example, peasants, workers, soldiers, intelligentsia, and so on) but also the social groups that did not, the political and social context, the movement's ideology, and other factors that contributed to its formation.

In essence, the analysis of a revolutionary movement involves breaking it into its key component parts so that it no longer appears to be an amorphous, teeming mass of revolutionaries, but rather can be seen as a combination of key elements and conditions. These elements can be viewed in isolation from one another, and they also can be understood in the context of the other parts. For example, the ideology of the movement could be examined both in isolation (What are the key ideas behind the movement?) and in the context of the major groups involved in the movement (How do these key ideas resonate with the concerns of each group within the movement?). This understanding of the term *analysis*—studying something in terms of its aspects or parts—is necessary background for the concept of *analytic frame*, a key focus of this chapter.

The analysis of social phenomena, while important, is only part of the dialogue of ideas and evidence. The other important part involves the synthesis of evidence. **Synthesis** is the counterpart to analysis. Analysis involves breaking things into parts (in the example above, the constituent elements of a revolutionary movement); synthesis involves putting pieces together to make sense of them. When social researchers synthesize evidence, they form a coherent whole out of separate parts, making connections among elements that, at first glance, may seem unrelated. These connections may lead to further insights into the phenomena they are trying to understand. For example, based on a preliminary examination of evidence from a college sorority, a researcher might develop an initial portrait of it as a type of self-help group. This portrait might be based on interviews with members or observation of the internal support system of the sorority as shown at the start of meetings, where members may be invited to share feelings and personal news, while others actively listen and engage in helping other members as needed. This preliminary synthesis of evidence, in turn, would illuminate other aspects of the sorority, which could then be targeted for further study—for example, how competition between members is contained.

The process of synthesizing evidence is an important part of the dialogue of ideas and evidence. In this chapter, synthesis is presented as a process of forming evidence-based images of the research subject. In social research, representations of social life emerge from the interplay between analytic frames (which are derived from ideas) and images (which are derived from evidence).

It is important to examine the different ways the dialogue of ideas and evidence can take shape, because the character of the representations of social life that result from different ways of practicing social research is strongly influenced by the nature of this dialogue. For example, the representation of what it is like to be a private in the U.S. Army constructed by a researcher who lives with a group of five privates is likely to differ substantially from the representation constructed by a researcher who uses a questionnaire to survey a random sample of 1,000 privates. In both types of research, there is a dialogue of ideas and evidence, but the two dialogues differ dramatically.

This chapter explains how the dialogue of ideas and evidence in social research is carried on through analytic frames and images. First, the chapter sketches a simple model of the process of social research as a way to introduce its four basic building blocks:

- Ideas
- Analytic frames
- Evidence
- Images

This sketch is presented as a map of the ensuing discussion; it is not a full elaboration of the main points of the chapter. Subsequent sections discuss these four building blocks in detail, especially the two that require the greatest clarification: images and analytic frames. The last section of the chapter addresses differences in the interplay of images and analytic frames across three common strategies of social research: the qualitative study of commonalities, the comparative study of diversity, and the quantitative study of covariation.

The Interpretive Model of Social Research

Figure 3.1 shows the understanding of the process of social research that guides the discussion in this chapter. At the base of the model is evidence/data. *Evidence* is the everyday word for what social scientists mean when they use the term *data*. Social researchers use a lot of evidence. Studies are often based on the examination of detailed, in-depth information on a small number of cases (as in the qualitative study of commonalities), a moderate amount of information on an intermediate number of cases (as in the comparative study of diversity), or a limited amount of information on many cases (as in the quantitative study of covariation). Ideas are at the top of the model. *Idea* is the everyday word used for what social scientists call "social theory." Social researchers draw on a pool of ideas when they conduct research, to help them make sense of the things they study.

Figure 3.1   The Interpretive Model

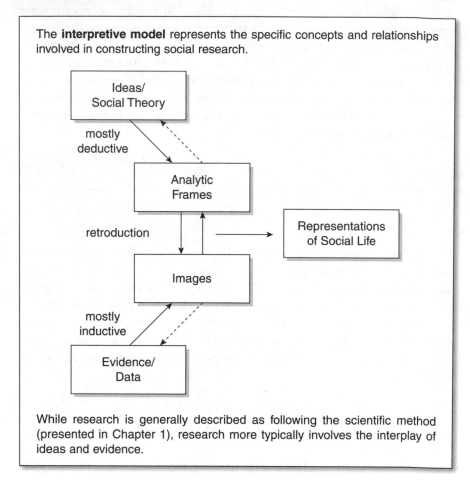

The **interpretive model** represents the specific concepts and relationships involved in constructing social research.

Ideas/
Social Theory

mostly
deductive

Analytic
Frames

retroduction

Representations
of Social Life

Images

mostly
inductive

Evidence/
Data

While research is generally described as following the scientific method (presented in Chapter 1), research more typically involves the interplay of ideas and evidence.

Ideas and evidence interact through images and analytic frames, as shown in Figure 3.1. Think of an **analytic frame** as a detailed sketch or outline of an idea about some phenomena. Ideas are elaborated through analytic frames. Frames constitute ways of seeing the things they elaborate.

An analytic frame might be used, for example, to articulate the *idea* of a table. People can recognize a table when they see one, even though tables differ greatly, because they have an implicit analytic frame for tables. They understand the category "table," and they can describe how tables vary—in size, color, material used to construct them, shape of surface, and so on.

The analytic frames of everyday life—like the one for table—are implicit; only rarely are they fully articulated or contested. The analytic frames that guide social research, however, are carefully specified and debated because social researchers must be precise when they define and characterize the phenomena they study. Much of the work of social research centers on debating, clarifying, and using analytic frames to represent social life. These frames make it possible for social researchers to see social phenomena in ways that enhance their relevance to social theory. The analytic frame for revolutionary movements sketched in the introduction to this chapter, for example, provides a brief specification of some of its key components—the different groups involved, their ideologies, and other elements.

Images, by contrast, are built up from evidence. Based on observations of workers who run their machines so fast that they break, for example, a researcher might develop an image of these workers as troublemakers or insurgents who subvert production while appearing to work hard. To construct images, researchers synthesize evidence—they connect different parts or elements of the things they study in order to create more complete portraits based on some idea of how these parts are or could be related. Initial images suggest new data collection paths. For instance, the researcher working on an image of workers as insurgents who break machines to disrupt work might study the timing of these disruptions. At what points in the workday, the workweek, or even in the life of a labor contract do these production breakdowns occur? Initial images lead to the collection of more evidence and to a progressive refinement of the image. This image of some workers as insurgents, for example, might lead the researcher to look for other manifestations of subtle subversions of production in this work setting. In short, building images is primarily *inductive.*

This process of synthesizing an image from evidence and refining it goes hand-in-hand with the process of analyzing the evidence using analytic frames. In essence, by articulating ideas, analytic frames direct an investigation down specific data collection paths. Suppose, for example, in the research just sketched, the researcher had started with an analytic frame for "resistance" that specified a variety of different conditions for its appearance (perhaps drawing on the ideas of Burawoy 1979 or Hodson 2001). This frame might prompt the researcher to consider the subversion of production as a possible form of resistance. The evidence collected, along with other data, might support the image of some workers as insurgents. Once images are built up from evidence, they may confirm or amend an analytic frame, or they may summon new ones. For example, the image of workers as insurgents might be amended to distinguish between collective actions (such as work slowdown resulting from complete adherence to regulations) and individual actions (such as theft) that are responses to perceived lower pay relative to one's coworkers rather than a response to the perceived exploitation of self along with one's coworkers.

Sometimes the researcher seeks simply to find a good fit between the images constructed from the data and the analytic frames derived from theories. Often, though, the fit is not right, and the researcher must determine whether different images can be constructed from the data or whether different analytic frames can be derived from theories. Alternatively, the researcher may use the images constructed from the data to devise new analytic frames or revise old ones. The interaction between analytic frames and images lead both to progressively refined images of social life and to better-specified analytic frames.

This process of refining images culminates in the representation of social life the researcher offers in a report of the results of the study. A social scientific representation thus can be seen as a product of the interaction between images and analytic frames. It is evidence that has been shaped by ideas, which in turn may have been selected and perhaps revised in response to evidence. The subsequent sections of this chapter elaborate the model in Figure 3.1. Of special importance in this discussion are the less familiar notions of images and analytic frames.

Ideas

Ideas about society come from everywhere: everyday life, a novel, an unusual event, an analogy, a misunderstanding, a slip of the tongue, a silly joke. Some ideas seem to appear more or less spontaneously. Most ideas turn out to be wrong or to be dead ends. For example, social scientists once thought that temperate climates caused higher forms of civilization to develop. As it turns out, this idea of climactic determinism does not do a very good job of explaining civilization. More than anything else, this thinking showed that those living in temperate climates were ignorant of non-Western cultures and of the complexity of most cultural forms.

Good ideas, or those that at least stand up under scrutiny, become part of the stock of knowledge that is passed from one generation of scholars to the next. In social science, abstract knowledge about social life is called social theory. Most people actually know a lot of social theory without studying it. They know, for example, that bureaucracies can become cumbersome and even choke on their own paperwork and procedures. They don't need to study organizational theory—a branch of social theory—to understand this. They also know that most people most of the time act in ways to maximize their material gains and other self-interests. They don't need a theory of rational choice—another branch of social theory—to understand this. Still, social theory is valuable because this body of thinking explores these and other ideas in depth: What are the types of factors that prevent bureaucracies from choking on their own procedures? Under what general conditions do people make what seem to be obvious irrational choices? Or, even more fundamental, is it always possible to tell which choices are rational and which are not?

The task of making sense of social life is daunting. The accumulated knowledge of social life represented in social theory offers an important resource. Some social research, as noted in Chapter 1, seeks to improve this body of knowledge by testing ideas derived directly from theory or by identifying general patterns that elaborate theoretical ideas. Not all research, however, is theory centered in this way. Social researchers who seek to interpret culturally or historically significant events, for example, view social theory as a reservoir of possible interpretations. Likewise, researchers who seek to give voice, another key goal of social research (as described in Chapter 2), recognize that their research cannot proceed without some theoretical guidance, yet their primary theoretical objective is to contribute to theory by learning more about phenomena and groups that have been ignored or misrepresented. However, even researchers who are more concerned with contributing new knowledge to this pool of ideas than with using existing ideas participate fully in the dialogue with ideas.

Analytic Frames

When most researchers approach the pool of ideas known as social theory, they usually have a specific research question or problem in mind. For example, a researcher might be interested in understanding why people vote the way they do. What theoretical ideas (that is, ideas from the pool of social theory) might help in this research? Different ideas lead to different ways of framing and using evidence.

For example, one very simple theoretical idea is the notion that people act in ways that maximize their self-interests—they make rational choices. This theoretical idea sees the question of voting as an individual-level decision based on a sober assessment of the costs and benefits for the person. The researcher would thus see the act of voting as a calculation of individual gains and losses given different outcomes, a calculation that would vary across individuals depending on their characteristics (for example, income or family size). In short, the idea of rational choice would lead the researcher to construct a particular analytic frame for understanding voting, which, in turn, would cause the researcher to see voting in a specific way. For instance, if the researcher notices that income has an effect on voting, a rational choice perspective might lead the researcher to expect that a politician's stance on taxation would motivate voters differently based on their respective incomes. A different idea implemented through a different analytic frame might lead to a dramatically different view of voting, a different way of breaking it into its key components. For example, a theory that emphasized processes of social influence would turn the investigator's focus to the nature of each voter's social networks. So a researcher using this frame might center her analysis on the political beliefs of the voter's parents, spouse or partner, or close friends.

Thus, analytic frames are fundamental to social research because they constitute ways of seeing. While this notion may seem abstract, consider the operation of analytic frames in everyday life: As people go through their lives, they classify and characterize the things around them. For example, they know how to distinguish between "people standing around in a room" and "a party" because they understand and can use the term *party*. They also generally know what makes a party fun—which ingredients in what quantities, and so on—which is another way of saying they know how to characterize parties in different ways. Another way to describe people's understanding of parties is to say that they have an implicit *analytic frame* for parties. An analytic frame defines a category of phenomena (for example, parties) and provides conceptual tools for differentiating phenomena within the category (what makes them more and less successful; more and less formal; more this, less that; and so on). In short, analytic frames articulate ideas, in this case the *idea* of a party.

The person who is ignorant of the term *party* may not be able to tell the difference between a conference and a party. Both involve rooms full of people who are talking, often at the same time, often without listening to each other, often with laughter, and so on.

Now consider a related example from social research (Smith-Lahrman 1992) that further illustrates the frame as a way of seeing. In some coffee houses, people spend a lot of time *avoiding* interaction. They use posture and props such as newspapers and books to maintain social boundaries and social distance. In this sense, their noninteraction is intentional and therefore is a *social accomplishment*. A quiet coffee house is not a social vacuum; it is teeming with purposeful social behavior.

Armed with the proper analytic frame—one emphasizing nonverbal communication—it is possible for social researchers to *see* that the noninteraction is "accomplished." Without this frame, it might appear simply that "nothing is happening," when in fact significant efforts to achieve noninteraction are being exerted throughout the coffee house. In short, without a frame for accomplished noninteraction, researchers might be blind to its occurrences. They might also fail to consider similarities and differences among its occurrences across broad social spaces (for example, differences in how it is accomplished in trains, airports, elevators, and so on; differences in how tweens and teens accomplish it; and other important considerations).

The process of using analytic frames to classify and characterize phenomena is carried out explicitly and formally in social research. Sometimes a social researcher will study something because it is unclear what it is or how it should be characterized. Is the movement toward "political correctness" a fad? Is it a social movement? Is it a new religion? Is a wave of anorexia among young women a response to fashion? Is it internalized misogyny? Is it an effort to erase gender differences by starving off secondary sex characteristics? Is it an emergent form of mass protest against traditional gender roles—a hunger strike? Which analytic frames work best? A researcher may try several frames to see which makes the most sense of the phenomenon and leads to new insights.

Consider a more detailed example: The decision by same-sex couples to hold a commitment ceremony could be understood as a "political act," and thus a researcher might study these ceremonies as one might study hunger strikes. Alternatively, a researcher might use the frame of "traditional cultural expression of love." When people decide to make a long-term commitment, a ceremony announces and publicly solidifies such intent as traditional, conventional, and potentially legally binding. To study commitment ceremonies is to examine the meaning of this act for the individuals involved. The researcher who uses the analytic frame of "political act" constructs a very different representation of the intention behind commitment ceremonies than the one constructed by the researcher who uses the frame of "traditional expression." In fact, ambiguities about the meaning of same-sex unions culturally, politically, and legally led Kathleen Hull to write the book *Same-Sex Marriage: The Cultural Politics of Love and Law* (2006). She interviewed 71 individuals in same-sex relationships to expand the body of knowledge concerning marriage rights beyond the context of constitutional, historical, or faith-based arguments by studying the people actually affected by the evolving legal system.

By debating, using, and formalizing analytic frames, researchers are able to relate their work to that of other researchers and to accumulate general knowledge about social life from their separate, individual efforts. For example, the researcher who uses the frame of "political act" to study same-sex marriages contributes to the body of knowledge concerned with the basic mechanisms of social change. The researcher who uses the frame of "traditional expression" contributes to the body of knowledge that addresses cultural rituals. This is not to say that researchers must select fixed analytical frames at the outset of their work; in fact, Kathleen Hull (2006) used a qualitative approach for her project specifically because this would allow her to uncover new perspectives that would not arise if she fixed her analytic frame in one way or the other.

Because analytic frames both classify and characterize social phenomena, they have two main components. When researchers use concepts to *classify* the phenomena they study, they **frame by case.** When they use concepts to *characterize* these cases, they **frame by aspect.** Both components of analytic frames are important parts of the dialogue of idea and evidence in social research.

Framing by case. When a social researcher states that most of what occurs in coffee houses is "accomplished noninteraction," he or she classifies the phenomenon. In essence, the social researcher answers the question, "What is this—the phenomenon being studied—a case of?" The social life of a coffee house provides a case of accomplished noninteraction. Framing by case (that is, answering the question, "What is this phenomenon a case of?") is an essential part of the process of social research (Ragin and Becker 1992).

When researchers claim that the people and events they are studying are an instance, or "case," of something wider and more important, a larger category, they offer a frame for their research. For example, to argue that it is important to study the genocide in Darfur, Sudan, as "a case of ineffective international intervention" is to frame this study as an instance of a more general category. Implicit in this statement is the idea that there are many such instances of "ineffective international intervention" and that the study of the genocide in Sudan should make a contribution to that general body of knowledge. Defining the case in conceptual terms—as an instance of something broader—is the most important part of the framing of a study. When more than one case is studied, they are often seen as multiple instances of the same larger category. For example, a comparative study of several instances of ineffective international intervention might examine specific United Nations resolutions that attempted to address the conflicts in Haiti, Rwanda, Sudan, and the former Yugoslavia.

The broad conceptual categories that frame social scientific studies do not always involve large units such as countries or abstract units such as social interaction. The units can be almost any size. For example, a researcher might frame a study of the conflict between the pro-choice and pro-life movements as an instance of "polarized social movements." Another case of polarized social movements in the United States might be the conflict between organizations representing unions and those representing corporations over "right-to-work" legislation seeking the elimination of compulsory union membership.

Still smaller units are involved when a researcher frames fraternities and sororities as instances of "same-sex communal groups." And even smaller units are involved when interaction rituals such as greetings are studied as instances of "efforts to cultivate relationships." All these examples involve framing by case. Even large-scale survey research involves framing by case. When a survey is used to examine the relation between economic interests and voting preferences, for example, the frame treats survey respondents as rational actors.

Framing by aspect. Specifying the broader category that is relevant to an investigation is only part of the process of analytic framing. Framing also involves specifying the key features or aspects that differentiate the cases in a broad category. Framing by case establishes an important category, or set of phenomena; framing by aspect indicates how the cases within a category vary.

For example, social situations that qualify as sites of accomplished noninteraction (a category that includes coffee houses, airports, buses, elevators, waiting rooms, some types of bars, and so on) vary in important ways. How do people accomplish noninteraction in all these different settings? What verbal, nonverbal, and other behavioral cues are used? What features of settings influence which cues are used and how they are used? The list of relevant aspects of settings that should be considered in this frame is very long. Sometimes noninteraction is accomplished among strangers and sometimes among acquaintances. The settings where it is accomplished vary by social density: Sometimes people are spread out and can move about (as in an airport), and sometimes they are tightly packed (as in a plane). Some social spaces are closed (buses, for instance); some are open (parks). Social settings that manifest high levels of accomplished noninteraction vary in many other ways, as well. Each of these features may have an important impact on how noninteraction is accomplished in each setting. Once social researchers answer the question, "What is this a case of?" (that is, once they frame by case), they use theory and other ideas to identify the major features of cases in the frame, and thus frame by aspect.

Consider again the study of the conflict in Darfur, Sudan. To state that this conflict is an instance of "ineffective international intervention" only partially frames this case. It is also necessary to elaborate the important aspects of the instances within this category. There may be many different forms of international intervention with varying degrees of effectiveness, and each method of intervention may involve putting together a different combination of mobilization resistance, trade embargoes, United Nations resolutions, sanctions, non-governmental organization (NGO) interference, and regionally developed policies and strategies. Further, strategies that work well in some contexts may not work at all in others. In short, there are many different aspects to "ineffective international intervention." The researcher's analytic frame for the study of ineffective international interventions should embrace all of these aspects.

Framing by aspect helps social researchers see both what is present and what is absent in a given case. For example, assume that the analytic frame for "ineffective international intervention" is applied to the conflict in Sudan. This frame guides the researcher both to examine specific phenomena that were present in Sudan (such as strong NGO interference and global awareness of the conflict) and to consider the impact of features that were absent in this case (such as a UN consensus on the nature of the conflict) but present in other cases covered by the analytic frame (Rwanda, for instance). Would NGO involvement and worldwide awareness have dampened the conflict if the United Nations had reached a consensus on the nature of it?

In all social research, some sort of guide is needed to see what is present and what is absent in a given case. Sometimes the things that are absent in a case help the most in explaining why it is one way and not another. Note, however, that it is easy to miss what is absent without an analytic frame to guide the analysis. Without this guidance, the tendency is to focus only on what is present.

Together, framing by case and framing by aspect constitute two key conversations that take place in the dialogue of ideas and evidence. How and when these conversations take place differ greatly from one research strategy to the next (Diesing 1971). Sometimes the analytic frame for a research project exists before the research begins and structures most aspects of the research; other times the frame is articulated in the course of the research. The interplay of analytic frames and research strategies is addressed in the final section of this chapter.

Evidence

When most people think about social scientific evidence, they usually think of questionnaires and telephone surveys. After all, social scientists conduct huge surveys on all aspects of social life and then publish their findings—the percentage of people who think this or that or who do this or that, broken down by gender, race, age, education, income, or whatever. However, social scientists are not limited to survey data. In fact, only a relatively small proportion of social scientists are survey researchers. Many study phenomena that cannot be adequately addressed with questionnaires.

All facets and features of social life offer evidence; virtually everything to a social scientist is "data," at least potentially. Some social researchers observe social life as it occurs in everyday settings. They take reams of **field notes** on people's daily routines of family, work, and play in their various locales: street corners and kitchens; offices and factories; country clubs and churches; bars, back alleys, and emergency rooms. Others conduct in-depth interviews with people from different walks of life and try to stimulate their subjects to be more introspective about their lives, to analyze their own thoughts and actions. A researcher interested in labor control, for example, might interview 50 employees of a factory, drawn from all levels and divisions of its workforce. Other researchers study past events, using historical documents and records from libraries and archives. Still other researchers study patterns across whole cities and countries, using official statistics published in the reports of government and international agencies. There are many, many sources of evidence about social life, and social researchers have explored virtually every type.

Not only are there many different sources of data, but each instance of social life potentially offers an infinite amount of information. The **empirical** world is limitless in its detail and complexity. Social research thus necessarily involves a *selection of evidence*. Most evidence must be ignored as irrelevant; otherwise, research would be impossible.

Consider the seemingly simple task of taking notes on what occurs in a classroom during an hour-long lecture. First of all, it's necessary to set the stage properly with a physical description of the lecture hall, its atmosphere, the number of people in attendance, their distribution in the lecture hall, and so on. This description could easily fill one notebook. Next, there is the lecture itself. Exhaustive notes on the content of an hour-long lecture could fill another notebook. But then there's also the lecture as a performance, which includes nonverbal behavior (gestures and other bodily movements) and the interplay of the verbal material and nonverbal behavior. This information could easily fill several notebooks. There should also be notes on the reactions of students in the audience. Of course, with enough resources, it would be possible to monitor the behavior of each person throughout the hour, including his or her verbal and nonverbal behavior, note taking, social interaction, and so on. This would yield enough information to fill at least one notebook for every person in attendance. And don't forget that it is also possible to take notes on the interaction between the lecturer and the cues—verbal and nonverbal, conscious and unconscious—that the listeners send to the lecturer. A videotape of this interaction could be studied for many years and yield many more reams of field notes. In short, to try to capture the full details of social life—even a very small slice of it—is a colossal undertaking.

Because every slice of social life potentially offers an unlimited amount of evidence, researchers must be selective in their use of evidence. It would take an infinitely long research report to use all the evidence a typical case offers. Although social researchers usually collect large volumes of evidence, the quantity they collect can, at best, constitute only a tiny fraction of the evidence they *potentially* could collect. They try to focus on only the most significant portions, using their ideas, analytic frames, interests, past studies, and so on to help them assess what seems most important to their research questions. The problem of selecting evidence returns us to ideas and analytic frames. Without some sort of sensitizing ideas or concepts, the world seems an amorphous blob. We perceive evidence and select some of it as especially relevant because of our ideas and frames. As will become evident in the next section, however, the images social scientists construct from these bits of evidence may not conform to the initial ideas and frames that defined the evidence as relevant in the first place.

This need for selectivity introduces a problem: When a writer becomes an advocate for a particular point of view, he or she "selects" for reporting only the bits of evidence that support that position. This kind of selectivity involves an ignorance of evidence, either willful or unconscious, that favors opposing points of view. Ignoring evidence is not always willful, however; sometimes it is a product of limited awareness or limited resources and thus is unintentional. For example, before the rise of feminist perspectives in the social sciences, many researchers did not see the pervasiveness of sexism in everyday life. Thus, evidence bearing on sexism was often missed in studies of a wide range of social relations. Many other forms of ignorance and unrecognized bias infect all research. While it would be great if every social scientist had some way to recognize the impact of such bias on his or her own research, there is no automatic safeguard. Social scientists are only human, and they can't designate evidence as relevant if their unrecognized biases persuade them to ignore it.

The only real safeguard to unrecognized bias is the fact that social science is *communitarian* (Merton 1973). Social scientists write for other social scientists and they judge each other's work. They try to detect bias. Often a social scientific representation of social life is evaluated by other social scientists before it is published or made public in some way. This, however, is less true with the dramatic increase in blogging and self-publication. Many well-respected social scientists have discussed ideas and presented data analyses in blogs with peer response rather than peer review. The debates that used to occur around university seminar tables now frequently take place in cyberspace. Peer-reviewed work is usually subjected to close scrutiny both before and after it is published. In fact, social scientific representations are subjected to more scrutiny than most other representations of social life. Of course, if all or even most social scientists share the same unrecognized biases, as is sometimes the case, then the influences of biased selection of evidence will not be immediately recognized. However, social scientists believe that future generations of social scientists will uncover and correct the unrecognized biases of preceding generations.

Images

Ideas and analytic frames direct the researcher's attention to specific kinds and categories of evidence. From an ocean of potential data, the researcher selects what seem to be the most relevant portions. Once a sufficient body of relevant evidence has been collected, the researcher's next task is to make sense of it and at the same time relate it back to the ideas and frames that motivated the collection of evidence in the first place.

Researchers make sense of their evidence by constructing images of their cases from the data they have collected. In effect, an image is constructed by the investigator when he or she brings together, or synthesizes, evidence. Images often imply motives or say something about causation. When a researcher notes that people with more income tend to vote for the Republican Party, for example, he or she creates part of an image of how a preference for Republicans comes about. Thus, an image is the product of the effort to bring coherence to data by linking bits of evidence in meaningful ways.

Consider an extended example: The researcher who wants to understand how medical students become doctors may start the research with specific ideas about the professions and the nature of professional socialization. One common notion is that each profession upholds certain values or principles and that professional socialization involves learning how to apply these principles in everyday situations. For the medical profession, one central value might be that the health of the patient comes before all else. Because this analytic frame emphasizes the application of abstract principles, the researcher might initiate data collection by observing medical students in clinical practice, with special attention to whatever general principles seem important in these settings. A few weeks of fieldwork in the clinics of a teaching hospital would no doubt result in a huge volume of notes on what was observed. During the process of digesting his or her observations, the researcher may ask questions about the relationship between these abstract principles and professional socialization such as the following: What images of medical students and their professional training emerge from this fieldwork? Which images make the most sense of this new body of evidence? Which aspects of the professional socialization of medical students should be investigated next?

Images are formed from evidence in order to make sense of it, summarize it, and relate it back to the ideas that initially motivated the collection of evidence. To construct images, researchers connect different aspects of cases to form coherent portraits. Suppose the researcher studying medical students found that clinical decision making revolved less around the best interests of patients, and more around the needs of doctors and hospital officials to protect themselves from charges of malpractice. The *image* of professional socialization that emerges from this connection is that training centers on getting medical students to exaggerate the correspondence between this need for protection from malpractice charges, on the one hand, and the best interests of patients, on the other. After all, charges of malpractice can be avoided in part by exercising extraordinary caution—for example, by ordering many laboratory tests on each patient so that every possible diagnosis is covered. This excessive use of laboratory tests could be construed as "thoroughness" or "expert care" and thus "in the patient's best interest," even though testing is often invasive, unpleasant, expensive, and may cause serious reactions and even secondary illnesses.

This image of professional socialization, built up from evidence, both elaborates and challenges the initial frame. The initial frame emphasized the importance of abstract professional values in professional socialization (for the medical profession, "putting the patient first"). The image constructed from evidence, however, indicates that, in everyday settings, professional values are learned primarily in the context of practical and institutional concerns (for example, avoiding charges of malpractice). In other words, practical and institutional concerns *modify* how professional values are understood and implemented. This image of the training of medical students, built up from observations of decision making in clinics, organizes the evidence the researcher has collected in a way that highlights its relevance to the original analytic frame.

Consider another example of images in social research: Researchers have noted that many inner-city neighborhoods have lost their middle-class families to more prosperous, outlying areas, and that these losses have accelerated the decline of these neighborhoods (W. Wilson 1980, 1987). This connection between the loss of middle-class residents and accelerated neighborhood decline contrasts two images. The first is a "thriving minority community"—what it presumably was like before the flight of the middle class: a neighborhood composed of individuals with different income levels (poor, working class, and middle class), with the more successful members offering community leadership, role models, information on how to get ahead, jobs in locally owned businesses, and many other resources for less fortunate members. The second image—the post-flight community—is an "inner-city ghetto" and offers a striking contrast: uniformly poor members with high rates of unemployment, crime, violence, drug addiction, welfare dependence, teenage pregnancy, despair, and so on. Linking these two images is the "exodus" of the minority middle class. This example of the construction of images can be used to illustrate three of their important qualities:

1. Images are **idealizations** of real cases. Every real neighborhood is complex and ever-changing. It is doubtful that any neighborhood perfectly fits either of the two images just elaborated, the "thriving minority community" or the "inner-city ghetto," at least not for any great length of time.

Images are exaggerations because they are necessarily constructed from selected pieces of information; they cannot reproduce real cases because these are infinitely detailed and complex. Thus, images should be seen as pure or idealized cases (Weber 1949). These two terms—*idealized* (as in idealized cases) and *idealization* (the process)—are used here not to indicate desirability, as in the statement, "This area offers an ideal climate for year-round outdoor sports." Rather, they are used to indicate that images are *abstractions*. Unlike theoretical ideas, however, they are abstractions that have a specific grounding in a body of evidence. The process of constructing idealized cases (idealization) involves abstracting from information about empirical cases to conceptually elaborated images. As idealized cases, images can be linked to theoretical ideas expressed in analytic frames.

2. Most images imply or embody *explanations*. Most explanations are *causal*, which means simply that they offer accounts of why things are the way they are, emphasizing connections among different phenomena. When we explain the accelerating decline of inner-city neighborhoods by pointing to the exodus of the minority middle class, we pinpoint a causal connection. The key part of a causal explanation is its *cause* words. Cause words, such as *exodus,* are the most important part—the action part—of the images that social scientists construct. Exodus connotes collective, willful abandonment of a specific locale. It's packed with meaning. Words like exodus link images to analytic frames, ideas, and ultimately to social theory. There are social scientific theories, for example, that seek to conceptualize the variety of push-and-pull factors that cause people to move from one community to another. These theories are relevant to many kinds of migrations: the exodus of minority middle-class people from inner-city neighborhoods, the gentrification of other urban neighborhoods, and the back-and-forth migration of Mexicans to and from particular villages in Mexico and specific communities in the United States.

3. Images are *guides* to further research; they suggest new research questions and new avenues to explore. Images help researchers see what they might otherwise miss and thus lead them to examine social life in a more systematic way. For example, we can ask the following questions: Have we omitted any important aspects in either of these two images? For instance, do most "inner-city ghettos" also lack grassroots political organizations? Are there important differences between those with such organizations and those lacking them? Here is another example: Are there inner-city minority neighborhoods with a good cross-section of income groups (poor, working, and middle class) that nevertheless developed high rates of crime, violence, drug addiction, teenage pregnancy, and so on? If so, why didn't the existence

of middle-class role models, leaders, and so forth forestall these develop-
ments? For still another example, would the return of middle-class minority
members to an inner-city ghetto help roll back the rising tide of violence,
drug addiction, welfare dependence, and the like? These questions follow
directly from the two images constructed.

Once formed, images interact with analytic frames. The process of constructing images (or **imaging**) complements the process of deriving analytic
frames from theory (or framing by case and framing by aspect). While these
two activities, framing and imaging, seem to correspond to deduction and
induction, it would be a mistake to limit them in this way. Even though
imaging is mostly inductive, it uses evidence that has been defined as relevant by the ideas and frames the researcher brings to the study. It is difficult
to form an image from evidence without first using some sort of initial analytic frame to highlight or define relevant evidence.

Likewise, even though framing is mostly deductive, the body of knowledge
from which frames are derived summarizes accumulated, evidence-based
knowledge about social life. Thus, framing is based on a vast body of system-
atized evidence. Furthermore, at the start of most research projects, the analytic
frame for the research is usually only half-developed, at best. Social theory is
abstract, general, and often vague, so much so that several different frames can
be derived from the same set of ideas. In the course of the research, if the images
formed from evidence are compatible with the initial analytic frame, then they
can be used to clarify and refine it. However, sometimes the images formed
from evidence reject the initial framing and force the investigator to seek out or
develop new frames (Walton 1991, 1992). This interaction between images and
frames is best understood as a process of *retroduction* (see Chapter 2).

Representations

The dialogue of ideas and evidence culminates in representations of social
life (see Figure 3.1). In social research, analytic frames and images interact
to produce a progressively refined portrait or picture, which becomes the
representation (and the explanation) that the researcher offers.

In many ways, social scientific representations can be compared to photographs. The photographer selects an image to be represented, taking care
to ensure that the right elements are brought together in the image. By bringing together these elements, the photographer conveys the message or idea
he or she intends. The image in the photograph is framed in several ways.
Within the photographic image itself, it is framed by focus—some parts of

the image are foregrounded and the focus is sharp, while others are backgrounded and out of focus. The photographic image is framed as well by its boundaries. It can be cropped in a variety of ways; each cropping has a different effect on the meaning of the image. Consider the fact that the world around the photographic image is seamless—it goes on forever. The frame established by the photographer limits the context of the image. Images are unclear if they are not properly framed.

So it is in social research. The main part of the representation is the image, which is built up from evidence. Researchers link pieces of evidence together to make images. The analytic frame provides the context for creating and understanding the image, establishing conceptual boundaries around the evidence-based image. It is important to understand that in both social research and photography, representations appear to audiences as finished products, complete with images and frames. However, these finished products result from a long process. There is interplay of possible frames and potential images in the construction of every representation.

At the core of every social scientific representation is an explicit or implicit explanation of some major aspect of the phenomena it represents. The explanation is what gives the representation coherence, because it is very difficult to "tell about" social life (that is, represent it in some way) without giving some kind of account of it (that is, explain it). For example, the researcher who studies interaction in a coffee house explains how people accomplish noninteraction; the researcher who studies ethnic tensions in a range of countries explains how conflict may be prevented or at least postponed; the researcher who studies medical students explains how they come to see a correspondence between the practical concerns of doctors and hospitals and their professional commitments to patients; and finally, the researcher who studies inner-city neighborhoods explains how their loss of middle-class members contributed to their decline.

Ways of representing the final product of the interaction of frames and images in social research are varied, and the intended audience for a representation has a strong impact on how it is presented. While it is possible to imagine a variety of ways of representing the results of social research (documentary films, dramatic performances, text mixed with still photographs and sound recordings, multimedia presentations, and so on), social researchers tend to use academic books, journal articles, textbooks, and an occasional article in a mass-circulation magazine. In other words, they use traditional academic outlets almost exclusively. Within each of these media, however, different formats may be employed: tables, charts, equations, transcripts, narratives, vignettes describing typical or exemplary cases, and so on.

Analytic Methods	
Deduction	The process of deriving more specific ideas or propositions from general ideas, knowledge, or theories, working out their implications for a specific set of evidence or specific kinds of evidence.
Retroduction	The interplay of induction and deduction, and is central to the process of scientific discovery. The process of constructing representations from the interaction between analytic frames and images involves retroduction.
Induction	The process of using evidence to formulate or reformulate a general idea. The process of constructing images via the synthesis of evidence is mostly inductive.

Processes and Strategies of Social Research

While all social research involves interaction between images and analytic frames, the nature of this interaction can differ significantly from one research project to the next. A key consideration in understanding these differences is the role of analytic frames in research. In some research, frames are **fixed** at the start of the study, while in others they may be either **flexible** or **fluid** and change in the course of the investigation.

Analytic frames may be elaborated at the outset of a research project and remain more or less the same throughout the study. This use of fixed analytic frames is often necessary, for example, in studies that seek to test theories. In essence, the analytic frame implements a hypothesis to be tested. If images constructed from the evidence are inconsistent with the hypothesis, then the hypothesis is rejected. Fixed frames are also common in research that seeks to make predictions based on current trends and in studies that seek to document broad patterns.

Fixed frames are most compatible with quantitative research on covariation (see Chapter 7). In research of this type, there is sometimes a close correspondence between the analytic frame developed at the outset of the research and the data set that the researcher then constructs. Recall that analytic frames elaborate ideas by specifying both a category of phenomena and the major ways phenomena within the category vary. For example, a frame that looks at voters as rational actors sees voters as the category and their individual-level differences (such as their different educational backgrounds or income levels) as aspects that might explain their different choices. This analytic frame readily translates to a survey format, where potential voters are queried about their demographic characteristics and their voting behavior (see Page and Shapiro 1991). This simple translation from the analytic frame to survey data permits a direct test of the idea that inspired the frame in the first place—that voters make rational choices. If the images constructed from the data do not correspond to the idea of rational choice, then the hypothesis is rejected.

In other studies, the analytic frame is flexible; it is elaborated as a guide for research, showing which kinds of factors might be relevant in which contexts. A flexible frame is useful, for example, in studies that seek to explore diversity or advance theory. A flexible frame shows the researcher where to look and what kinds of factors to look for without forming specific hypotheses about relationships among factors.

Flexible frames are common in comparative research (see Chapter 6), especially when the goal is to make sense of a range of diverse cases. Consider a researcher who is interested in tyranny and explores it by studying many of the major tyrants of the 20th century (Joseph Stalin, Adolph Hitler, François "Papa Doc" Duvalier, Rafael Trujillo, Saddam Hussein, and so on; see Chirot 1993). The analytic frame might direct the researcher to examine a range of factors: how these tyrants came to power; what good, if any, they accomplished; who supported them, both domestically and internationally; what ideologies they used, if any, to justify their cruelty; how much suffering they caused; and so on.

Examination of this evidence might lead the researcher to differentiate types of tyrants. For example, the evidence might show that the more ideological tyrants (Hitler and Stalin, among others) caused more suffering than the less ideological ones. In this way, the researcher could elaborate the analytic frame, used initially as a way to guide the research, with these evidence-based images (the two main types of tyrants—more ideological and more abusive versus less ideological and less abusive). Thus, the research could offer important leads for the advancement of theories of political oppression (Chirot 1993).

Finally, in some research, analytic frames are fluid. Researchers who seek to give voice (one of the goals of research discussed in Chapter 2), for example, may want to limit the influence of pre-existing ideas. Of course, they must have some initial ideas about their research subjects; otherwise, the research could not be started. But these ideas might be quickly set aside once the research is underway. Alternatively, the researcher might start with several frames and move fluidly among them, depending on the nature of the evidence as it accumulates. The use of multiple, fluid frames is especially appropriate when researchers seek to give voice because a fixed analytic frame might prevent them from hearing the voices of the people they study.

Fluid frames are most common in qualitative research (see Chapter 5). Often researchers will not know what their case is "a case of" when they first start their investigation. When there are many possible framings, each can be explored to see which help make the most sense of the evidence. Sometimes multiple frames are retained throughout a project and included in the representation, especially if these different framings illuminate the subject in complementary ways. The American Civil War can be framed in many different ways: as a fight over slavery, as a fight over states' rights in a federal system of government, as a struggle between a plantation society and an emerging industrial society, and so on. These different frames can be integrated into a single, encompassing portrait.

Framing a case in different ways enriches our understanding of the case when each frame offers insights for other frames. When this occurs, the case or cases that are the focus of the study are said to be "rich" because they provide so much raw material for the advancement of social thought. Unfortunately, this creative interaction among frames is relatively rare in social research. Typically, in qualitative research investigators struggle simply to come to terms with their cases. Existing frames may not work well at all, and the case becomes a platform for developing new ideas and new frames.

The Challenge of Social Research

Ideas and evidence are everywhere. It's no great surprise, then, that there are so many people busy constructing representations of social life, from poets and painters to playwrights and political scientists. Different ways of constructing representations require different kinds of regimen. The regimen of poetry, for example, is to construct representations that make the most of as few words as possible. The regimen of social research is also strict, though quite different, and it is reinforced by the primary audience for social research—social scientists.

The regimen of social research demands both clear specification of the ideas that guide research and systematic examination of the evidence used to build images and representations. The challenge of social research is to construct powerful and instructive representations of social life that contribute to social theory (the ongoing conversations about social life), and at the same time embrace a breadth or depth of evidence about social life in a systematic way. This challenge can be met by building a dialogue of ideas and evidence—analytic frames and evidence-based images—into the process of social research.

4

The Ethics of Social Research

Introduction

The ethical norms for a social scientist studying human behavior generally conform to those held by individuals within society. For example, any type of physical or verbal abuse directed by the researcher toward a person or group of people being studied is considered unethical. In addition to general ethical norms, social scientists also are expected to meet particular research standards. Further, just as there is general agreement in society about when some norms have been violated and there is debate about other norms, social scientists also find that there is general agreement about how to meet some research standards and in other cases, ethical standards are less clear. In this chapter, we explore *ethical dilemmas,* instances in which implementation of ethical principles in research is unclear or debatable. Let's examine two cases.

First, consider an ethical dilemma faced by an individual stationed at the Abu Ghraib prison in Iraq in 2003. U.S. Army Specialist Joseph Darby, a reservist, made the decision to turn over a file containing photos of the abuse of Iraqi prisoners to the Army's Criminal Investigation division (Hersh 2004). He acted ethically in accordance with military standards. The photos were ultimately leaked to the CBS network by an unknown source and aired on *60 Minutes II* (Dao and Lichtblau 2004). Like many other whistle-blowers, Darby experienced a backlash, as many people felt his decision was unpatriotic and contemptible. His actions were interpreted as fueling anti-American sentiment in Iraq and undermining the war effort—so much so that Darby's family spent 6 months under armed protection because of fears of retaliation, after receiving death threats and having property vandalized

> *A democracy, like science, functions best only when all actions are open to question, and when we require the highest levels of accountability. If there is a risk that politics is being placed above empirical truth on issues of vital national importance, inaction by scientists may be unethical.*
>
> —Lawrence M. Krauss
> ("The Citizen Scientist's Obligation" 2003)

("Abu Ghraib Whistleblower" 2007). In contrast, Darby was viewed as a hero by many other people. He was awarded the John F. Kennedy Profile in Courage Award in 2005. His actions led to an investigation of the abuses, increased scrutiny of the military's shifting policies on interrogation techniques, and international outrage over the violation of the human rights of detainees. Even though Darby adhered to codified standards, whether his decision was right or wrong can be debated.

Now, consider a research-related example: When qualitative sociologist Sudhir Venkatesh (2008) studied the organizational life of gang members, was it unethical that he did not report the crimes (including physical violence) that he observed to the police? What about when he *participated* in the criminal activity? Many argue that it is not unethical to observe illegal, unethical, or otherwise abhorrent behavior as a researcher because the objective of some research is to understand the underground organizational life of subsets of society who are engaged in illicit behavior. A researcher might feel strongly that this basic knowledge could then be used for the benefit of society as a whole (e.g., to reduce the violence committed by gang members). Indeed, it may be considered unethical if a researcher were to *report* any criminal activity to the authorities. For example, Venkatesh might feel it is ethical for him to protect the names of the gang members—similar to a journalist protecting his or her sources. He might also have concerns about potentially unfair treatment by our police and legal system for the gang members and their families.

As the title of his recent book, *Gang Leader for a Day,* implies, Venkatesh (2008) wrote about his participation in illegal drug sales. There is an ethical dilemma here—a trade-off between gaining a full understanding of a drug king's leadership role and participating in illicit activity. However, Venkatesh's choice to step into a leadership role could also be viewed as an *ethical failure* where he had stepped *outside* of his professional role by placing himself in a position of power over those he was studying and where his actions could lead directly to their harm. Let's address this often blurry boundary between ethical dilemmas and ethical failures in greater detail.

Ethical Dilemmas and Failures

An **ethical dilemma** is when an individual or organization is faced with a situation in which there is a tension between two or more ethical principles. With ethical dilemmas, there exists a debatable set of actions that may or may not be viewed as ethically responsible. An **ethical failure** is when an individual or organization makes a decision that is at odds with professional standards of ethics.

Within the realm of social science research, ethical failures would include the following: deliberately publishing made-up data, plagiarizing the work or ideas of others, taking credit for others' work, giving undue credit to someone who did not contribute to the work, mistreating collaborators and research participants, or concealing known concerns about the research process and results. It seems fairly easy to identify an ethical failure; however, it is not always as easy as it seems. For example, is shoddy research, which is obviously a professional failure, also an ethical failure?

Addressing such failures and dilemmas does not begin to cover the myriad ethical principles, frameworks, and distinctions, but is intended to be a starting point. This chapter elucidates some of the many questions that are involved in doing ethical social research. Before looking more closely at some ethical dilemmas faced by social scientists today, we consider the historical context out of which current ethical principles have arisen, and we describe the ethical principles used by institutions to evaluate proposed and ongoing research projects.

The Troubled History of Human Subjects Research

Interest in the ethics of human subject research in the 20th century emerged from mistreatment of people in various biomedical studies— mistreatment that has continued well past the notorious examples we discuss below. The inhumane medical experiments performed by Nazi doctors in concentration camps, brought to light in the Nuremberg war crime trials, are some of the most notorious violations of the "do no harm" set of ethical principles followed by medical practitioners. Nazi Germany was not, unfortunately, an aberration in terms of their unethical research practices. In this section, we outline six examples of post–World War II research that generated public outcry and increased skepticism of research-related activities. The first three studies are biomedical; the designs of these three studies clearly introduce a high level of risk for the subjects with limited possibility for benefit to them. The latter three studies are social science projects, and all three have more room for debate in terms of whether or not they were ethical.

Tuskegee Syphilis Trials, 1932–1972

The U.S. Public Health Service (PHS) began a study of the long-term effects of untreated syphilis in the early 1930s. Initially, 399 African American men with syphilis from rural Alabama were enrolled *unknowingly* in this study, which became known as the Tuskegee Syphilis Trials. The astounding part is that even after 1947, when penicillin could be used to effectively treat syphilis, treatment was withheld from these men so that researchers could continue their study of the long-term consequences of untreated syphilis. In fact, the researchers took extra efforts to make sure the subjects did not see doctors outside of the study who would, of course, diagnose and treat them (Reverby 2000). The PHS continued to deny treatment to these men until 1972 when an employee leaked the story to the press. By this time, over two-thirds of the men had died from syphilis or syphilis-related complications. (The 1997 film *Miss Evers' Boys*, directed by Joseph Sargent, is based on the Tuskegee experiment.)[1]

Willowbrook Hepatitis Study, 1963–1966

In 1963, Dr. Saul Krugman, director of research at Willowbrook State School for the Retarded, initiated a research project in order to study the effects of hepatitis in a somewhat controlled setting. Some of the cognitively impaired children were placed in a special unit and deliberately infected with hepatitis (while simultaneously protected from other diseases, such as measles). In addition, when the rest of the school was filled to capacity and no longer accepting new residents, space was available in the hepatitis unit and so admission to the school was in essence contingent on participation in the experiments. The study was halted in 1966 due to public outrage. The rationale for infecting these children with hepatitis was that outbreaks were common within the school, so given that the children were likely to get the disease, it would be better for them to contract it while under medical supervision (Krugman 1986). The legality of intentional transmission of hepatitis has been questioned on the grounds that the risks to these children's health and well-being far outweighed any benefit they could possibly get from being a part of this study (Beecher 1966). A key point of contention with this study was whether parental consent was acceptable when an individual child would receive no realized or potential therapeutic benefit for his or her involvement.[2]

MKULTRA Project, 1953–1964

The Central Intelligence Agency's Project MKULTRA remains an elusive part of U.S. history, with evidence of CIA misconduct including experimental drug administration and radiation exposure to unwitting subjects from 1953–1964 (Goliszek 2003). The CIA's goals for the project were twofold: first, to develop ways to protect their own operatives and employees from the effects of interrogation techniques, and second, to develop drugs and procedure to increase the efficacy of behavioral modification and interrogation techniques on persons of interest to the CIA. There were 149 projects under the MKULTRA umbrella. The late Senator Ted Kennedy ("Project MKULTRA" 1977) summed up the episode: "The Central Intelligence Agency drugged American citizens without their knowledge or consent. It used university facilities and personnel without their knowledge. It funded leading researchers, often without their knowledge" (p. 4). The majority of the MKULTRA files were destroyed in 1973 as ordered by then-CIA Director Richard Helms.[3]

The unifying theme of these research projects is the exposure of individuals, who are often marginalized or otherwise seen as expendable, to grievous or even fatal risks for a supposedly greater good. The medical research might be seen as more defensible than the politically motivated research, but all three of these studies are viewed as extremely unethical by contemporary standards. By contrast, the social science studies discussed below still have many defenders today, including the original researchers and even some of the subjects. They are overall more difficult to dismiss on ethical grounds, perhaps because there was a much lower risk of physical harm to the subjects. In any case, these three projects are seen as particularly influential in shaping the debate about research ethics. The first two, the Milgram Experiment and the Stanford Prison Experiment, overlap considerably with the CIA's agenda of better understanding behavior modification and the nature of compliance and social control. Like some of the CIA's studies, the third study, Humphreys' *Tearoom Trade*, also involved individuals who were studied and placed at risk without their consent or knowledge.

Milgram Experiment, 1961–1962

In 1961, social psychologist Stanley Milgram, then at Yale University, began a series of experiments. The participants, paid volunteers, were told they would be taking part in a learning experiment. They were not told that Milgram's primary interest was in obedience to authority, as this would have obviously biased the participants' behaviors. The participants were ordered to administer electrical shocks to another person at increasingly intense voltages (up to 450 volts) if the person did not provide the correct answer to a question. That person, an actor working with Milgram, was not actually harmed. During one of his first experiments, 65% of the participants were willing to deliver the final and highest level of shock simply because the authority figure told them to continue. In this condition, the "shock victim" was in a separate room and answered the questions through a signal box. The victim could not be seen and did not vocalize at all; however, the participant could hear pounding on the wall with increasing intensity as the shock levels increased. For subsequent experiments, participants were subjected to slightly different conditions (e.g., having the participant hear the cries of the victim through the wall, having the participant in the same room as the victim, requiring the participant to force the hand of the protesting victim onto a shock plate while administering the shock, and moving the experiment to a location off of Yale's campus to reduce the degree to which the researcher was seen as an authority figure). Many participants experienced extreme duress and emotional breakdowns during and following the experiments and some even begged not to have to deliver the shock, but then complied anyway. Those who refused to continue also experienced psychological strain, perhaps because of their defiance, their unwillingness to complete the experiment, or the pain they believed they had previously administered. Further discussion of the results and details of Milgram's experiments can be found in his 1974 book, *Obedience to Authority*.[4]

Stanford Prison Experiment, 1971

In 1971, a group of researchers headed by social psychologist Philip Zimbardo set up an experiment to investigate what happens to otherwise well-adjusted individuals when they take on the role of either a prisoner or prison guard. This study became known as the Stanford Prison Experiment. The paid male volunteers, all Stanford University students, were informed that they would be involved in a study of the psychological effects of prison life. The application process included instructions that each participant could leave the study through "established procedures" at any time but by doing so, the person would forfeit his or her pay. They were also told that the prisoners should expect some harassment and violations of their civil rights and privacy while in the makeshift prison. Each of the nine randomly selected "prisoners" was "arrested" unexpectedly at his home by actual Palo Alto police officers, put through booking procedures at the local police station, taken to the "prison" (in the basement of a campus building), and subjected to additional admissions procedures designed to humiliate him. The guards were instructed to maintain order, create a sense of helplessness among the prisoners, and strip them of their individuality. Within days, the guards began harassing and abusing the prisoners through a variety of tactics, including arbitrarily assigning special privileges to a few, waking prisoners several times a night to make them recite their prison numbers and the prison rules, and punishing them for minor infractions. The punishments included ordering them to do push-ups, subjecting them to strip searches, making the prisoners simulate sexual acts, and putting them in solitary confinement. This type of abuse escalated throughout the study and was particularly brutal at night and other times when the guards felt no one was monitoring them. The experiment was halted on day 6 of the study (8 days early) when an outside researcher who came to interview the guards and prisoners expressed outrage at the sadistic treatment on the part of the guards and concern for the pathological reactions being exhibited by some of the prisoners. Many other individuals who were not directly involved had visited the experiment; none of them had expressed any objection to what they had seen (Haney, Banks, and Zimbardo 1973).[5]

Humphreys' *Tearoom Trade,* Mid-1960s

In his book *Tearoom Trade: Impersonal Sex in Public Places,* Laud Humphreys (1970/1975) presents the results of his mid-1960s dissertation research on men who met in public restrooms for casual sexual encounters. Humphreys gained access to these men by volunteering to be the "watch queen," a voyeur charged with signaling the men if police arrived. When the men left these encounters, he recorded the license plate numbers of their cars. He then obtained their home addresses through a police department contact. A year later, he went in disguise to their homes to conduct interviews claiming he was doing market research for an insurance company. While his work was influential in terms of expanding the then-limited knowledge of closeted homosexuality (as over half of his subjects lived their public lives as heterosexual men), he was heavily criticized by the academic community for not obtaining consent, using the men's license plate information illegally, risking exposure for the men who were not openly gay, and for conducting the final interviews under false pretenses.

The ethical problems with these three studies are often presented as self-evident; however, each of these researchers felt the research was, at least in part, justified. Humphreys (1970/1975) addressed many of the ethical criticisms of his work in the second edition of his book. He provided further explanation of how he protected the confidentiality of his subjects and why this information would have been difficult to obtain without some form of deception. He also acknowledged that his research design placed his subjects at greater personal risk than he recognized at the time. Milgram (1974) stated that the key ethical complaint regarding his work had to do with his surprising results, which he could not have foreseen. However, the study was not halted, even after it was clear that individuals were experiencing high levels of psychological distress. Milgram claimed the continuation of the experiments was justified because "there was no indication of injurious effects in the subjects; and as the subjects themselves strongly endorsed the experiment" during the post-experiment debriefing (p. 194). After the results of the first few experiments, it seems reasonable for Milgram to have implemented some process that might have minimized the possibility of longer-term psychological issues (e.g., pre-screening the participants for mental health, having a clinical psychologist onsite to intervene). At a minimum, it appears that Milgram did not fully process the implications of what was happening. Finally, Zimbardo (2007) acknowledged that he was caught up in the dynamics of his makeshift prison and his role as the prison superintendent and was unable to separate himself from the situation.[6]

The Current Ethical Standards and Institutional Oversight

Due to the widespread attention given to the unethical Nazi experiments, international, national, and professional standards for protecting human subjects were developed. The most influential were the Nuremberg Code (1949) and the Declaration of Helsinki (World Medical Association 1964). In 1966, the United States' National Institutes of Health (NIH) established policies for the protection of human subjects based on both Nuremberg and Helsinki. The NIH began requiring that all institutions receiving its funding establish **institutional review boards (IRBs)**. IRBs, typically consisting of faculty members within a university or college, one community representative, and one non-scientist representative, are charged with evaluating and either approving or rejecting research proposals involving human subjects. IRBs are also charged with the oversight of all research involving human subjects conducted by the institution's faculty, staff members, and students.

In 1974, what was then the U.S. Department of Health, Education, and Welfare (HEW) elevated the NIH policies to cover all federally funded research. Currently, the **Office of Human Research Protections (OHRP)** within the U.S. Department of Health and Human Services is responsible for overseeing compliance with the federal regulations by individuals and institutions receiving federal funding. Most universities require that all individuals planning research involving human subjects, regardless of the source of funding, secure approval from their IRB.

One of the primary issues with these regulations is that they were developed to address problems with medical and psychological experiments, rather than to provide guidance for the broad range of research done with human subjects, including within social science disciplines such as sociology, anthropology, economics, and political science. We'll look closely at one of the central documents, the **Belmont Report,** which continues to guide the efforts of IRBs in assessing and determining if a research proposal is acceptable.

The Belmont Report

In 1978, the U.S. Department of Health, Education, and Welfare (later renamed the Department of Health and Human Services) convened a commission to develop and document ethical principles and practices with the intent to prevent the mistreatment of human subjects. This commission issued the Belmont Report, which delineates three major ethical principles along with their applications:

Principle	Application
Respect for Persons	Informed Consent
Beneficence	Assessment of Risks and Benefits
Justice	Fair Selection of Subjects

This report continues to guide institutional review boards, charged with the oversight of research involving human subjects, in terms of how they determine if a research proposal is acceptable.

In 1978, the Belmont Report was written by a commission charged by the HEW to develop and document ethical principles and practices to prevent mistreatment of human subjects. The report delineates three major ethical principles (respect for persons, beneficence, and justice) along with the applications of these principles (informed consent, assessment of risks and benefits, and fair selection of subjects). This report was never intended to solve all of the problems of social research, but rather to provide "an analytical framework that will guide the resolution of ethical problems arising from research involving human subjects" (National Commission for the Protection of Human Subjects of Biomedical and Behavioral Research

Participants or Subjects?

The dominant focus of ethical guidelines on the individuals participating in research experiments has led to the replacement of the label "research subject" with that of "research participant." The ethical concern is that by calling a person a "subject," the researcher may view the individual as an object rather than as an individual; however, the "participant" label only works when the individual being studied is active in the research. For this reason, we have not adopted the new standard consistently throughout this text. It makes no sense to talk about a research "participant" when the individual is unaware of the research (e.g., ethnographic fieldwork); when the individual is not living; or when the research subject is not a person but an organization, group, country, or some other entity. In some of these cases, it may even be misleading to use such a term.

[NCPHS] 1978:1). Contrary to our broad definition of social research, the Belmont Report's principles and guidelines apply to "research," which is defined as an activity "designed to test an hypothesis, permit conclusions to be drawn, and thereby to develop or contribute to generalizable knowledge (expressed, for example, in theories, principles, and statements of relationship)" (p. 3). In addition, the Belmont Report clearly states that it addresses problems related to biomedical and behavioral research, and that policy relating to other types of social research should also be developed. This additional policy was not developed; instead, these principles have been applied, without modification, to social research.

As you will see below, the Belmont principles do not neatly align with many of the methods used in social research. At best, this means that many social researchers do not get sufficient direction from these principles. At worst, their ability to do social research is thwarted because they attempt to conform to standards that were never intended to apply to their work. More and more universities are responding to this mismatch by establishing separate institutional review boards for the social sciences. After briefly discussing each principle and application below, we will consider several problems within the current system of oversight. Then we turn to dilemmas facing individual researchers as they attempt to do ethically responsible research.

The first Belmont principle, **respect for persons,** recognizes each person's autonomy and his or her ability to deliberate about personal goals and to act accordingly. Furthermore, it recognizes that not every human being has this ability and that persons of diminished autonomy (e.g., children) must be protected. Respect for persons requires that autonomous human subjects enter research "voluntarily and adequately informed," and that those with diminished autonomy are protected accordingly or perhaps left out of the study entirely. To prove that individuals are entering research studies voluntarily and adequately informed, researchers are often required to obtain **informed consent** from all participants or the participants' legally authorized representatives. To obtain informed consent, researchers must communicate the research procedure, purposes, risks, and benefits to the participants in "jargon-free" language. Also, researchers must clearly communicate that participation is voluntary and that the participant can withdraw at any time. Signed informed consent forms, documenting that participants have been informed of the study details and are voluntary participants, have become a standard requirement of most research proposals.

The **beneficence principle** adds to the respect for persons principle by requiring researchers to ensure the well-being of the human subjects involved. Beneficent actions in research are defined as those that *do no harm* and *maximize possible benefits and minimize possible harms*. Researchers are obligated to complete an **assessment of risks and benefits** to justify that the benefits to be gained by the study outweigh the risks to the subjects. The Belmont Report acknowledges a tension here between the benefits to the individual (that is, the subjects of the study) and the benefits to others down the road.

The **justice principle** addresses the issues regarding equal distribution of benefits and burdens of the research. The report specifies that the populations studied must reap the rewards of the research in which they are involved, while recognizing that there are multiple acceptable distribution methods: "(1) to each person an equal share, (2) to each person according to individual need, (3) to each person according to individual effort, (4) to each person according to societal contribution, and (5) to each person according to merit" (NCPHS 1978:9). Furthermore, all benefits of research supported by public funding must be shared with the public, and not just with those who can afford the benefits. The application of this principle, the **fair selection of subjects,** requires that researchers demonstrate that the subjects of their proposed studies are being selected for research reasons and not because of their "easy availability, their compromised positions, or their manipulability" (p. 10).

Ethically Questionable Research
A Thing of the Past?

In spite of the standards and policies developed to better ensure ethically responsible research, contemporary biomedical and social researchers continue to generate controversies. Here are two examples of questionable social scientific research:

• A study conducted by Kennedy Krieger Institute and funded by the U.S. Environmental Protection Agency (EPA) in the early 1990s involved renting partially lead-abated housing—housing where lead contamination had been partially reduced—to families with young children and infants so as to monitor the lead levels of the children. Parents signed consent forms, but they were not advised of the hazards of dust in contributing to lead poisoning in children. The "greater good" argument here is that landlords would be more willing to pay for lead abatement in their buildings if they can do a partial (and less expensive) abatement. The U.S. Court of Appeals ruled in 2001 that a parent cannot provide consent for a child to participate in nontherapeutic research.

> Otherwise healthy children, in our view, should not be enticed into living in, or remaining in, potentially lead-tainted housing and intentionally subjected to a research program, which contemplates the probability, or even the possibility, of lead poisoning or even the accumulation of lower levels of lead in blood, in order for the extent of the contamination of the children's blood to be used by scientific researchers to assess the success of lead paint or lead dust abatement measures. Moreover, in our view, parents, whether improperly enticed by trinkets, food stamps, money, or other items, have no more right to intentionally and unnecessarily place children in potentially hazardous nontherapeutic research surroundings than do researchers. In such cases, parental consent, no matter how informed, is insufficient. (*Grimes v. Kennedy Krieger Court of Appeals* 2001)

• In 2001, an assistant professor at Columbia University began a study to examine how restaurants handled customer complaints. Apparently without the university's knowledge, Frank Flynn sent identical letters to 240 New York restaurants claiming he had gotten severe food poisoning at that restaurant during an anniversary dinner (Appelbaum 2001). The letter also implied that Flynn would report the restaurant to the Better Business Bureau if it did not respond accordingly. The restaurant owners later stated that the complaint letter had cost them time, money, and peace of mind, as they, along with their staff, tried to track down the source of the food poisoning and determine when and what Flynn had eaten at their restaurant. Some of the restaurants got together and sued (unsuccessfully) the university for $100 million for libel, emotional distress, and negligent misrepresentation.

Ethical and Professional
Dilemmas Facing Social Researchers

The ambiguity of expectations and requirements often leaves researchers on their own to work through the ethical and professional dilemmas they face when conducting research. The second half of this chapter addresses these dilemmas and problems. First, we discuss the problems faced by researchers as they attempt to reconcile the Belmont principles and applications with social research realities. Second, we examine several professional dilemmas created by IRB oversight. Third, we consider how accountability to different individuals and institutions can create conflict and result in a set of ambiguous choices for researchers. Finally, our last section considers several dilemmas that arise from the interactions between researchers and their subjects.

Reconciling the Belmont Principles
With Social Research Realities

A major dilemma facing social scientists is how and whether to comply with ethical guidelines that often don't address or don't apply to the realities of social research. Here we examine several quandaries that arise from each of the three Belmont applications.

Respect for Persons and Informed Consent Issues. Informed consent for certain social research strategies does not make sense. A problem arises for researchers when they are required to obtain signed informed consent forms in situations where they feel the spirit of the principle is better served with some other method (e.g., verbal consent). In fact, the federal guidelines allow for informed consent to be waived when

> the research involves no more than *minimal risk* to the subjects; the waiver or alteration will not adversely affect the rights and welfare of the subjects; the research could not practicably be carried out without the waiver or alteration; and whenever appropriate, the subjects will be provided with additional pertinent information after participation. (U.S. Department of Health and Human Services 2009, emphasis added)

However, a waiver may or may not be granted in actuality. The guidelines for informed consent are open to interpretation by the institutional review boards. There are many research projects for which obtaining a signed informed consent form could jeopardize the integrity of the research. For example, it is often inappropriate to request a signed form when participants want to maintain their anonymity, are illiterate, are skeptical of legal documents, or are fearful of the future implications of their participation (e.g., in situations of state repression or blacklisting). Given that social scientists can have their records subpoenaed, this is of particular concern for researchers studying illicit activities, such as gang life or organized racism. Mandating a signed consent form in such inappropriate situations can undermine the relationship between participants and researchers, affect the interactions going forward, or derail the entire project. Also, astute participants realize that the rationale for a signed consent form may not be just about informing them of the study, but may also be about protecting the universities, external funding agencies, and researchers from litigation. Ironically, completion of the form can become a risk for the research participants.

Ethnography and Ethics

Mitchell Duneier (2001) describes fieldwork as "a morally ambiguous enterprise" in part due to the intimate relationships that evolve when a researcher immerses himself or herself into the lives of others (p. 336). In his book *Sidewalk,* he took two unusual steps to address this ambiguity. First, he used the real names of the Greenwich Village street vendors he was studying, when standard practice in social research is to use pseudonyms. Second, he is sharing royalties with the 21 people on whose lives the book is primarily based, though this is not a standard or expected practice in his discipline.

A second problem revolves around the quantity and quality of information about the study given to potential participants before data collection. The appropriate balance between fully informing participants about all aspects of a study and protecting the integrity of the research is an issue. The requirement of an individual's signature on a consent form impacts the degree to which a participant feels like his or her confidentiality will be maintained. Excessively detailed information also might deter certain people from participating, as it may result in an inflated view of the risks involved or the degree to which involvement might result in a subsequent hassle. Consequently, using a consent form that fully informs participants and is signed by them may result in a sample that does not represent a given population. Some research involves deception from the outset, as the findings would be impossible to obtain if the purposes of the research were disclosed up front. This type of deception is common in experimental psychology.

For example, the participants in Milgram's study could not have been told about his interest in obedience without rendering the results meaningless. Other researchers use deception to "catch" people in behaviors they would otherwise not admit to if they knew they were part of a research study. For example, Monica McDermott (2006) spent a year working as a convenience store clerk in order to better understand race relations among working-class individuals. By working undercover, she was able to observe everyday interactions. The process of getting informed consent, including the detailed procedures and disclaimers, is also likely to affect the subjects' behaviors and responses. Thus, the way that informed consent shapes the research introduces another variable. Psychologists have demonstrated that research participants often alter their behavior to do what they feel is expected of them rather than what they would do normally (Orne 1962). It seems possible, then, that fully informed consent could produce questionable research results.

A third problem with the respect for persons principle centers on defining who is autonomous and who is vulnerable. If a researcher wants to conduct in-depth interviews with survivors of the World Trade Center attacks, is this acceptable according to the principles laid out by the Belmont Report? Some of these survivors are likely to become upset during the interview. Is the autonomy of these individuals considered "diminished"? At what point will they regain "full autonomy"? Should participation be decided by the individuals asked to participate (assuming they are competent adults) rather than a removed committee, as this research might give the survivors an opportunity to shape the handling of future tragedies? In addition, by ruling out participation of these survivors, the researcher might deny them the opportunity to give voice to their losses as well as their experiences dealing with a highly visible tragedy—a process that could have significant benefits for the survivors. Ironically, researchers studying IRBs run into an interesting circumstance. They need to get IRB approval for certain aspects of their research such as talking to IRB members. The IRB then determines if other IRB members are capable of making their own decision about participation (e.g., Doherty and Kramer 2005; Stark 2007).

Beneficence and Exposing Injustices. The underlying ethic of "do no harm" to research subjects embodied in the beneficence principle does not make sense when we consider evaluation, participatory, action, and policy-oriented research whose goals often include calling attention to injustices such as domestic abuse, political corruption, or police brutality. The very act of engaging in the research in the first place occurs in order to bring situations to light, which may trigger a chain of events that would negatively impact the lives of some of the individuals involved (e.g., the firing of a corrupt leader). When the role of the researcher is to expose injustice, perhaps the ethical principles followed by investigative journalists are more appropriate.

The "do no harm" principle assumes that the human subjects will be somehow medically treated or psychologically manipulated, yet much social scientific research involves observation, archival work, in-depth interviews, and surveying, for which there is little risk of psychological harm and virtually no risk of physical harm. When IRBs disallow research that might cause nonphysical harm to some participants, they enter the murky waters of impinging on academic freedom. When researchers want to better understand religious extremists, survivors of war atrocities, or corrupt politicians, it is likely that there will be stressful moments during the interviews. The potential for psychological distress seems likely, so does this mean these areas of research are off-limits or that they must be studied by some means other than talking directly to the individuals involved? The lack of professional agreement on what constitutes minimal nonphysical harm results in an IRB having tremendous power over what is or is not studied within its institution.

Justice and Distribution of Benefits. Evaluation, participatory, action, and policy-oriented research are clearly in sync with the notion that some type of benefit or improved quality of life should be a goal of the research. What, though, is the obligation to give back to the community or individuals in the study? In some cases, researchers hope for direct positive results from their work. For other researchers, however, their work may only have an indirect impact by influencing research down the road. Should researchers simply avoid research projects that do not have the potential for some kind of social or common benefit? And who determines what constitutes a social or common benefit? Researchers also may benefit from successful research by promotions, job opportunities, prestige, and book royalties. Does the principle of justice imply that these benefits be shared? Should researchers whose work results in royalties be required to share these with the people they observed? If so, how much is appropriate? As noted in the earlier text box, Mitchell Duneier's (2001) unusual step of sharing royalties with some of the individuals in his book is a prominent and rare example of a researcher attempting to address this principle by sharing the rewards of the research.

Problems With Institutional Oversight

Beginning in the late 1990s, universities became increasingly risk averse and intensified their scrutiny of all research conducted by their faculty, staff, or students. The reasons for this were not driven by ethicists or social researchers;

rather, this increase in oversight was an institutional response to a wave of biomedical research scandals. The gene therapy trial at the University of Pennsylvania in 1999, which resulted in the death of Jesse Gelsinger, 18 years old, was one of several questionable biomedical studies that drew widespread public attention. The U.S. Office for Protection From Research Risks at the National Institutes of Health withdrew all federal research support, suspended trials midstream, or issued fines at many prestigious universities where ethical lapses and questionable oversight practices had come to light. In addition, many of the cases resulted in litigation. For example, the Gelsinger family sued the university and later settled for an undisclosed amount. The negative public attention, the threat of losing all federal research funding, and the threat of litigation all contributed to the increased scrutiny, extended jurisdiction, and heightened bureaucratic demands of university IRBs.

A recurring criticism is that this intensified regulatory environment has not yielded many, if any, benefits within the social sciences. Nonetheless, social researchers have had to deal with this environment. It is viewed by many as one "in which review of research becomes an exercise in avoiding sanctions and liability rather than in maintaining appropriate ethical standards and protecting human participants" (Burris and Walsh 2007). Many social scientists have written about their increasing frustrations with the current research review process (see "Symposium on Censorship and Institutional Review Boards" 2006). The increased institutional oversight and frustrations with it have certainly shaped how individual researchers are conducting their work. This section covers three issues with the current system of oversight: freedom of inquiry, conflicts of interest, and self-censorship.

Freedom of Inquiry. IRB oversight has been used inappropriately to censor research. Some IRB members feel it is part of their job to deny approval to "bad" research designs or topics that they do not consider to be worthwhile. This strikes at the heart of academic freedom. (For numerous real-world examples, see Zachary Schrag's blog at www.institutionalreviewblog.com.) As discussed earlier, IRBs indirectly impinge on academic freedom by attempting to comply with the Belmont principles. Professor of law Philip Hamburger (2004) makes a strong case that IRBs operate as a licensing agency and end up violating the First Amendment rights of researchers. Court rulings so far have not supported the idea that social scientists have a constitutional right to conduct research. Hamburger's ideas, however, are shaping the debates about IRB oversight and the ways in which it limits academic inquiry.

Conflicts of Interest. There are institutional incentives in place that predispose IRBs to overregulate—a "better safe than sorry" mentality dominates

(Carpenter 2007). A major reason for this mentality centers on the competing interests of the IRB. The members of an IRB face pressure to protect the university from scandal litigation. Larger research universities may hire an IRB director who is evaluated on his or her ability to either bring a university into compliance or maintain its compliance. Thus, a university and its IRB have a major incentive to be risk averse to avoid fines, citations, or the withdrawal of funding from the U.S. OHRP. A major scandal can lead to termination of the problematic study and potentially to all studies receiving OHRP funding. In addition, universities and researchers often have a personal financial stake in their project. Within the social sciences, this is typically limited to book royalties, speaking fees, or small ventures (such as the development of surveying technology). Within the world of biomedical research, however, the financial stakes can be huge. For example, a chemist at Northwestern University developed the drug pregabalin to treat fibromyalgia nerve pain (marketed by Pfizer as the blockbuster drug Lyrica). Sales of this drug have bought in tens of millions of dollars to the university as well as enormous wealth to the chemist who developed the product. In another example, both the University of Pennsylvania and the researchers there had financial interests in the gene therapy study that resulted in Jesse Gelsinger's death.

The role of direct corporate funding introduces another potential conflict of interest. Some corporate funders have required that all research from a given study receive their approval before being published. The current system does not fully appreciate how the relationships between industry and universities have become inextricably bound together. Conflicts of interest have the potential to shift the focus of an IRB from protecting the subject or the academic freedom of the researcher to pleasing funding agencies and university administrators. Financial conflicts of interest also may distort a researcher's decision making about what is ethical. These are already major issues within the biomedical world and ones we anticipate will increase in the social sciences.

Self-Censorship. The dilemma here is whether to tackle risky, risqué, or politically sensitive research topics, which might become bogged down in the IRB review process. Researchers may also modify their topics to gain IRB approval and move forward in a timely fashion. This self-censoring could have an adverse effect on the quality of research being undertaken. Many researchers admit to this type of reaction. For example, professor of journalism Margaret Blanchard (2002) has shifted her focus from the 20th century to the 19th, as she feels research on deceased subjects will elicit less IRB interference. She has summed up her frustration with her IRB as follows: "A better formula for demoralizing graduate students and faculty members could not be imagined. A better formula for stultifying research is beyond contemplation" (p. 68).

Researchers are also likely to self-censor when selecting a research strategy. Quantitative research, which tends to be more deductive and adheres more closely to the scientific method, gets IRB approval more easily. This is because the analytical frame for this type of research is largely fixed in advance of the data collection. When the quantitative research is initiated, there is a clear and predictable process. The interactions with subjects are often highly scripted, as in a telephone survey. When other research strategies are used, especially qualitative, the researcher is uncertain of what might unfold. The higher degree of certainty for any given study makes the ethics review process smoother. Only three of the seven goals of social research, identifying broad patterns, testing/refining theory, and making predictions, are suited to the current IRB model because they align with more quantitative research strategies (see Chapter 2).

Ethics on a Small Scale

A model of social research that centers on ethics will generate changes even in seemingly inconsequential research projects. For example, a researcher was doing a small study of four separate marketing flyers in conjunction with a women's self-defense nonprofit to determine which of four images was most compelling and why. Graduate students participated anonymously and voluntarily, randomly getting one of the four versions along with the same set of survey questions. While the content of the flyers was in no way violent, the researcher felt that two of the questions (Have you or someone close to you ever been sexually assaulted or attacked? Have you ever defended yourself against a sexual assault?) could have brought up thoughts and feelings about negative experiences for some students. To address this, the survey included a separate sheet with information on where students could find support in general and support geared toward those experiencing or recovering from domestic violence or sexual assault (e.g., the counseling center, medical emergency and campus safety information). The entire exercise took no more than 10 minutes during a class break. The researchers easily could have conducted this study without any thought to the students' reactions and most likely no lasting harm would have occurred; however, by adding information about sexual assault resources, the researchers thought beyond their goals for the research and considered the experience of the researched. Consequently, this small study may have yielded some benefit to the participants.

There are several ways in which researchers attempt to resolve this dilemma. One way is to steer clear of institutional oversight entirely. Some do this by determining that their work is outside the boundaries of the federal definition of "research." Research is vaguely defined in the federal regulations code as "systematic investigation, including research development, testing and evaluation, designed to develop or contribute to generalizable knowledge" (HHS 2009). Others believe that their work is exempt because it is not federally funded, when in reality, most universities require IRB oversight for all research involving human subjects regardless of the source of funding. Still others do not see IRB oversight as legitimate and therefore have an easy time deciding that they are not under an IRB's jurisdiction. For example, if his sociological projects are challenged by an IRB, Howard Becker claims he'll say that they are conceptual art, because universities "don't hassle artists" (quoted in Shea 2000).

A second way to address the dilemma involves the focus researchers place on various aspects of their study design when filing the required document for IRB approval. The researcher may provide explanations of the aspects of his or her intended study that best fit with expectations while neglecting to mention or skimming over aspects that are not. For example, qualitative researchers might emphasize their informed consent procedures, the questions that they might ask during in-depth interviews, how they will ensure that their field notes are secure and the confidentiality of their subjects protected, while glossing over other aspects such as potential interactions with children, the possibility of witnessing illegal behaviors, or the degree to which some of their questions might cause a participant stress. This "low-level cheating" is not a well-concealed practice (Swidler, quoted in Shea 2000). In fact, a great deal of negotiating with IRB members occurs prior to the submission of an application.

This brings us to a third way of handling this dilemma, which rests on actions by IRB members themselves. IRB members generally want their peers to be productive, and so they work with the researchers to wordsmith their applications and informed consent forms to satisfy the IRB's interpretation of the regulations. Also, an IRB member might fully understand the inductive nature of a colleague's work, but adopt willful ignorance so the research can be conducted without requiring the researcher to change the research design, complete protocol amendments, or experience multiple delays of his or her work (Bledsoe et al. 2007).

Issues of Accountability

During the course of a single research project, a researcher may feel accountable to various parties, including funders, employers, colleagues, assistants, research subjects or participants, themselves, and society at large. These competing obligations can pose dilemmas in terms of what is or is not ethically responsible.

The issue of researcher accountability depends in part on the researcher's view of science. In the essay "The Meaning of 'Ethical Neutrality' in Sociology and Economics," Max Weber (1917/1949) articulated a value-neutral approach to social inquiry in which a researcher is obliged first and foremost to develop knowledge about reality based on observed social facts. If a researcher believes that creation of objective knowledge is his or her primary obligation, then the role of objective and uninvolved observer is the ethically responsible and professionally legitimate one. This value-neutral approach has been challenged by many social scientists as problematic. Feminists, critical theorists, and action researchers point out that the object of study is inextricably bound up with the individuals doing the studying. In this light, social scientific representations are not unbiased truths but are imbued with the values guiding the research, the researcher, and the researched. If a researcher is skeptical of the distance between the observer and the subject of observation, the proper role of the researcher may not be to simply observe but to interact, even intervene.

An interview setting can be used to illustrate this issue. Take a situation where a researcher is interviewing parents about their experiences with health care professionals in a hospital setting. If the researcher has information that would help these parents better navigate the bureaucracy or better understand the needs of their child, what is that researcher's obligation? If he or she intervenes, then the social process may not unfold in the same manner and the intervention threatens the research. Are there alternatives that would balance the goals of the research with the obligation to the participants? Given that most social science researchers are not trained to offer advice or guidance on substantive issues outside of their particular area of expertise, an obligation to intervene in a productive manner would render much social research impossible.

The issue of researcher accountability should also be informed by disciplinary professional codes of ethics. If a researcher suspects that one of the subjects is extremely depressed, the researcher may or may not feel an obligation to help him find support. If the researcher suspects a subject is being physically abused or physically abusing someone else, the obligation to act might increase considerably. But in both of these situations, the decision is left to the researcher. Unlike physicians, psychiatrists, teachers, and social workers, there are no clear rules for social researchers or for journalists, social commentators, or historians, for that matter. It seems clear that lawyers are more involved in crafting these guidelines to ensure that the professional association or research institution is legally protected. Ethics have been displaced by a fear of litigation. Take as a case in point this segment from the American Sociological Association's (1999) *Professional Code of Ethics*:

> Sociologists may confront unanticipated circumstances where they become aware of information that is clearly health- or life-threatening to research participants, students, employees, clients, or others. In these cases, sociologists balance the importance of guarantees of confidentiality with other principles in this Code of Ethics, standards of conduct, and applicable law. (p. 10)

Let's turn to a case where the question of accountability shifts from the individual to the organizational level. In *The Basics of Social Research*, Earl Babbie (2008) discusses an ethical dilemma arising from his plan to collect data from law students about their legal education in order to make recommendations to law schools to improve legal education in the state of California: "[T]he plan was to prepare a questionnaire that would get detailed information about the law school experiences of individuals. People would be required to answer the questionnaire when they took the bar exam" (pp. 65–66). Babbie cancelled the project after a colleague pointed out that the law students would not be voluntary participants, and so the study was unethical. It seems like a clear-cut case; however, the California Bar Association also has a responsibility to those who will be using the services provided by those attorneys it deems qualified to join its profession. Studying law programs and determining areas of inadequacy are crucial to maintain the quality of legal practice in California. In this case, is the consent of the bar association, as a gatekeeper, sufficient to require individuals taking the bar to complete a survey about their legal education? Accountability to the legal profession could be viewed as sufficient rationale for requiring individuals who are seeking admission to the legal profession to complete a survey. These are not unwitting subjects; they are adults who are seeking to join an elite profession. Asking them to provide confidential information about their learning experiences to help improve the process, particularly if they are allowed to leave questions blank, seems reasonable. In fact, it could be viewed as negligent on the part of the California Bar Association *not* to take measures to improve the legal training in the state.

Researchers may find themselves in a double bind in which acting responsibly with respect to one party conflicts with what is needed to act responsibly toward another. Our next section focuses on the tensions surrounding a researcher's relationship with a subject or participant. These tensions are heightened when a research design calls for a high level of interaction with those being studied, such as with qualitative research.

Relationship Between Researcher and Subject

For many research projects, there is interaction between the researcher and participant. (A few exceptions—**archival research** and **meta-analyses**—come to mind.) What, then, is a researcher's responsibility for the content or consequence of this interaction?

For certain types of research techniques, such as the survey, the researcher-participant interaction is often not given much consideration by the researcher. Perhaps more attention is warranted. Although less visible, even researchers using "less intrusive" methods are indeed interacting with, intruding on, and influencing participants. For example, a longitudinal study of children of divorced parents involves interviewing the children annually, through to adulthood, to assess their overall health, the health of their relationships with their parents, and the ways in which the children believe their parents' divorce affected them. When a large percentage of these children say their parents' divorce had a huge impact on who they are today, it seems reasonable to us that their participation in the recurring interviews could have influenced their responses.

Another researcher might be interested in children's perception of various social factors. The researcher devises a survey instrument to be given to children, with a school board's permission. Many adults will review and approve the survey questions. The most interesting and valuable questions are likely to be those that tap into complicated topics (e.g., social comfort in minority/majority settings). If a researcher exposes a child to a particular issue (e.g., his or her level of social comfort in a setting where he or she is a minority) that the child had not previously considered, then taking a survey is a far more meaningful interaction than it might appear on the surface. The question hinges on the degree to which we think these researchers are affecting the individuals and environments under study.

On the other side of the spectrum are researchers who immerse themselves in their field of study. Such researchers will have given these interactional dynamics considerable attention. In particular, they have focused on the consequences of being both an observer and a participant. There are a limitless number of ways to do fieldwork, ranging from "fly on the wall" observation at one extreme to full participation at the other. The closer to the participant end of this observer-participant continuum a researcher situates himself or herself, the more likely he or she is to get an insider's perspective. Developing the type of rich knowledge gained from immersing oneself deeply into a field site is a hallmark of ethnography. Intimate knowledge is seen as more authentic and valued. Ethnographers are often cautioned to remain partially outside so that they can critically assess and reflect on their experiences. While this poses a dilemma for researchers, it is more of a professional dilemma than an ethical one. Yet from this tension arises a number of related ethical dilemmas with respect to reconciling the intrusion of oneself into people's lives. Researchers find themselves facing complicated questions such as how to conduct research on individuals or groups whose values, beliefs, or actions are considered by the researcher to be undesirable or amoral; how to protect the privacy of the participants and the information they provide; and how to manage relationships with key informants. These questions are often most pressing when the researcher fully immerses himself or herself into the field. Let's look more closely at them.

Working With Undesirables. In order for most people to share personal information about their lives with someone, there must be a certain level of trust. The process of gaining an individual's trust is referred to as **building rapport** among social scientists. The better a researcher's rapport with an individual, the greater will be the access to the underlying meanings the individual attributes to his or her ideas and actions. When the participants' worldviews and behaviors are judged as undesirable, even reprehensible, by the researcher, he or she faces an ethical dilemma: how to remain true to his or her own convictions while simultaneously building sufficient rapport so participants share details of their lives. Kathleen Blee (2003) was concerned about how her research with women active in neo-Nazi, Ku Klux Klan, and Christian Identity organizations might give voice to these individuals and their causes. She also had concerns about her own safety, about her attention being seen as acceptance or tacit support for their racist views, and about the potential that her representation of the individuals within the world of organized racism might garner additional sympathy for their ideas. Blee had to balance these concerns with her goal of interpreting culturally significant phenomena, particularly in the closed groups she aimed to penetrate.

Protecting Privacy. Kathleen Blee (2003) did not worry about providing any benefit to those groups whose actions and ideas she found reprehensible. Her concern for those she interviewed was limited to protecting their confidentiality so that her field notes could not be used for prosecutorial purposes. In fact, some of the women did not want her protection. They wanted their informed consent forms modified to require her to use their real names. She refused to do so. Researchers who get to know their participants intensely may later be called upon to provide information about those participants' actions or statements. Ethnographers and anthropologists frequently write up extensive notes describing their observations, encounters, and initial reactions to what they experienced. They may also make audio and video recordings of events and interactions. These notes and records can be viewed as valuable evidence when a legal dispute arises or when a criminal investigation is underway. The researcher may also be called upon to provide an eyewitness account of what he or she observed. In these situations, a researcher faces a difficult dilemma regarding the extent to which he or she should cooperate with the investigators.

For example, medical anthropologist Sheldon Zink spent over a year and a half with James Quinn, a patient who underwent experimental surgery to replace his fatally diseased heart with an experimental mechanical one. When Quinn's quality of life following the surgery fell short of what his wife felt had been promised during the informed consent process, she sued the mechanical heart maker and members of the hospital staff. Zink's field notes were subsequently subpoenaed by the defense attorneys. She refused to turn over her field notes on the grounds that it violated the American Anthropological Association's code of ethics and her First Amendment rights. She was present during Quinn's ordeal and his surgery so as to gather data pertaining to her research topic (which was how new technology affected organizations and individuals). Quinn agreed to Zink's presence because he trusted her to protect his privacy. She was faced with the prospect of being jailed for contempt or betraying his privacy (R. Wilson 2003).

While social scientists like Zink have been threatened with imprisonment for refusing to turn over their notes, we are aware of only two who were actually incarcerated, both for refusing to answer a grand jury's questions. In 1972, political scientist Samuel Popkin was jailed for a week (Meislin 1972). Popkin did not even know why he was called before a grand jury, which was charged with investigating the leak of a major governmental report. He further indicated that their questions did "not reveal a clear pattern of what they were after" (quoted in Meislin 1972). Sociologist Rik Scarce was jailed for 5 months. Scarce refused to answer questions about the activities of an animal rights activist whose organization Scarce had been studying during the period under investigation. Scarce (2005) has continued to advocate for a federal shield law, which would protect social scientists from subpoenas and imprisonment by providing a legal safeguard for all information obtained during a researcher's study.

There are several problems with the use of pseudonyms for the people and places being studied. In some research, particularly social history, a project is concerned with documenting and interpreting historical events. In these cases, the standard should be to use real names. Citing sources and attributing quotes to specific people is standard practice in journalism unless there is a compelling reason for withholding this information. Other research has the goal of giving voice to a particular group. The use of pseudonyms here may actually reduce the value of the research. Even without concerns for historical preservation or other research goals, Mitchell Duneier (2001) feels that if he had used pseudonyms for his book on Greenwich Village sidewalk vendors, he would have had more to gain from this than the vendors. He argues that anonymity limits the ability of others to verify his accounts, and so using real names holds him "to a higher standard of evidence" (p. 348).

Managing Relationships. The last dilemma we will consider here, management of one's relationships with participants, revisits the issue of accountability. Two factors within a research design play a role in how we might judge a researcher's responsibility to a community or to a key informant. The first factor is whether the researcher is participating in an intense or meaningful moment in a person's life (e.g., adoption of a child). The second factor is whether the researcher is immersing himself or herself in the field for an extended period of time (e.g., relocation to a gentrifying community). There are certainly cases where a social researcher is in the field when both factors are present, such as Sheldon Zink's experience with James Quinn. Zink did not take her responsibility to Quinn and his family lightly. Prior to the subpoenas and 2 months prior to Quinn's death, Zink switched from her role of anthropologist to one of patient advocate at the request of Quinn's family (R. Wilson 2003). Some may view Zink's decision to switch roles as evidence that she was no longer an objective observer and thus, her increased involvement in the case undermines her research results. Others may not even agree with us that there is any ethical dilemma. The degree to which a researcher has responsibility to people in the field, in particular those key informants with whom the researcher may have developed close friendships, will be viewed differently by different people. For those who see an ethical dilemma, it is intensified by a researcher's willingness to fully integrate his or her life with those in the selected field site, his or her ability to fit in, and whether or not people remember or are reminded that the researcher is studying their lives.

The discomfort of being in the field in an intense fashion and the subsequent departure from the field are often personalized in ethnographic and anthropological accounts, instead of being seen as something commonly experienced within the profession. Since researchers view this tension as emerging from their personal and distinctive experiences, there is limited general discussion of this aspect of doing social research within the social sciences.

The Problem of Representation

Let us consider one last issue at the center of the construction of social research: To what extent is the researcher's voice and interpretation privileged relative to those being studied? As a researcher observes, interprets, and analyzes social life, he or she is also making decisions with respect to what is included and omitted—what (or who) gets attention and what is ignored—in the final representation. Even those researchers who literally turn the camera over to their subjects often make decisions about what footage to include, in what order, with what accompanying sounds, and so on. How does the representation capture, omit, or suppress the diversity of voices, experiences, and meanings that emerged as part of the research process?

Some researchers view themselves as capable of capturing social life in an unbiased, undistorted fashion, and are often comfortable using their expert authority and observational skills in crafting a final representation. Yet many others are wary about determining what material gets included, what matters, and what it all means. They are concerned that this exercise of "power" might undermine their efforts to give voice to the subjects. These researchers view this problem of representation as an ethical dilemma.

Social researchers use their best judgment in terms of what to emphasize and what conclusions to include in their representations because "there is no way to stuff a real person between the covers of a text" (Denzin 1989:82). Furthermore, researchers continue to develop and use novel approaches for creating a "dialogue based on the authority of the subject rather than the researcher" (Harper 2002:15). For example, researchers may review their work with the people they are studying prior to publication (as Mitchell Duneier did by reading passages to all the individuals who were discussed at any length in his book *Sidewalk* [2001]) and engage subjects directly in the interpretation of the evidence (as Douglas Harper did by asking those he was studying to provide their interpretation of various photographs in his book *Changing Works* [2001]). Regardless of whether or not a researcher views representation as an ethical issue, conveying an authentic portrayal of people studied is a high priority of most researchers, particularly those using a qualitative approach.

Conclusion

Some researchers continue to do ethically questionable research in spite of the appalling history of abuse of human subjects, the current ethics review system, and the expansive literature on research ethics and ethical lapses. Hopefully, the most disturbing examples discussed in this chapter serve as reminders that social researchers are not above unethical behavior whether due to hubris, a misguided focus on self-interests, or an overemphasis on a "greater good." Getting IRB approval is one way researchers have been encouraged to consider the "worst case scenarios" for their subjects. The IRB process can encourage researchers to do a better job of adhering to ethical standards even for small, inconsequential studies. Yet the process is now dominated by a regulatory frame of reference emphasizing compliance. As a result, there are ethical issues with certain research designs that rightly should be addressed but are neglected. For example, issues of accountability and responsibility for relationships in the field are not addressed by the current system of oversight.

Social researchers must push for normative models centering on ethics rather than compliance. It is too easy for the process to be co-opted. A good example of this co-optation comes from looking at informed consent processes. IRBs initially required signed consent forms as evidence that participants were fully informed of what their participation would entail. Evidence of informed consent is still the stated purpose for the signed form; however, forms have frequently included language that serves to protect the institutions and researchers from liability. In spite of federal guidelines prohibiting the use of such provisions, some panels have moved so far from the initial charge of ethics review that they require projects to obtain approval from the university's risk management and legal departments.

Ethical and professional standards are evolving. Some of the problems of ethical oversight are likely to be resolved by refining our practices. Henry Beecher (1966), the physician who exposed 22 unethical medical studies (including the Willowbrook Hepatitis Study), expressed doubt about formal rules for ensuring ethical research practices (p. 1360). We agree that the ethical and professional dilemmas mentioned in this chapter, along with the many others that arise from conducting social research, will not be solved by changes to the oversight system.

Just like non-scientists, social researchers will make questionable decisions they perhaps will later regret. Also, the problem of representation is not likely to have a single answer. There are many philosophical arguments associated with the ethics involved with balancing a researcher's voice and interpretation with those of the people being studied. Some research decisions will be condemned and others debated. Just as with Venkatesh's decision to play gang leader for a day, people will disagree on what is the right or wrong course of action for the many decisions facing social researchers.

With the increase in the number of cross-cultural studies being conducted, new dilemmas are arising (e.g., if local ethical belief systems conflict with those of the researcher, which system should take precedence?). Likewise, the increase in research involving new social media on the Internet has created more discussions around privacy, disclosure, and consent. No matter how comprehensive any given set of codes or rules, research projects take place in different contexts in which various dilemmas will arise. It is ultimately up to social researchers, individually and collectively, to consider these research-related dilemmas and work to resolve them in a conscientious manner.

Notes

1. For a detailed account of the Tuskegee Syphilis Trials along with other instances of gross mistreatment of African Americans by medical researchers, see Harriet Washington's book *Medical Apartheid* (2008).

2. To learn about recent controversies with research involving children, see Chapter 4 of Lainie Ross's 2008 book, *Children in Medical Research*.

3. Theodore Kaczynski (known as the Unabomber and hunted by the FBI for almost 2 decades until his arrest in 1996 for killing 3 people and injuring 23 by mailing bombs) was among the many Americans involved as subjects in MKULTRA-related projects. He participated in one of Henry Murray's CIA-backed, stress-related experiments during his first year at Harvard University (Chase 2000). Given the pervasiveness of what is known and the destruction of the remaining records, conspiracy theories about MKULTRA and other CIA-backed experiments have thrived. For further discussion of what is known about MKULTRA, see John Marks' 1979 book, *The Search for the "Manchurian Candidate,"* which is based on the documents he eventually obtained through the Freedom of Information Act.

4. In 2006, Jerry M. Burger (2009) conducted a partial replication of Milgram's study with some significant changes to attend to ethical issues. He found that obedience rates in his study were just slightly lower than those from the experiments conducted in the early 1960s.

5. In December of 2001, another prison experiment was conducted by researchers in the UK in conjunction with the BBC, which aired 4 one-hour programs based on the experiment. Like the Stanford Prison Experiment, this experiment was cut short because of concerns for the psychological well-being of the "prisoner" participants; however, many changes were made and safeguards put in place to ensure that the study was ethical (e.g., the researchers did not assume prison management roles; the prison was monitored around the clock; a separate committee could, by majority vote, call off the experiment if they felt at any time the participants were at risk; Reicher and Haslam 2006). These researchers argue that the participants' shared identities and group memberships were the primary drivers of the behaviors on the part of the guards and prisoners during their study, in contrast to the Stanford researchers' argument that the negative behavior by the guards in their study was due to the power inherent in their assigned roles.

6. Zimbardo continues to study the incremental process of dehumanization, which he views as a central mechanism explaining how ordinary people (like the Stanford students playing the role of prison guards and the military guards at Abu Ghraib) can participate in or fail to intervene in acts of atrocity. He devotes two chapters in his 2007 book, *The Lucifer Effect*, to understanding the abuses at Abu Ghraib.

PART II

Strategies of Social Research

The diverse goals of social research favor strikingly different research strategies. The goal of identifying general patterns, for example, suggests a research strategy appropriate for the study of many cases. When many cases are studied, it is difficult to study each case in depth. Typically, only a relatively small number of features across many cases can be incorporated into a representation. Thus, studies that examine many cases tend to focus on select aspects of them (that is, on a specific set of "variables"). By contrast, consider the goal of assessing historical or cultural significance. Usually, this strategy focuses on a small number of cases, sometimes only one, and researchers examine each case in great detail. This intensive strategy attempts to construct a full portrait through close analysis of the links among many different aspects of a case or cases. Studies that focus on a small number of cases tend to examine many features of those cases.

More generally, there is a trade-off between the *number of cases* and the *number of features of cases* social researchers typically can study and then represent. At one extreme is most qualitative research: few cases, many features. At the other extreme is most quantitative research: many cases, few features. In between these two extremes is comparative research. The comparative study of diversity across a moderate range of cases strikes a balance between in-depth knowledge of cases and broad knowledge of relations among variables (Ragin 1991). It is the best strategy when there are too many cases for close, detailed investigation of each case, but too few for quantitative analysis.

These three strategies are the primary concern of Part II of *Constructing Social Research*. Chapter 5 presents the qualitative study of commonalities as a strategy that is best suited for clarifying categories and concepts. Chapter 6 presents comparative research as a strategy oriented toward identifying and unraveling complex patterns of similarities and differences. Chapter 7 discusses quantitative research as an approach that most often focuses on the covariation of features across many cases.

Each of these strategies offers a different approach to evidence, and each has core data procedures that investigators use when they construct images from evidence. These different data procedures structure the interaction between researchers and their evidence, allowing them to digest large quantities, pinpoint decisive bits, or identify subtle patterns. Procedures differ from one strategy to the next because the nature of the evidence and the goals of research can vary so greatly. After all, a research strategy that uses a relatively small amount of information on each of a thousand cases calls for data procedures that differ dramatically from one that involves sifting through mounds of detailed information on a small number of cases.

Of course, all researchers work with evidence in many different ways—they use whatever procedures help them make sense of the evidence they collect. However, it is easier to grasp the three strategies discussed in Part II if each is presented along with the data procedures that are most compatible with the goals and logic of that strategy.

Qualitative methods are appropriate for in-depth examination of cases because they aid the identification of key features. Most qualitative methods *enhance* data. Comparative methods are appropriate for the study of diversity because they are sensitive to complex differences among cases. Comparative methods can be used to *elucidate* subtle patterns in the data. Finally, quantitative methods are appropriate for the study of relationships among variables because these methods can be used to assess the correlation between two or more features across many cases. Quantitative methods can *condense* data on the relations between two variables across many cases into a single number.

While the differences among these three strategies are emphasized, it is important to remember that they all involve a dialogue of ideas and evidence, as described in Chapter 3. Further, all three approaches are used to construct social scientific representations of social life, the primary goal of social research.

5

Using Qualitative Methods to Study Commonalities

Introduction

In some respects, qualitative research does not seem as scientific as other kinds of social research. Usually when we think of social science, we think of sweeping statements like, "People with more education tend to get better jobs," and "Poor countries tend to have more social conflict and political instability than rich countries." These statements offer "big picture" views that say nothing about individual cases. In these big-picture views, a single statistic or percentage can summarize a vast amount of information about countless cases.

But a lot may be missed in the big picture. Often, researchers do not want these broad views of social phenomena because they believe that a proper understanding can be achieved only through in-depth examination of specific cases. Indeed, qualitative researchers often initiate research with a conviction that big-picture representations seriously misrepresent or fail to represent important social phenomena. Consider the researcher who wants to understand how individuals make sense of their own and others' gender identities. A big-picture view might show that most people view gender identities as stable and intrinsic. But does the big-picture view say very much about individuals at the boundaries of gender, such as "gender benders"? What's the best way to study and understand the gender identities of gender benders—individuals who consciously challenge the traditional social norms associated with gender identities and gender roles by behaving in ways that transgress these boundaries (e.g., dressing in a manner inconsistent with their gender)?

A lot can be learned simply by talking to a group of gender benders. As discussed in Chapter 1, Leila Rupp and Verta Taylor (2003) went to Cabaret 801 in Key West to study the complex lives of a subset of gender benders, drag queen entertainers. In order to truly encompass gender identity issues and other factors affecting the lives of the drag queens, the researchers wanted to gain an in-depth understanding of the performers, their impact on their audience members, and their ideas about gender identity. How did they get started in drag performances? How long have they been involved in the show, and how often do they perform? What is involved in getting ready to perform? What types of gender identity issues do they face, and how do they personally describe their own gender identity? How do they think audience members feel about gender identity before and after seeing a show? In what ways, if any, do they think drag queens fit into the frequently interrelated lesbian, gay, bisexual, and transgender rights movements?

Using evidence from intensive interviews, Rupp and Taylor (2003) built an image of one category of gender benders—drag queen entertainers—by crafting a composite image of the performers. This composite image was then fleshed out further by studying the audience members and others involved in various ways. Along with their interviews (with 12 drag queens, the cabaret owner, the manager, two boyfriends, and two mothers), the researchers made audio recordings of 50 drag performances and conducted focus groups to gather audience interpretations. The key was to obtain as much in-depth knowledge as possible and look for common patterns among drag queens and their social worlds.

Sometimes the emphasis of the qualitative approach on in-depth knowledge means the researcher examines only a single case (for example, the life history of a single individual or the history of a single organization). Knowing as much as possible about one case is not easy because every case, potentially at least, offers information that is infinite in its detail. Much of this information is not useful because it is redundant or irrelevant, given the researcher's questions and purposes. In the qualitative approach, researchers must determine which information is useful in the course of the investigation, and they become more selective as additional knowledge about each case is gained. In the course of learning more about the research subject, the investigator sharpens his or her understanding of the case by refining and elaborating images of the research subject and relating these to analytic frames (see Chapter 3). These emerging images serve to structure inquiry further by marking some data collection paths as promising and others as dead ends.

Qualitative research often involves the clarification of the researcher's image of the research subject on the one hand, as well as the concepts that frame the investigation on the other. Images are built up from cases, sometimes by looking for similarities among several examples of the phenomenon that seem to be in the same general category. These images, in turn, can be related to concepts. A *concept* is a general idea that may apply to many specific instances. Concepts offer abstract summaries of the properties shared by the members of a category of social phenomena. They are the key components of analytic frames, which in turn are derived from ideas—current theoretical thinking about social life (see Chapter 3).

Let's revisit an example from Chapter 2: "Interactional vandalism" is a concept developed by Duneier and Molotch (1999) to describe a violation of conversational norms by an individual in a less powerful social position toward an individual in a more powerful one. The "street men"—sidewalk vendors, scavengers, and panhandlers—in their study persist in clearly unwelcome discussions with female passersby by breaching conversational expectations. An example of interactional vandalism is when a vendor, ignoring linguistic cues that a conversation is wrapping up, continues to ask questions of a female passerby. This study involved a mutual clarification of the category "street men" and the concept of "interactional vandalism." The researchers clarified the image of these men's lives on the street (an empirical category) as they clarified the concept of interactional vandalism. Their analysis makes it clear that this negative type of interaction is but one part of these men's complex relationships with people in the neighborhood and their customers. A relatively small number of these men were responsible for the instances of interactional vandalism, which were regarded as problematic by the other men. The concept, interactional vandalism, summarizes a lot of the interaction from the perspectives of both the passersby and the street men. It recognizes that the individual who is initiating an unwelcome conversation or otherwise breaching conversational norms is, in fact, doing more than behaving rudely. He is demonstrating his ability to upset the social order, create tension, or simply create a distraction to help pass the time. In addition, it captures the way in which this type of troubled interaction can be perceived as threatening by the receiver. This process of clarification is ongoing and culminates in the representation of the research that the investigator offers at the conclusion of the study. The newly refined concepts—those that were elaborated in the course of the study—are featured in the representation of the results of qualitative research.

The Goals of Qualitative Research

Because of its emphases on in-depth knowledge and on the refinement and elaboration of images and concepts, qualitative research is especially appropriate for several of the central goals of social research. These include giving voice, interpreting culturally or historically significant phenomena, and advancing theory.

Giving Voice

There are many groups in society, called *marginalized groups* by social scientists, that are outside of society's mainstream. Often, these groups lack voice in society. Their views are rarely heard by mainstream audiences because they are rarely published or carried by the media. In fact, their lives are often misrepresented—if represented at all.

Techniques that help uncover subtle aspects and features of these groups can go a long way toward helping researchers construct better representations of their experiences. By emphasizing close, in-depth empirical study, the qualitative approach is well suited for the difficult task of representing groups outside the mainstream. Shiori Ui (1991) was interested in studying women in a Cambodian immigrant community in the United States—a classic example of a marginalized social group. During her initial conversations with Cambodian community leaders in the San Francisco Bay Area, she was told that women did not hold any significant leadership roles. This is consistent with the conventional viewpoint that ethnic enclaves preserve traditional customs and family-member roles. However, once Ui began her in-depth study of another Cambodian community, she found that women were frequently taking on leadership roles in the community as well as within their households. Ui discovered that many factors (lack of jobs for men, women's participation in the informal economy, increased likelihood of learning English, and the socioeconomic background of the Cambodian immigrant community) contributed to the atypical presence of these Cambodian women in leadership roles. Thus, a great deal was learned about this Cambodian community on the whole, and about the more subtle ways in which leadership opportunities are enabled and constrained by structural factors.

Interpreting Culturally or Historically Significant Phenomena

How we think about an important event or historic episode affects how we understand ourselves as a society or as a nation. For example, in the mid- to late 1800s, the United States was involved in a series of territorial struggles with Mexico. These struggles can be interpreted as part of the inevitable westward expansion of European Americans across a vast, sparsely populated continent. Or perhaps they can be seen as part of a pattern of unjust bullying of a generally peaceful neighbor. As the United States has been gaining an ever-larger Hispanic population over the past few decades, a revision of our understanding of these earlier territorial struggles may help us adjust our view of the diverse collection of people who make up American society.

Methods that help us see things in new ways facilitate this goal of interpreting and reinterpreting significant historical events. Of course, if the evidence does not strongly support a new image, or offers better support to existing images, then new ways of understanding past events will not gain wide acceptance. The important point is that the qualitative approach mandates close attention to historical detail in the effort to construct new understandings of culturally or historically significant phenomena.

Advancing Theory

There are many ways to advance theory. New information about a broad pattern that holds across many cases (for example, a strong correlation; see Chapter 7) can stimulate new theoretical thinking. However, in-depth knowledge—the kind that comes from case studies—provides especially rich raw material for advancing theoretical ideas. When a lot is known about a case, it is easier to see how the different parts or aspects of the case fit together—how they relate.

For instance, it is difficult to know if or how the structure of a nun's daily routines of prayer, work, and community life help her maintain her deep religious commitments without collecting detailed observations of the lives of nuns. This in-depth knowledge is useful for elaborating concepts such as "commitment" and for direct examination of the connections among the phenomena that the researcher believes illustrate and elaborate the concept—for example, the daily routines of those with strong commitments.

The value of qualitative research for advancing theory also follows directly from practical aspects of this type of research. It is impossible to decide which bits of evidence about a case are relevant without clarifying the concepts and ideas that frame the investigation. The initial goal of knowing as much as possible about a case eventually gives way to an attempt to identify the features of the case that seem most significant to the researcher and his or her questions. This shift requires an elaboration and refinement of the concepts that prompted the study in the first place or the development of new concepts. Researchers cannot forever remain open to all the information that their cases offer. If they do, they are quickly overwhelmed by a mass of indecipherable and sometimes contradictory evidence.

Finally, qualitative research also advances theory in its emphasis on the commonalities that exist across cases. In some studies, cases may be selected that at first glance may seem very different. Identifying commonalities across diverse cases requires that the investigator look at them in a different way and perhaps discover new things about them. For example, David Shulman's study *From Hire to Liar* (2007) focuses not only on the deceptive practices of private investigators but also on the informal deceptions playing out among employees across 30 different organizations. Despite significant differences in the nature of the work across these venues, Shulman draws parallels in the ways deception is routinely used as a tool for the successful completion (or appearance of completion) of day-to-day work. By looking for similarities in unexpected places, social researchers develop new insights that advance theoretical thinking.

The Process of Qualitative Research

Qualitative research is often less structured than other kinds of social research. The investigator initiates a study with a certain degree of openness to the research subject and what may be learned from it. Qualitative researchers rarely test theories. Instead, they usually seek to use one or more cases or categories of cases to develop ideas. The qualitative researcher starts out by selecting relevant research sites and cases, then identifies "sensitizing concepts," clarifies major concepts and empirical categories in the course of the investigation, and may end the project by elaborating one or more analytic frames.

Selecting Sites and Cases

Qualitative research is strongly shaped by the choice of research subjects and sites. When the goal of the research is to give voice, a specific group is chosen for study. When the goal is to assess historical or cultural significance, a specific set of events or other slice of social life is selected. When the goal is to advance theory, a case may be chosen because it is unusual in some way and thus presents a special opportunity for the elaboration of new ideas.

Sometimes, however, cases are chosen not because they are special or unusual or significant in some way, but because they are typical or undistinguished. A researcher interested in U.S. migrant communities in general, for example, might select a neighborhood that is typical or average, not one with the highest or lowest proportion of migrants (see, for example, Levitt's 2001 study, *The Transnational Villagers*). To select a neighborhood at either extreme might limit the value of the study for drawing conclusions about migrant communities in general. In short, because qualitative researchers often work with a small number of cases, they are sometimes very concerned about establishing the *representativeness* of the cases they study (see Chapter 1; see also Small 2009 for a detailed discussion of case selection issues in qualitative research).

In-depth knowledge is sometimes achieved through the study of a single case. Often, however, it is best achieved by studying several instances of the same thing because different aspects may be more visible in different cases. Consider Monica McDermott's research, published in her book, *Working-Class White* (2006). By working as a convenience store clerk, she was able to observe racial interactions so as to develop a detailed representation of black and white race relations. (The ethics of this type of "undercover" ethnography are worth debating. See the discussion of informed consent in Chapter 4.) Much can be learned from studying interactions at a single convenience store in a given city. In fact, it is only through in-depth study such as McDermott's that working-class views regarding racial identity and stereotypes could be so thoroughly documented. However, McDermott deepened her research by selecting two convenience store locations, one in Boston, the other in Atlanta. Both stores were located in working-class white neighborhoods adjacent to working-class black neighborhoods. By comparing her observations and experiences in the two stores, McDermott was able to explore the ways in which white racial identity is contingent on location.

When qualitative researchers collect data on many instances of the phenomena under study, they focus on what the different instances have in common. Examining multiple instances of the same thing (for example, observing street men and passersby) makes it possible to deepen and enrich a representation (for example, a representation of interactional vandalism). A study of environmental activists might focus on the life experiences they share. A study of racist organizations might focus on their recruitment efforts. A study of immigrant neighborhoods might focus on the different ways immigrants establish and use interpersonal networks to facilitate their adjustment to new surroundings.

When many instances of the same thing are studied, researchers may keep adding instances until the investigation reaches a point of **saturation.** At that point, the researcher stops learning new things about the case, and recently collected evidence appears repetitious or redundant in light of previously collected evidence. It is impossible to tell beforehand how many instances the researcher will have to examine before the point of saturation is reached. In general, if the researcher learns as much as possible about the research subject, he or she will be a good judge of when this point has been reached.

Of course, if the cases selected for study are not sufficiently representative of the category the qualitative researcher hopes to address, then the point of saturation may be reached prematurely. For example, a study that seeks to represent the work of taxi drivers in New York City may reach saturation (no new things are being learned) after the researcher interviews 10 taxi drivers who are recent immigrants from Haiti. However, these 10 Haitian taxi drivers are probably not representative of *all* New York taxi drivers. The researcher should seek out taxi drivers with different backgrounds.

Even when qualitative researchers study many instances of the same thing (as when 50 small-town mayors are interviewed, for example), they often describe the case as singular ("the case of a small-town mayor") because the focus is on commonalities—aspects that the instances share. By contrast, a quantitative researcher (see Chapter 7) interested in systematic differences (say, the covariation between time in office and use of non-standard policies among these same mayors) would emphasize the fact that the research summarizes information on many cases (50 mayors). Statements about patterns of covariation (for example, "mayors serving more than two terms are more likely to adopt non-standard policies") are more likely to be accepted if they are based on as many cases as possible.

This distinction is subtle but very important. The qualitative researcher who interviews 50 small-town mayors seeks to construct a full portrait of "the small-town mayor" and the degree to which such mayors act in novel ways. It may be that the images that emerged changed very little, if at all, after the tenth mayor was interviewed, and not much was learned from the remaining 40 mayors. The difference between 10 and 50 is not important; what matters is the soundness of the portrayal of this case (the small-town mayor). If a study is done properly and is based on a sufficient number of interviews, it can be used for comparison with other cases (for example, comparing small-town mayors with the mayors of suburban villages). The important point is that even though many examples of the same thing may be examined, research that emphasizes similarities seeks to construct a single, composite portrait of the case.

Use of Sensitizing Concepts

It is impossible to initiate a qualitative study without some understanding of why the subject is worth studying and what concepts might be used to guide the investigation. These concepts are often drawn from half-formed, tentative analytic frames, which typically reflect current theoretical ideas. The analytic frames are fluid. These initial, sensitizing concepts get the research started, but they do not straightjacket the research. The researcher expects, at a minimum, that these initial concepts will be significantly altered or even discarded in the course of the research.

For example, a researcher studying hospital patients may bring "social class" as a sensitizing concept to the research and expect to find that patients from families with more income receive better care. However, the concept of social class, as expressed in family income, might prove to be too limiting as a frame for the research and be supplanted by an emphasis on some other aspect of family social status, such as occupational prestige of the adults in the household. Sometimes concepts that seem important or useful early in the study prove to be dead ends, and they are discarded and replaced by new concepts drawn from different frames. Armed with these new concepts, the researcher may decide that some of the evidence that earlier seemed irrelevant now needs to be reexamined.

For example, John Walton (1991, 1992) studied the conflict over water rights in Owens Valley, California, a struggle that pitted local residents against water-hungry Los Angeles in the 1930s. The battle over water rights dragged on for decades and generated so much mass protest and collective violence that it became known as "California's dirty little civil war." At first, Walton tried to use concepts that centered on social class and class conflict to understand this struggle. These were his initial, sensitizing concepts. However, he found that these concepts did not help him make sense of the evidence that he collected, nor did they direct him down data collection paths that advanced the study. Eventually he came to understand the struggle more in terms of collective responses, anchored in local conditions, to changing governmental structures, especially the growing influence and power of the federal government. These new concepts directed him to important historical evidence that he might have overlooked otherwise.

Clarifying Concepts and Categories

Qualitative research clarifies *concepts* (the key components of analytic frames) and empirical *categories* (which group similar instances of social phenomena) in a reciprocal manner. These two activities, categorizing and conceptualizing, go hand-in-hand because concepts define categories and the members of a category exemplify or illustrate the concepts that unite them into a category.

Generally, the members of a category are expected to be relatively homogeneous with respect to the concepts they exemplify. For example, since Duneier and Molotch (1999) found that only *some* street men engage in interactional vandalism, it would be wrong to use the concept to characterize *all* street men. Suppose they found that only those men who grew up outside of the neighborhood engaged in interactional vandalism. It might be possible to trace this to a difference in the level of belonging (or feeling of legitimacy) felt by the individual. The lack of fit between the concept "interactional vandalism" and the broad category "all street men" in this event would enrich the study, making it possible to narrow the relevant category to a subset of street men—those who grew up elsewhere—and showing a direct connection to a sense of social belonging.

This example shows the importance of examining the members of a category to make sure that they all display the concepts they are thought to exemplify. Researchers develop concepts from the images that emerge from the categories of phenomena they examine. They then test the limits of the concepts they develop by closely examining the members of relevant categories. In the example just presented, the concept of interactional vandalism emerged from images of some street men constructed by the investigators. Additional examination of all street men—to see if they all engage in interactional vandalism—establishes the limits of the relevant category.

Consider a second example of the interaction of categories and concepts: Howard Becker's (1953) classic study of becoming a marijuana user. Becker studied several marijuana users and found that each went through a process of *learning* to become a user—of learning *how* to enjoy marijuana. This led him to speculate that all *marijuana users* (the category) go through a *social process of learning* (the concept) to enjoy marijuana. He elaborated the key steps in the process of becoming a user by interviewing more than 50 users in the Chicago area in the early 1950s. He found that most of them went through the same process of learning how to enjoy marijuana.

However, Becker (1953) did encounter a few users who did not go through this process of learning how to use marijuana, and, although they were users, they said that they did not enjoy the drug. Becker described them as people who used marijuana for the sake of appearance—in order to appear to be a certain kind of person or to "fit in" with the people around them. Did this invalidate the idea that all users go through the same learning process? Becker solved the problem by narrowing the relevant category. He argued that the social process of learning how to enjoy marijuana applied only to those who used marijuana for pleasure, a category that embraced most, but not all, users. This narrowing made it possible for him to establish a closer correspondence between category (those who use marijuana *for pleasure*) and concept (the social process of learning how to use marijuana).

These examples show that the core issue in the clarification and elaboration of categories and concepts is the assessment of the degree to which the members of a category exemplify the relevant concept. Are the same elements present in each instance in more or less the same way? When encountering contradictory evidence (for example, street men who do not engage in interactional vandalism or marijuana users who did not go through the social process of learning how to enjoy marijuana), researchers have two choices: They can discard the concept they were developing and try to develop new ones—concepts that do a better job of uniting the members of the category—or they can narrow the category of phenomena relevant to their concept and try to achieve a better fit.

Elaborating Analytic Frames

Because categories and concepts are clarified in the course of qualitative research, the researcher may not be certain what the research subject is a "case of" until all the evidence is collected and studied. Deciding that the research subject is a case of something and then representing it that way is often the very last phase of qualitative research.

The open character of qualitative research can be seen clearly in the role played by analytic frames in this strategy. In some research strategies (for example, quantitative research; see Chapter 7), the main purpose of the analytic frame is to express the theory to be tested in terms of the relevant cases and variables. In qualitative research, by contrast, there is often only a tentative, vaguely formulated analytic frame at the outset because it is developed in the course of the research.

As more is learned about the cases and as categories and concepts are clarified, the researcher can address basic questions: What is this case a case of? What are its relevant features? What makes the chosen research subject or site valuable, interesting, or significant? As qualitative researchers elaborate analytic frames, they also deepen their understanding of their cases. For example, to describe some behavior of male street vendors as "cases of interactional vandalism" suggests that there are other instances of interactional vandalism in other situations, such as interactions between telemarketers and people just sitting down to dinner or between sales representatives and customers. The interactional vandalism frame developed in the study of male street vendors and female passersby may be applied to these and other social settings.

Not all qualitative researchers develop analytic frames. Sometimes they leave this task to other researchers studying related cases. The development of analytic frames is challenging because it requires the extension of the concepts elaborated in one case to other cases. Many qualitative researchers are content to report detailed treatments of the cases they study and leave their analytic frames implicit and unstated. They feel that their cases speak well enough for themselves.

This unwillingness to generalize is found in all types of qualitative research, from observations of small groups to historical interpretations of the international system. For this reason, qualitative researchers are often accused of being "merely descriptive" and not "scientific" in their research.

As should be clear by now, however, the process of representing research subjects, with or without generalization, is heavily dependent on the interaction between concepts and images, regardless of whether this interaction is made explicit by researchers when they represent their subjects. Without concepts, it is impossible to select evidence, arrange facts, or make sense of the infinite amount of information that can be gleaned from a single case. Like other forms of social research, qualitative research culminates in theoretically structured representations of social life—representations that reflect the regimen of social research.

Using Qualitative Methods

There are many textbooks on qualitative methods, and they describe such methods in a variety of ways (see, for example, Denzin 2006; Denzin and Lincoln 2005; Emerson 2001; Luker 2008; Rossman and Rallis 2003). In part, this diversity of views follows from the emphasis on in-depth investigation and the fact that there are many different ways to achieve in-depth knowledge. In sociology, anthropology, and most other social sciences, qualitative methods are often identified with **ethnographic study** and **in-depth interviewing.** Both methods seek to uncover the meaning and significance of social phenomena or subjects for people in a given research setting.

Ethnographic study emphasizes the immersion of the researcher in the research setting. It might involve living in an isolated village in some faraway part of the world. Consider anthropologist Katherine Hoffman's work, *We Share Walls* (2008), which details the impact of migration and politics on people's lives in rural Morocco. Ethnographic study might also involve long periods of observing and talking to people in a local setting, such as Erving Goffman's sociological research on the staff and patients of a mental institution in Washington, D.C., reported in his classic study *Asylums* (1961).

In-depth interviewing emphasizes the building of relationships and exploration of ideas with the individuals being studied. Rather than observing and participating in experiences, a researcher conducts interviews to hear how the people in the research setting make sense of their lives, work, and relationships. For example, as noted in Chapter 4, Kathleen Blee (2003) interviewed women who were active in racist and anti-Semitic groups. The women told stories of pivotal moments when their personal convictions were transformed, and also described ways in which their involvement with these groups increased incrementally. If Blee had observed or participated in the events and meetings of these groups, she might have noted the ways in which events and meetings were organized to reinforce group identity and incrementally increase member loyalty, but this approach would not have yielded the rich biographic details that the members revealed during the in-depth interviews. The interview setting allowed her, without seeming out of line, to delve further into ideas with the people in her study, deepening her understanding of their account of things.

Both techniques are unconstrained by the researcher's initial expectations or set of questions and are best for studying social situations at the level of person-to-person interaction. The organizing principle of this type of research is the idea that the kind of in-depth knowledge needed for a proper representation of the research subject must be based on the perspectives of the people being studied—that their lives and their worlds must be understood "through their eyes." In short, the emphasis is on immersion and empirical intimacy (Truzzi 1974).

The goal of this presentation of qualitative methods, however, is to address procedures that are relevant to all types of qualitative research, not simply the work of those who seek to represent social life as it appears through the eyes of participants. Researchers who seek to represent historically significant events, for example, cannot hope to see these events through the eyes of the participants if these events occurred in the distant past (the French Revolution, for example, or slavery in the U.S. South). Still, these historical researchers, like others who use qualitative methods, value and seek in-depth knowledge about cases, and they attempt to piece together meaningful images from evidence with the help of concepts and analytic frames.

The key features common to all qualitative methods can be seen when they are contrasted with quantitative methods. Most quantitative data techniques are data *condensers*—they condense data in order to reveal the big picture. For example, calculating the percentage of unionized workers who vote for the Democratic Party condenses information on thousands of individuals into a single number showing the link between these two attributes (union membership and party preference). Qualitative methods, by contrast, are best understood as data *enhancers*. When data are enhanced, it is possible to see key aspects of cases more clearly, depending on how the researcher searches for "hidden meanings, non-obvious features, multiple interpretations, implied connotations, unheard voices. While quantitative research is focused on summary characterizations and statistical explanations, qualitative research offers complex descriptions and tries to explicate webs of meaning" (ten Have 2004:5).

In many ways, data enhancement is like photographic enhancement. When a photograph is enhanced, it is possible to see certain aspects of the photographer's subject more clearly, depending on how it is done. When qualitative methods are used to enhance social data, researchers see things about their subjects that they might miss otherwise. Data enhancement is the key to bringing in-depth knowledge to light.

Almost all qualitative research seeks to construct representations based on in-depth, detailed knowledge of cases, often to correct misrepresentations or to offer new representations of the research subject. Thus, qualitative researchers share an interest in procedures that clarify key aspects of research subjects—procedures that make it possible to see aspects of cases that might otherwise be missed. While there are many such procedures, two that are common to most qualitative work are emphasized here: analytic induction and theoretical sampling. Both techniques are data enhancers.

Analytic Induction

Analytic induction means very different things to different researchers. Originally, it had a strict meaning and was identified with the search for "universals" in social life (Cressey 1953; Lindesmith 1947; Robinson 1951; Turner 1953). Universals are properties that are invariant. For example, if *all* upper-middle-class white males over the age of 50 in the United States voted for the Republican Party, then this would constitute a universal. However, if even one person in this category voted for some other party, the pattern would not be universal and thus would not qualify as a finding, according to a very strict, very narrow application of the method of analytic induction. Today analytic induction is often used to refer to any systematic examination of similarities that seeks to develop concepts or ideas.

Rather than seeing analytic induction as a search for universals, and one that is likely to fail, it is better to see it as a research strategy that directs investigators to pay close attention to evidence that challenges or disconfirms whatever images they are developing from their evidence. As researchers accumulate evidence, they compare incidents or cases that appear to be in the same general category with each other. These comparisons establish similarities and differences among incidents and thus help to define categories and concepts. Sociologists Barney Glaser and Anselm Strauss (1967) have called this process the **constant comparative method.** Evidence that challenges or refutes images the researcher is constructing from evidence provides important clues for how to alter concepts or shift categories.

For example, a study in a hospital might examine the care given to dying patients along the lines of Glaser and Strauss. By comparing cases of this type, the researcher can identify common features and the major dimensions of variation among incidents. Based on hours of observing the care of dying patients, a researcher might find (1) that nurses and other hospital personnel implicitly evaluate the potential "social loss" represented by each patient—if the patient were to die, (2) that a small number of patient characteristics enter into this evaluation (for example, the age and education of the patient), and (3) that the quality of patient care depends on the potential social loss inferred by the hospital personnel.

Incidents that challenge either the generality of the evaluation of the social loss of dying patients or the impact of this evaluation on the care patients receive would be especially important for refining these ideas. In the next phase of the research, the investigator might seek out disconfirming evidence (for example, a patient who is judged to be not much of a "social loss" but nevertheless receives excellent care) to test out these initial images and see how they need to be revised or limited. If, for instance, the researcher found that hospital personnel ignored the social loss represented by accident victims, then he or she would be forced either to reformulate the image to accommodate accident victims or else limit its applicability to non-accident patients.

In effect, the method of analytic induction is used both to construct images and to seek out contrary evidence because it sees such evidence as the best raw material for improving initial images. As a data procedure, this technique is less concerned with how much positive evidence has been accumulated (for example, how many cases corroborate the image the researcher is developing) and more with the degree to which the image of the research subject has been refined, sharpened, and elaborated in response to both confirming and disconfirming evidence.

Analytic induction facilitates the reciprocal clarification of concepts and categories, a key feature of qualitative research. When Howard Becker (1953) narrowed his category from "all marijuana users" to "those who use marijuana for pleasure," for example, he used the technique of analytic induction. Essentially, the technique involves looking for relevant similarities among the instances of a category, and then linking these to refine an image (such as the image of how one becomes a marijuana user). If relevant similarities cannot be identified, then either the category is too wide and heterogeneous and should be narrowed, or else the researcher needs to take another look at the evidence and reconceptualize possible similarities. Negative cases are especially important because they are either excluded when the relevant category is narrowed or they are the main focus when the investigator attempts to reconceptualize commonalities and thereby reconcile contradictory evidence.

Consider a more detailed example: Jack Katz (1984) studied legal assistance lawyers—those who help low-income people. He found that many of these lawyers burn out quickly—in less than 2 years—and abandon this kind of work, often for more lucrative legal careers. Katz wanted to understand why by studying those who stayed with legal assistance work despite its drawbacks. He assembled evidence on the legal assistance lawyers in the group he studied and checked out several of his initial ideas by comparing those who had quit before 2 years of service with those who had stayed on for more than 2 years.

One of the first ideas Katz examined was based on his initial impressions of these attorneys. He speculated that legal assistance lawyers who were former political activists did not burn out like the others. A systematic examination of the evidence on many lawyers provided some support for this speculation. However, the fit was far from perfect. There were some who stayed with legal assistance work who were not former political activists, and there were former political activists who left legal assistance work before 2 years had elapsed.

Katz examined these negative cases closely and found some problems with his initial formulation. Some former activists left for obvious reasons. They were offered positions that were clearly a step up career-wise. Some who were not former activists stayed because they lacked alternatives—they couldn't get better jobs as lawyers—or because they had positions in the organization that they liked (such as administrative positions).

It was clear to Katz that his categories "staying" and "leaving" had to be refined and that his search for adequate explanatory concepts was far from over. First, he narrowed the category that interested him most—those who stayed. However, clearly he was not interested in *all* stayers. Some stayers, after all, had interesting work within the legal assistance organization he studied. Rather, he was interested in people who stayed despite being involved in frustrating or limiting work. He restricted his focus to this subset of stayers and searched for relevant similarities within this group.

With this shift, he became less interested in all stayers versus all leavers and more interested in differences between categories of stayers—those who stayed despite frustrating work versus other types of stayers. In short, the focus was on *how* people stayed, and he had straightforward explanations for many stayers (for example, those with interesting work). As it turned out, this tighter category—stayers with frustrating work—also proved to be too broad, and he later narrowed it further to legal assistance lawyers who were involved in low-status work. After all, some lawyers doing high-status work, he discovered, were nevertheless frustrated with their work.

The search for explanatory factors became more focused as the main category of interest narrowed. After rejecting "activist background" as an explanation for staying, Katz tried to distinguish lawyers who were more oriented toward using the legal system for reform from those who were less so. He also looked at the participation of lawyers in social activities that celebrated reform work (for example, progressive political groups). This search for important commonalities among stayers went hand-in-hand with narrowing the relevant category of stayers from all stayers to those who were involved in low-status work.

The process of narrowing and refining is depicted in Table 5.1, which shows the process of analytic induction in tabular form, based on Katz's description. The table reports hypothetical information on 30 lawyers to illustrate the general process he describes, not his specific conclusions. The first three columns show the narrowing of the category of stayers, from all stayers (column 1; 18 out of 30 lawyers) to stayers with frustrating work (column 2; 13 out of 30 lawyers), to stayers involved in work that carried no status (column 3; 10 out of 30 lawyers). Columns 4 through 6 show the various ways Katz tried to explain staying—his various images of the "stayer." As his focus shifted from column 1 to column 2 and then to column 3, he became more interested in how and why people stayed and less in the difference between stayers and the 12 leavers at the bottom of the table. In other words, he came to view staying as an accomplishment for those doing low-status work and studied how it was accomplished.

First, he tried to construct an image of staying as a continuation of a commitment to political activism (column 4). As the hypothetical data in Table 5.1 show, this image fails. Of the 18 lawyers who stayed more than 2 years, only 7 were former activists, and of the 12 who left the organization, 4 were former activists. Next, Katz studied his negative cases closely (especially non-activists who stayed) and found that his categorization of stayers versus leavers was too crude. He reasoned that what really interested him most was people who stayed despite their involvement in frustrating work. He then tried to find commonalities among this subset of stayers, looking at their reform orientations and their participation in a social life supportive of reform work. The fit was still not close enough. There were some lawyers who did frustrating work, for example, who were not reform oriented.

Examination of negative cases led to a further narrowing of the category (to lawyers involved in low-status work) and further refinement of the image (to participation in a social environment that glorified reform work). These further refinements resulted in a good fit. The data in the table suggest that legal assistance lawyers will do low-status work if they participate in a social environment that glorifies the idea that important social reforms can be achieved through the legal system.

Columns 3 and 6 correspond perfectly. In fact, most qualitative researchers are satisfied with less than a perfect fit. There is usually at least a handful of extraneous evidence that neither fits nor challenges a particular image. The goal is not perfect fit per se, but a conceptual refinement that

Table 5.1 Hypothetical Example of Analytic Induction

| | Categories | | | Explanatory Concepts | | |
| | 1 | 2 | 3 | 4 | 5 | 6 |
Case	Stayed More Than 2 Years?	Works in a Frustrating Place?	Involved in Low-Status Work?	Activist Background?	Reform Oriented?	Social Life Supports Reform Orientation?
1	yes	yes	yes	yes	yes	yes
2	yes	yes	yes	yes	yes	yes
3	yes	yes	yes	yes	yes	yes
4	yes	yes	yes	yes	yes	yes
5	yes	yes	yes	yes	yes	yes
6	yes	yes	yes	yes	yes	yes
7	yes	yes	yes	yes	yes	yes
8	yes	yes	yes	no	yes	yes
9	yes	yes	yes	no	yes	yes
10	yes	yes	yes	no	yes	yes
11	yes	yes	no	no	yes	no
12	yes	yes	no	no	no	no

13	yes	yes	no	no	no	no
14	yes	no	no	no	no	no
15	yes	no	no	no	no	no
16	yes	no	no	no	no	no
17	yes	no	no	no	no	no
18	yes	no	no	no	no	no
19	no	no	no	yes	no	no
20	no	no	no	yes	no	no
21	no	no	no	yes	no	no
22	no	no	no	yes	no	no
23	no	no	no	no	no	no
24	no	no	no	no	no	no
25	no	no	no	no	no	no
26	no	no	no	no	no	no
27	no	no	no	no	no	no
28	no	no	no	no	no	no
29	no	no	no	no	no	no
30	no	no	no	no	no	no

provides a deeper understanding of the research subject. Basically, the greater the effort to account for or understand negative cases or contrary evidence, the deeper the understanding of the research subject. The technique of analytic induction thus facilitates the goal of in-depth knowledge.

Jack Katz (1984) comments that analytic induction is poorly labeled because it is not a technique of pure induction. Researchers work back and forth between their ideas and their evidence, trying to achieve what Katz calls a "double fitting" of explanations and observations (that is, ideas and evidence). This process of double fitting is best understood as retroduction, a term (discussed in Chapter 3) that describes the interplay of induction and deduction in the process of scientific discovery.

Theoretical Sampling

Sometimes qualitative researchers conduct investigations of related phenomena in several different settings. Most often this interest in a broader investigation follows from a deliberate strategy of **theoretical sampling** (Glaser and Strauss 1967) to describe the process of choosing new research sites or cases to compare with one that has already been studied. For example, a researcher interested in how environmental activists in the United States maintain their political commitments might extend the study to (1) environmental activists in another part of the world (such as China) or perhaps to (2) another type of activist (such as religious activists in the United States).

The choice of the comparison group (for example, comparing environmental activists in the United States with either environmental activists in China or with people in the United States who maintain radical religious commitments) can vary widely depending on the nature and goals of the investigation. Different comparisons hold different aspects of cases constant. Comparing environmental and religious activists in the United States, for example, holds some things constant such as the impact of national setting, but allows the nature of the commitment to vary (environmental versus religious). Comparing environmental activists in the United States with environmental activists in China highlights the impact of the factor that varies most (national setting), but holds the nature of the commitment (environmental) constant.

This process of theoretical sampling occurs not only in the study of social groups (such as environmental activists) but also in the study of historical processes and episodes. For example, general questions that arise in a study of the Woodstock 1999 riot might be addressed by examining other entertainment riots such as those at the 1992 GNR (Guns N' Roses)–Metallica

Stadium Tour, the Los Angeles Lakers game in 2000, and in Montreal when hockey fans rioted following a round 1 playoffs victory by the Montreal Canadiens over the Boston Bruins. For example, there may be questions about the role of crowd density in Woodstock that could be answered by examining the GNR–Metallica case and comparing it to the sports cases.

When a researcher employs a strategy of theoretical sampling, the selection of additional cases is most often determined by questions and issues raised in the first case studied. Selection of new cases is not a matter of convenience; the researcher's sampling strategy evolves as his or her understanding of the research subject and the concepts it exemplifies matures. The goal of theoretical sampling is not to capture all possible variations, but to sample in a way that aids the development of concepts and deepens the understanding of research subjects.

A researcher studying how hospital personnel evaluate the potential social loss of dying patients and link the care they give to these evaluations might believe that this practice is caused by limited resources in the hospital studied. If the hospital had more resources (for example, more nurses), it might be able to provide better and more uniform care to all patients, regardless of their social value. To explore this idea, the researcher might study two additional hospitals, one with more resources and one with fewer resources than the first hospital. If the reasoning based on the first hospital is correct, then the staff of the hospital with more resources should spend less time evaluating the social loss of dying patients and provide more uniform care, while the staff of the hospital with less resources should spend more time evaluating social loss and should adjust their care in more strict accordance with these evaluations.

This expansion of the study to two new sites is a straightforward implementation of the idea of theoretical sampling. The selection of the new sites follows directly from ideas developed in the first site and provides an opportunity to confirm and deepen the insights developed in that setting. Of course, if research in these new settings were to contradict expectations based on research in the first hospital, then the researcher would be compelled to develop a different understanding of how and why hospital personnel varied their care of dying patients.

This example of theoretical sampling also shows that it is a **data triangulation** technique (Denzin 2006). Triangulation is a term that originally described how sailors use stars and simple trigonometry to locate their position on earth. More generally, triangulation can be understood as a way of using unrelated pieces of information to get a better fix on something that is only partially known or understood. In the example just presented, the researcher used evidence from two other hospitals, one with more resources and one with less, to get a better fix on the first hospital. By comparing the three hospitals, arrayed along a single continuum of resources, the researcher could assess the validity and generality of findings from the first hospital.

Theoretical sampling is also a powerful technique for building analytic frames. For example, journalist Hunter S. Thompson, after spending a year with the motorcycle gang Hell's Angels, introduced the concept *edgework* to refer to voluntary activities that include a strong element of risk taking (Thompson 1966, cited in Lyng 2005:19). Sociologist Stephen Lyng (1990) further elaborated the concept by focusing on people in other walks of life, such as skydivers, who also seek out dangerous situations. Lyng, along with other researchers, then applied this concept to still other forms of voluntary risk taking to further develop it, distinguish it from related concepts, and explain its causal connections to other concepts. Each study offered evidence on a different type of edgework. The end product of this collective strategy of theoretical sampling is a fully developed analytic frame for edgework (Lyng 2005). ·

Here is another example: Howard Becker (1963) studied a variety of groups classified as deviant in addition to marijuana users. He joined these different cases together in a single analytic frame and called all these groups "outsiders." His frame emphasized a dual process of social learning (people learn "deviant" behaviors from others in social settings) and labeling (society's tendency to label some groups deviant furthers their isolation from the larger society). His work challenged conventional thinking that certain types of people were at a greater risk of becoming deviant and focused subsequent research on social processes. In a similar manner, Erving Goffman (1963) studied a wide variety of stigmatized people, from those with physical deformities to prostitutes. From a consideration of many different types, he developed a powerful analytic frame for understanding how stigmatized individuals deal with their discredited identities.

While the strategy of theoretical sampling is an excellent device for gaining a deeper understanding of cases and for advancing theory (one of the main goals of social research), many qualitative researchers consider the representation of even a single case sufficient for their goals. Some consider the addition of new cases—using the strategy of theoretical sampling—to be a useless detour from the important task of understanding one case well. They are content to leave the comparison of cases and the development of broad analytic frames to researchers more interested in general questions.

While this reluctance to broaden an investigation is common among qualitative researchers, the strategy of theoretical sampling offers a powerful research tool. As Glaser and Strauss (1967) argue, theoretical sampling

offers the opportunity to construct generalizations and to deepen understanding of research subjects at the same time.

The Study of a Single Case

The techniques of analytic induction and theoretical sampling work best
when there are multiple instances of the phenomenon the researcher is studying. The study of the care of dying patients just described, for instance,
involves observing how patients are treated. Each patient provides another
instance to examine. What techniques can researchers use when they study
only a single instance—for example, one person's life or a single historical
event? While it is true that most data procedures are designed for multiple
instances, the study of a single case is not haphazard and unstructured
(Feagin, Orum, and Sjoberg 1991). In fact, the single-case study is structured
in ways that parallel analytic induction.

For illustration, consider a researcher who seeks to evaluate the historical
significance of the resignation of President Richard Nixon in the middle of his
second term. Suppose the goal of the researcher in this investigation is to try
to interpret this episode as a serious blow to the authority of the U.S. government, at least in the eyes of the American people. Because of what tran-
spired, according to this interpretation, the American people could never
again trust government leaders and officials to tell them the truth.

Of course, there are many different ways to interpret each historical
episode, and each interpretation is anchored in a different analytic frame.
The interpretation just described sees the events surrounding the resignation
of President Nixon in terms of the authority and legitimacy of governments.
What kinds of conditions and events enhance a government's authority?
What kinds undermine its authority?

In order to evaluate this interpretation, the researcher would have to
assemble facts relevant to the analytic frame (ones that emphasize factors
influencing a government's authority) and see if they can be assembled into
an image that supports the interpretation just described. Of course, there are
many facts, and not all will necessarily be consistent with the initial interpretation. The key question is this: Among the relevant facts, which are consistent and which are not? Analytic frames play an important part in this
process because they define some facts as relevant and others as irrelevant,
and different frames define different sets of facts as relevant.

In many ways, this evaluation of facts is like analytic induction. In analytic induction, the goal is to see if all the relevant instances are the same
with respect to some set of causes or characteristic, as in Jack Katz's (1984)

research on legal assistance attorneys. In the study of a single case, the problem is to see if all the relevant facts—those that are relevant in some way to the suggested frame—agree with or support an interpretation. Thus, the different facts in the study of a single case are like the different instances in analytic induction.

Often the facts relevant to a particular frame, once assembled, do not provide strong support for the initial interpretation. As in analytic induction, the interpretation and the facts are "double fitted." That is, there is an interplay between the researcher's interpretation and the facts, an interaction that moves either toward some sort of fit or toward a stalemate. As in the study of many instances (for example, the care of many different patients in a hospital), the interplay between evidence-based images and theoretical ideas expressed through analytic frames leads to a progressive refinement of both.

It is important to remember that each different interpretation is anchored in a different frame. Thus, the facts relevant to one frame will not overlap perfectly with the facts relevant to another. Thus, there can be many different ways to frame a single case, and each interpretation may be valid because of this imperfect overlap. Cases that can be interpreted in a variety of different ways are considered "rich" because they help researchers explore the interconnection of the ideas expressed through different frames.

Conclusion

Researchers use qualitative methods when they believe that the best way to construct a proper representation is through in-depth study of phenomena. Often they address phenomena that they believe have been seriously misrepresented, sometimes by social researchers using other approaches, or perhaps not represented at all. This in-depth investigation often focuses on a primary case, on the commonalities among separate instances of the same phenomenon, or on parallel phenomena identified through a deliberate strategy of theoretical sampling.

Qualitative methods are holistic, meaning that aspects of cases are viewed in the context of the whole case, and researchers often must triangulate information about a number of cases in order to make sense of one case. Qualitative methods are used to uncover essential features of a case and then illuminate key relationships among these features. Often a qualitative researcher will argue that his or her cases *exemplify* one or more key theoretical processes or categories. Finally, as qualitative research progresses, there is a reciprocal clarification of the underlying character of the phenomena under investigation and the theoretical concepts that they are believed to exemplify.

6

Using Comparative
Methods to Study Diversity

Introduction

Comparative researchers examine patterns of similarities and differences across a moderate number of cases. The typical comparative study has anywhere from a handful to 50 or more cases. The number of cases is often limited because one of the concerns of comparative research is to establish familiarity with each case included in a study. Like qualitative researchers, comparative researchers consider how the different parts of each case—those aspects that are relevant to the investigation—fit together; they try to make sense of each case. Thus, knowledge of cases is considered an important goal of comparative research, independent of any other goal.

While there are many types of comparative research (for example, see Mahoney and Rueschemeyer 2003), the distinctiveness of the comparative approach is clearest in studies that focus on diversity (Ragin 2000). Recall that the qualitative approaches examined in Chapter 5 emphasize commonalities, and the primary focus is on similarities across instances (such as when hospital personnel assess the potential social loss of each dying patient). This concern for commonalities dovetails with an interest in clarifying categories and concepts (such as the concept of potential social loss and the situations in which it is assessed). In comparative research on diversity, by contrast, the category of phenomena that the investigator is studying is usually specified at the outset, and the goal of the investigation is to elucidate and explain the diversity within a particular set of cases. (This type of comparative research, which is the major focus of this chapter, is examined in detail in Ragin 2000.)

Consider the following example of comparative research on diversity. From the mid-1970s through the 1980s, many less developed countries experienced mass protest in response to "austerity programs" demanded by the International Monetary Fund (IMF). (These mass protests were similar to those that occurred in Greece in May of 2010 after that government reached an agreement with the IMF that included increasing taxes, cutting public spending, and freezing government wages and pensions for three years.) These countries had accumulated large public debts that they could not repay. In exchange for better terms (e.g., lower interest rates and longer repayment periods), the governments of these countries agreed to implement a variety economic policies designed to facilitate debt repayment. For instance, in some countries the IMF demanded that the government stop subsidizing the prices of basic commodities such as fuel and food. These austerity measures saved governments money and made debt repayment more feasible; they also provoked widespread protest among citizens faced with new challenges to their economic and social well-being (Walton and Ragin 1990).

A comparative researcher interested in these countries might contrast the different *forms* of protest that occurred in response to these austerity programs. In some countries, there were riots; in others, there were labor strikes led by unions; in others, there were mass demonstrations involving many different groups; in still others, opposition political parties organized protests; and so on. Why did different kinds of protest erupt in different countries? What causal conditions explain these different responses to austerity programs? And why did some countries with severe austerity programs experience very mild mass protest?

To explain this diversity, a comparative researcher would first group countries according to their different responses to austerity, placing all those with riots in one category, those with demonstrations in another, and so on. Next, the investigator would look for patterns of similarities and differences. What are the similarities among the countries with riots that distinguish them from the other countries? Perhaps the countries with riots also had repressive governments, widespread poverty, and serious crowding in major urban areas, and none of the non-riot countries had this specific combination of conditions. How did the countries with mass demonstrations differ from all the other countries with austerity programs? This systematic search for differences would continue until the researcher could account for the diverse responses to austerity found in these countries.

Thus, in research that emphasizes diversity, the focus is on the similarities within a category of cases with the same outcome (e.g., countries with riots) that (1) distinguish that category from other categories (countries with other forms of austerity protest) and (2) explain the outcome manifested by that category. In other words, the study of diversity is the study of patterns of similarities and differences within a given set of cases (in this example, countries with austerity protests).

Contrasts With Other Research Strategies

As already noted, the main difference between comparative research on diversity and qualitative research on commonalities is that their basic orientation toward cases differs. When qualitative researchers study commonalities, they usually view multiple cases as many instances of the same thing. A qualitative researcher who interviews many taxicab drivers, for example, uses these many instances to deepen the portrayal of this case—the taxicab driver.

Comparative researchers who study diversity, by contrast, tend to look for differences among their cases. Comparative researchers examine patterns of similarity and difference across cases and try to come to terms with their diversity. A comparative researcher might study the settlement of Somali refugees in the United States since the onset of the 1991 Somali Civil War, contrasting the ways they were received in a variety of different communities. It might be possible to distinguish four or five basic types of reception—from hostile to indifferent to open to paternalistic and so on—and then to pinpoint the factors (such as the size and wealth of a community) that determined these different receptions. Another comparative researcher might study bars in a community and contrast the different strategies they use to encourage and discourage drinking (for those patrons who have been overserved). Bars that cater to different customers (for example, bikers versus college students) surely use different techniques. In each of these examples, the research focuses on the diversity that exists within a specific set of cases.

Quantitative researchers (the focus of Chapter 7) also examine differences among cases, but with a different emphasis. In quantitative research, the goal is to explain the covariation of one variable with another, usually across many, many cases. A quantitative researcher, for example, might explain different levels of income across thousands of individuals included in a survey by pointing to the covariation between income levels and educational levels—people with more education tend to have more income. In quantitative research, the focus is on differences in levels and how different variables like income and education covary across cases. In comparative research, by contrast, the focus is on diversity—*patterns* of similarities and differences. In other words, the focus is on the various configurations of a set of attributes (such as the basic types of reception of Somali refugees in the United States).

Furthermore, a quantitative researcher typically has only broad familiarity with the cases included in a study. As the number of cases exceeds 50 or so, it becomes increasingly difficult to establish familiarity with each case. Imagine a survey researcher trying to become familiar with the lives of the thousands of people included in a telephone survey or a political scientist trying to keep up with major elections in all democratic countries. Neither task is feasible. There are practical limits to how many cases a researcher can study closely.

We emphasize how these three research strategies typically have different approaches toward case selection, use different techniques to collect and analyze evidence, and have different underlying research goals. Yet it is important to reiterate that there is a unity among these strategies, as they all involve the interplay of ideas and (large amounts of) evidence to produce representations. The distinctions we draw between these strategies are not absolute. Consider an example that blurs these distinctions. The 2007 book *Bargaining for Brooklyn: Community Organizations in the Entrepreneurial City*, by Nicole Marwell, is a qualitative study of eight nonprofit, community-based organizations in Brooklyn, New York. By developing in-depth knowledge of her cases, Marwell is able to uncover a range of organizational strategies used by community-based organizations in their attempts to help local residents move out of poverty. Her focus is on the patterns of similarities and differences across these cases, where diversity in organizational strategies emerges even though all the organizations operate in the same neighborhood. (For an example of quantitative researchers attending to diversity, see Grant, Morales, and Sallaz 2009.) As mentioned previously, researchers will use whatever procedures they believe will best illuminate their object of study. Many researchers use multiple strategies to study the same phenomenon. They hope that the weaknesses of one approach will be counterbalanced by the strengths of another (see, for example, Fernandez-Mateo 2007).

The Goals of Comparative Research

The emphases of comparative research on diversity (especially the different patterns that may exist within a specific set of cases) and on familiarity with each case make this approach especially well suited for the goals of exploring diversity, interpreting cultural or historical significance, and advancing theory.

Exploring Diversity

The comparative approach is better suited for addressing patterns of diversity than either of the other two strategies. Diversity is most often understood in terms of types of cases. The typical goal of a comparative study is to unravel the different causal conditions connected to different outcomes—causal patterns that separate cases into different subgroups. This explicit focus on diversity distinguishes the comparative approach from the qualitative approach. Recall that in qualitative research, the goal is often to clarify categories with respect to the concepts they exemplify by examining similarities across the instances of a category (such as taxicab drivers).

One common outcome of comparative research is the finding that cases that may have been defined as "the same" at the outset are differentiated into two or more categories at the conclusion of the study. For example, a researcher studying major U.S. cities that have elected African American mayors might conclude at the end of the study that there are two major types—those cities where interracial alliances resulted in the successful election of African American mayors and those cities where black voters, who happened also to constitute a majority of voters, made the difference in the election of African American mayors. The political dynamics and significance of the elections could differ considerably across the two types.

A researcher studying governments that terrorize citizens who oppose them might find that there are several main types, depending on the international standing of the government in question. For instance, when a government is supported by the United States and other major powers, its terrorizing may be overlooked. When a government lacks this support, its terrorizing may be considered repugnant. Governments in the second category would have to contend with the possibility that their actions might provoke international sanctions or intervention and therefore would likely practice more covert forms of terror.

While comparative researchers often discern *types* in the course of their examinations of patterns of diversity, they may also begin their research with a tentative delineation of types. A common strategy is to categorize cases according to their different outcomes. The goal of such a strategy is to unravel the causal conditions that generate various outcomes. If different causes can be matched to the different outcomes, then the research confirms the investigator's understanding of the factors that distinguish these cases. If not, then the frame for the research needs to be reformulated.

For example, a researcher might examine the causes of different types of government repression. Some repressive governments, for example, may simply harass their opponents—incarcerating them for short periods, subjecting them to frequent questioning, opening their mail, and so on. Other repressive governments may torture and kill their opponents (as Iranian President Mahmoud Ahmadinejad has done since his election in 2005 [McManus 2009]). Still other governments may focus their repressive energies not on opponents, but on purging the less committed from their own ranks—members of the ruling political party or clique (as did Saddam Hussein by executing hundreds of members of the Ba'ath Party in Iraq [Makiya 1998]. Still others may attack random members of society in order to maintain a general state of terror and obedience (as Joseph Stalin did in the Soviet Union during the 1930s [Gregory 2009]). It is important to understand different types of repression and the various conditions that explain the emergence of each type, particularly for researchers whose fundamental goal is to generate knowledge with the potential to transform society (see Chapter 2).

The goal of exploring diversity is important because people, including social researchers, sometimes have trouble seeing the trees for the forest. That is, they tend to assume uniformity or generality when, in fact, there is a great deal of diversity. Here is a simple example: Generally, governments that are less democratic tend to be more repressive. However, there are many instances of repression by democratically elected governments and many instances of politically tolerant and lenient governments that are not democratic. To understand government repression fully, it is necessary to go beyond the simple identification of political repression with an absence of democracy and examine the different forms of government repression that exist in all countries.

Interpreting Cultural or Historical Significance

Comparative researchers focus explicitly on patterns of similarities and differences across a range of cases. Relevant cases, in turn, are almost always drawn from a specific and known set. Recall that in qualitative research (Chapter 5), much energy is often devoted to coming to terms with the case: What is this case a case of? What concepts are exemplified in this case? Into which larger social scientific categories, if any, does it fit? In comparative research, by contrast, the researcher usually starts with a good sense of the larger category that embraces the cases included in the study because this category is usually specified beforehand (such as "countries with austerity protests").

For example, a researcher might focus on "military coups in Latin America since 1975" or "major cities in the United States that have elected African American mayors." In these examples, the relevant set of cases is defined in advance, and there is a finite, usually moderate number of such cases. Typically, the category that establishes the boundary of the set is historically and geographically delimited. In each of the examples just mentioned, time and place boundaries are either plainly stated ("Latin America since 1975") or implied ("recent U.S.").

This focus on circumscribed categories makes the comparative strategy well suited for the goal of interpreting historically or culturally significant phenomena, especially when there are a moderate number of cases, as in the examples just mentioned. The category "major cities in the United States that have elected African American mayors," for example, is historically significant in part because it is a relatively new and major phenomenon. Prior to the expansion of civil rights in the 1960s, there were no African American mayors in major U.S. cities. It is culturally significant because of the relevance of race and race relations to American society. Likewise, the category "military coups in Latin America since 1975" is significant to those concerned with the progress of democracy and human rights in this region.

Because the comparative approach focuses on differences between cases and the differentiation of types, it facilitates historical interpretation. Consider the category "revolution." Some revolutions simply change those who are in power or alter other political arrangements without implementing any major changes in society. The revolutionaries who overthrew Ferdinand Marcos in the Philippines, for example, did not attempt any fundamental changes in Philippine society. Other revolutions, by contrast, bring with them regimes that seek to alter society fundamentally: Kings are beheaded, property is confiscated, basic social patterns and relations are changed forever. Revolutionary social changes of this nature were attempted after the French Revolution of 1789, the Russian Revolution of 1917, and the Chinese Revolution of 1949.

Revolutions that attempt fundamental social change are treated as a distinct type by social scientists. These massive upheavals of society are called "*social* revolutions" to distinguish them from revolutions that simply change leaders or other political arrangements (Skocpol 1979). By differentiating social revolutions from all other kinds, researchers provide important tools for understanding and interpreting these massive social transformations. When a major upheaval occurs, researchers can assess whether or not it qualifies as a social revolution. If so, it can be compared with other social revolutions. If not, then some other category may be used (for example, coup d'etat) to interpret the event and to specify comparable cases. Generally, when a set of comparable cases can be specified, these cases aid the interpretation and understanding of the new case.

More generally, when social scientists categorize an event, they establish a primary analytic frame for its interpretation. Thus, the interpretation of historically or culturally significant events is often a struggle over the proper classification of events into broad categories—a key concern of the comparative approach.

Advancing Theory

Several basic features of the comparative approach make it a good strategy for advancing theory. These features include its use of flexible frames, its explicit focus on the causes of diversity, and its emphasis on the systematic analysis of similarities and differences in the effort to specify how diversity is patterned.

In comparative research, investigators usually initiate research with a specific analytic frame, but these initial frames are open to revision. The researcher interested in military coups in Latin America since 1975, for example, already has a frame for the research—the frame of military coups. Recall that the frames of qualitative research are fluid, and researchers may not finish developing their frames until after all the work of collecting and studying the evidence is complete. In comparative research, by contrast, frames are established at the outset of a research project, but they remain flexible. Comparative researchers expect their frames to be revised, and in fact conduct research in order to sharpen the ideas expressed in a frame.

A researcher interested in welfare states in advanced countries, for example, might start out with a frame that specifies two basic types of welfare states but then conclude with a specification of three or four types (Esping-Andersen 1999). Or, the researcher might conclude that there is only one main type and that all deviations are best understood as underdeveloped or incomplete expressions of the main type (J. Stephens 1979). By altering initial frames in response to evidence, comparative researchers refine and elaborate existing ideas and theoretical perspectives.

When conducting their research, comparative researchers are more explicitly concerned with causation and causal complexity than are most qualitative researchers. For example, when comparative researchers differentiate types (such as types of government repression), they also try to specify the combinations of causal conditions conducive to each type: What causes some regimes to concentrate their repressive efforts on regime opponents? What causes others to focus their efforts on purging troublesome members of the ruling party? And what causes still other regimes to cultivate a general state of terror in the population at large? This emphasis on causation is central to theory because most theories in the social sciences are concerned with explaining how and why—that is, with specifying the causes of social phenomena.

To assess causation, comparative researchers study how diversity is patterned. They compare cases with each other and highlight the contrasting effects of different causes. Comparative researchers view each case as a combination of characteristics (for example, conditions relevant to government repression) and examine similarities and differences in combinations of characteristics across cases in their effort to find patterns.

The Process of Comparative Research

The comparative study of diversity is neither as fluid as qualitative research nor as fixed as quantitative research. Comparative researchers typically start with a carefully specified category of phenomena that is intrinsically interesting in some way (for example, countries with austerity protests). They use analytic frames to help them make sense of their categories, and they revise their frames based on their examination of evidence.

In the course of their research, they focus on patterns of similarities and differences among cases and assess patterns of diversity. This assessment of diversity provides the foundation for improving or revising the analytic frame chosen at the outset of the study. Like qualitative research, the comparative approach stimulates a rich dialogue between ideas and evidence. Researchers generate images from their data and adjust their frames as they construct representations of their research subjects.

Selecting Cases

Comparative researchers usually initiate their research with a specific set of cases in mind. Most often, this set has clear spatial and temporal boundaries and embraces cases that are thought to be comparable with each other, as in the examples already described. The degree to which the cases that are selected actually belong to the same category (and therefore are comparable) is assessed in the course of the research. While conducting the investigation, the researcher may decide that some cases don't belong in the same category as the others and can't be compared. They also may reformulate the category as the research proceeds. Usually, however, such adjustments are modest.

Typically, the cases that comparative researchers select for study are specific to their interests and to those of their intended audience—for example, countries with mass protest against IMF-mandated austerity programs. This category of countries has clear spatial and temporal boundaries and embraces a set of comparable cases. It is also an intrinsically interesting set of cases. In short, it is just the kind of delimited empirical category that is well suited for comparative investigation.

The comparative approach can be applied to many different kinds of cases, not just countries. It is important, however, for the cases selected to be comparable and to share membership in a meaningful, empirically defined category. For example, the comparative approach can be applied to the fraternities on a college campus, to refugee groups living in a major urban area, to different religious congregations in a medium-sized town, to the truck stops along Interstate 55, or to the elections in the congressional districts of a large state. The set of cases must be coherent. Usually, the cases must also offer some potential for advancing social scientific thinking.

Using Analytic Frames

When researchers choose their cases, they also usually select their analytic frames. Essentially, a frame is chosen when the researcher specifies what about the cases is of interest. For example, the researcher wanting to study countries with austerity protests may be interested in the different forms that the protest took. This frame, which would be developed from the existing social science literature on mass protest, would specify how people respond to different conditions in different ways when they engage in political protest. In short, it would detail the different kinds of factors the researcher should examine in a comparative study of protest.

To continue this example, in some countries, opposition groups may have many resources; in others, they may have few. Groups with more resources are more likely to engage in organized activities such as strikes and in other activities that are relatively costly to participants. People on strike, for example, must give up their wages. Thus, this frame, which would be developed from the existing literature on social movements and collective action, would direct the researcher to focus on resource mobilization, among other things. Analytic frames help researchers see aspects of cases that they might otherwise overlook, and direct their attention away from other aspects.

Sometimes researchers are interested in many facets of their cases and don't select a frame until they are well along in their research. It might take awhile, for example, to determine what a comparison of countries with austerity protests might best offer in the way of general social scientific knowledge. Comparative researchers also may develop new frames from their evidence—for example, a new frame for the study of race and politics based on a study of cities where coalitions of white and black voters have elected African American mayors. This practice is less common in comparative research than in qualitative research, however, because comparative researchers start with a fairly good sense of their cases and the empirical category that embraces them (such as "countries that experienced mass protest in response to IMF-mandated austerity").

Analyzing Patterns of Diversity

In comparative research, the examination of diversity—patterns of similarities and differences—goes hand-in-hand with the study of causes. Generally, researchers expect different causal conditions to be linked to divergent outcomes in interpretable ways. Thus, the goal of the researcher's examination of patterns of similarities and differences is to identify causal links—how different **configurations** of causes produce different outcomes across the range of cases included in a study. The specification of different patterns of causation is the primary basis for the differentiation of types.

In a study of how sororities generate a feeling of group solidarity, for example, different ways of generating this feeling should affect the *nature* of the solidarity that is generated. The researcher might find that some sororities generate solidarity around special events and rituals, while others generate it through routine activities that bring members of the sorority together on a daily basis. These different ways of generating this feeling (that is, these different causes of solidarity) should have consequences for the nature of the solidarity observed. For example, solidarity in sororities of the first type may be more visible but also less durable, while in the second type, it may be more subtle but more enduring.

If causes and outcomes cannot be linked in interpretable ways, then researchers must reexamine their specification of causes and outcomes and their differentiation of types. In many ways, this process of differentiating types and specifying causal links specific to each type resembles the "double fitting" of categories and images that constitutes the core of qualitative methods (see Chapter 5). There is a dialogue between ideas and evidence that culminates in a meaningful representation of the research subject. The main difference is that in qualitative research, the emphasis is on clarifying a category and enriching its representation, whereas in comparative research, the emphasis is on using contrasts among cases to further the researcher's understanding of their diversity.

Using Comparative Methods

Comparative methods are used to study configurations. A **configuration** is a specific combination of attributes that is common to a number of cases. For example, if all the countries that experienced mass demonstrations in response to IMF-mandated austerity were similar in having low levels of economic development, high levels of urbanization, undemocratic governments, and poorly organized opposition groups, this would constitute a specific configuration of conditions associated with mass demonstrations as a response to IMF-mandated austerity. The examination of patterns of diversity essentially involves a search for combinations of conditions that distinguish categories of cases. Thus, researchers look for uniformity *within* categories and contrasts *between* categories in combinations of conditions.

Data procedures appropriate for the study of configurations, initially formalized by Drass and Ragin (1989), constitute the core of the comparative approach to diversity. Comparative methods are used to examine complex patterns of similarities and differences across a range of cases. Like quantitative methods (see Chapter 7), comparative methods are used to examine causes and effects, but the emphasis in comparative research is on the analysis of configurations of causal conditions.

Before examining data procedures specific to comparative methods, let's first consider an example that shows the main ideas behind the techniques.

An Overview of Comparative Methods

A hypothetical example, based on a study of the *repression* of austerity protests conducted by Walton and Ragin (1990), is used to illustrate general features of comparative methods. Table 6.1 presents hypothetical data on 16 countries that experienced austerity protests in the early 1980s. Eight of these countries had governments that became violently repressive in response to austerity protests; the governments of the other eight did not, even though they also experienced such protests.

The table shows differences and similarities among these 16 countries with respect to conditions believed to be relevant to repression, derived from an analytic frame for government repression. The conditions include the following:

1. Whether the country was politically aligned with the Soviet Union or with the United States and Western Europe in the 1980s

2. Whether or not the country had undergone substantial industrialization prior to 1980

3. Whether or not the country had a democratic government prior to the emergence of austerity protests

4. Whether or not the country had a strong military establishment prior to the emergence of austerity protests

The goal of comparative analysis is to determine the combinations of causal conditions that differentiate sets of cases. In this analysis, the goal is to find combinations of causal conditions that distinguish the eight countries with governments that became repressive from the other eight countries. Careful examination of the similarities among the countries with violently repressive governments shows that they do not share any single causal condition or any single combination of conditions. However, there are two combinations of conditions that are present in the set of countries that had repressive governments that are both absent from the set that did not. The 16 cases are sorted in the table to highlight these two combinations.

The first four cases share an absence of democratic government prior to the emergence of austerity protests combined with a strong military establishment. None of the cases in the lower half of the table (the eight countries lacking violent repression) has this combination. The second four countries with violent repression share two different conditions: a presence of democratic government prior to austerity protests combined with an absence of significant industrialization prior to the protests. Again, none of the eight countries lacking violent repression has this combination of conditions.

The results of the examination of similarities and differences thus lead to the conclusion that there are two different combinations of conditions (or causal configurations) that explain the emergence of violent repression in these cases. The first configuration (nondemocratic rule combined with a strong military) suggests a situation where the military establishment has gained the upper hand in part because of the absence of checks (democratic government) on its power. The second configuration (absence of significant industrialization combined with presence of democratic government prior to the emergence of violent repression) suggests a situation where a breakdown of democratic rule occurred in countries that lacked many of the social structures associated with industrialization (e.g., urbanization, literacy, and so on). These social structures are believed to facilitate stable democratic rule. Further research might show important differences between these two sets of cases with respect to the kind of repression that was inflicted on the protesters.

Table 6.1	Simple Example of Comparative Methods*

Case	Aligned With USSR	Industrialized	Democratic Government	Strong Military	Violent Repression[†]
1	0	0	0	1	1
2	0	1	0	1	1
3	1	0	0	1	1
4	1	1	0	1	1
5	0	0	1	0	1
6	0	0	1	1	1
7	1	0	1	0	1
8	1	0	1	1	1
9	0	0	0	0	0
10	0	1	0	0	0
11	0	1	1	0	0
12	0	1	1	1	0
13	1	0	0	0	0
14	1	1	0	0	0
15	1	1	1	0	0
16	1	1	1	1	0

*In the columns with causal or outcome conditions, the number 1 indicates the presence of a condition, or "yes"; 0 indicates its absence, or "no."
†The two combinations of conditions linked to violent repression are (1) absence of democratic government combined with strong military and (2) presence of democratic government combined with an absence of industrialization.

The cases are arranged in Table 6.1 so that the main patterns of similarity among the countries with violent repression are easy to detect, and the comparison of these cases with countries lacking violent repression is simplified. Specific procedures for assessing patterns of similarity and difference are detailed in the next section. Before examining these procedures, consider several general features of the comparative analysis just presented:

- Comparative analysis proceeds by comparing configurations of causes—*rows* of the table—and not by comparing the presence or absence of each causal condition (that is, each of the first four columns) with presence or absence of the outcome (the last column—repression).

- Comparative analysis allows for the possibility that there may be several combinations of conditions that generate the same general outcome (government repression in the example).

- Comparative analysis can address complex and seemingly contradictory patterns of causation. One causal condition (democratic government prior to the emergence of violent repression) is important in both its present and absent condition—it appears in both causal configurations, but contributes in opposite ways.

- Comparative analysis can eliminate irrelevant causes. One causal condition (whether the country was aligned with the Soviet Union) was eliminated as an important causal condition. Even though it was considered a possible factor at the outset, examination of similarities and differences among repressive and nonrepressive cases shows that this cause is not an essential part of either of the key causal combinations.

The findings in Table 6.1 are easy to see. Usually, however, the patterns are not so simple, and researchers must use more systematic comparative methods to help them analyze similarities and differences. These techniques, explained in the next sections, make it possible for researchers to find patterns that they would probably miss if they tried to unravel differences simply by "eyeballing" their cases.

Specifying Causes and Outcomes

In the comparative approach, each case is understood as a combination of causal conditions linked to a particular outcome. Thus, the selection of the outcome to be studied and the specification of causal conditions relevant to that outcome are crucially important parts of a comparative investigation.

Generally, in order to specify causes, the investigator must be familiar with the research literature on the outcome (for example, "government repression" in the study just described) and with the cases included in the study. In this early phase of the research, the investigator explores connections between social scientific thinking (for example, about government repression) and the evidence. These early explorations lead to a clarification of the nature of the outcome to be studied and a specification of the relevant causes.

The comparative methods described in this chapter use what social scientists call **presence–absence dichotomies**. This means that causal conditions and outcomes are either present or absent in each case and can be coded "yes" or "no," as in Table 6.1. Thus, instead of using a precise measure of industrialization (for example, the percentage of the work force employed in manufacturing) in the data analysis, an assessment is made of whether or not substantial industrialization has occurred. The use of presence–absence dichotomies simplifies the representation of cases as configurations of causal conditions. It is important to note, however, that comparative analysis is not limited to presence–absence dichotomies. In fact, any type of measure can be used in a comparative analysis. As Ragin shows in *Redesigning Social Inquiry* (2008), researchers can examine configurations of causal conditions that vary by level or degree. The key is to use measures that scale the degree of membership in sets, using scores that range from 0 to 1, instead of simply absent (0) or present (1)— the schema used in this chapter to illustrate the logic of comparative research. The use of measures that vary by level or degree is discussed as well in Chapter 7; however, Chapter 7 focuses on the correlations between measures, not on different configurations of conditions.

When using causal conditions expressed in presence–absence dichotomies, the number of conditions determines the number of causal combinations that are possible. For example, the specification of four causal conditions (as in the middle four columns of Table 6.1) provides for 16 (that is, 2^4) logically possible combinations of causal conditions (all 16 appear in Table 6.1). Specification of five causal conditions provides for 32 (2^5) combinations, six causal conditions provides for 64 (2^6) combinations, and so on. Causal conditions are not examined separately, as in studies focusing on covariation, but in combinations.

Once causal conditions have been selected, cases conforming to each combination of causal conditions are examined to see if they agree in terms of the outcome. In Table 6.1, there is only one case for each combination of causal conditions, so there is no possibility of disagreement. But what if there were two cases in the first row (that is, two countries that combined absence of alignment with the Soviet Union, absence of substantial industrialization before 1980, absence of democratic government, and presence of a strong military), but in one country protesters suffered violent repression and in the other they did not? The researcher would have to determine what additional factor (present in one country but absent in the other) caused repression. This new causal condition would then be added to the table for all cases.

If there are many causal combinations with cases that disagree on the outcome, then the investigator should take this as a sign that the specification of causal conditions is incorrect or incomplete. The close examination of cases that have the same presence–absence values on all the causal conditions yet have different outcomes is used as a basis for selecting additional causal variables. Investigators move back and forth between specification of causal conditions (using social science theory and their general substantive knowledge as guides) and examination of evidence to resolve these differences.

Constructing the Truth Table

Once a satisfactory set of causal conditions for a particular outcome has been identified, evidence on cases can be represented in **truth tables.** A truth table summarizes a **data matrix** (e.g., Table 6.1) by sorting cases according to their combinations of values on dichotomous (yes/no) causal variables. The use of truth tables facilitates the analysis of patterns of similarities and differences.

The first step in constructing a truth table is simply to list the evidence on the cases in the form of a data table. Consider, for example, the data presented in Table 6.2. This table shows hypothetical evidence on 30 suburban school districts surrounding a major metropolitan area. The outcome of interest here is whether or not the elementary schools in each district track students according to ability. When students are *tracked,* they are grouped together into relatively homogeneous classes. Students who learn things quickly are assigned to one class, while students who learn things at an average speed are assigned to another, and so on.

Having students of uniform ability together in the same room is thought to simplify teaching, making it more efficient. After all, it clearly would be a mistake to put first graders and eighth graders in the same classroom. Why not apply this same principle to students within grade levels? The usual objection is that students who are assigned to the "slow" group become branded low achievers and are rarely given the opportunity to prove otherwise. Plus, being surrounded by "faster" students can motivate a "slow" student to learn faster. Assigning students to the slow group may seal their academic fate.

The researcher in this example wanted to understand why some school districts track elementary school students and others don't. The middle columns

| Table 6.2 | Hypothetical Data on Tracking in School Districts[*] |

School District	Racial Diversity	Class Diversity	Competitive Elections	Unionized Teachers	Ability Tracking
1	0	0	0	0	0
2	0	0	0	0	0
3	0	0	0	0	0
4	0	0	0	1	1
5	0	0	0	1	1
6	0	0	1	0	0
7	0	0	1	1	1
8	0	1	0	0	0
9	0	1	0	0	0
10	0	1	0	0	0
11	0	1	0	0	0
12	0	1	0	1	1
13	0	1	1	0	0
14	0	1	1	1	1
15	1	0	0	0	1
16	1	0	0	0	1
17	1	0	0	1	1
18	1	0	0	1	1
19	1	0	0	1	1
20	1	0	0	1	1
21	1	0	1	0	0
22	1	0	1	0	0
23	1	0	1	0	0
24	1	0	1	1	0
25	1	1	0	0	1
26	1	1	0	1	1
27	1	1	0	1	1
28	1	1	1	0	0
29	1	1	1	1	0
30	1	1	1	1	0

[*]In the columns with causal or outcome conditions, the number 1 indicates the presence of a condition, or "yes"; 0 indicates its absence, or "no."

of the table list the causal conditions that the researcher, based on an examination of the relevant research literatures, thought might be important:

1. Whether the school district is racially diverse or predominantly white

2. Whether or not the school district has a broad representation of income groups (poor, working class, middle class, and upper middle class)

3. Whether or not the school board elections in the district are open and competitive, with good voter turnout

4. Whether or not the teachers in the district are unionized

The first two factors (racial and class diversity) show the social composition of school districts. These factors are important because where there is more diversity, members of dominant groups (for example, whites in racially diverse districts) generally believe that tracking will benefit their children most. The competitiveness of school board elections is important because the majority of voters usually disapprove of tracking in elementary schools. They believe this practice benefits only a small number of students. In districts where school board elections are routine matters that attract little voter interest, however, the small number of families that benefit from tracking might have more influence. Unionization of teachers is included because the researcher believes that teacher unions prefer tracking because it simplifies teaching.

The school districts are sorted in Table 6.2 according to the four causal conditions so that districts that are identical on these factors are next to each other. Inspection of the data shows that there are no districts that have the same combination of scores on the causal conditions but different outcomes. Districts 8–11, for example, all show the same pattern on the four causal conditions; they also are identical on the outcome—none of these districts tracks students according to ability. If the cases were not consistent on the outcome, it would be necessary to examine them closely to determine which other causal factors should be added to the table.

Listing the data on the cases, as shown in Table 6.2, is a necessary preliminary to the construction of the truth table. The idea behind a truth table is simple: The focus is on causal combinations. Each logical combination of values on the causal conditions is represented as one row of the truth table. Thus, truth tables have as many rows as there are logically possible combinations of values on the causal conditions. If there are four dichotomous causal conditions, as in Table 6.2, the truth table will contain $2^4 = 16$ rows. Each row of the truth table is assigned an outcome score (1 or 0, for presence or absence of the outcome) based on the cases in that row. The first three cases in Table 6.2, for example, have the same combination of scores on the causal conditions (absent on each of the four conditions) and the same outcome (absence of tracking). They are combined to form the first row of the truth table presented in Table 6.3. The number of districts that make up each row of the truth table is also reported in Table 6.3, so that the translation of Table 6.2 to Table 6.3 is clear.

Simplifying the Truth Table

The truth table (Table 6.3) summarizes the causal configurations that exist in a data table (Table 6.2). Listing configurations is not the same as identifying patterns, however. Usually, comparative researchers want to examine configurations to see if they can be simplified. When investigators simplify configurations, they identify patterns.

Here is a quick example of simplification: Look at rows 13 and 14 of the truth table reported in Table 6.3. Row 13 reports that school districts that combine the following four characteristics track students: (1) racial diversity, (2) class diversity, (3) an absence of competitive school board elections, and (4) an absence of teachers' unions. Row 14 reports that school districts that differed on only one of these four conditions—districts in this row had teachers' unions—also tracked students. The comparison of these two rows shows that when the first two causal conditions are present (race and class diversity) and the third is absent (competitive school board elections), it does not matter whether or not teachers are unionized; tracking by ability still takes place.

An easy way to represent this simplification is to use uppercase letters to indicate presence of a condition and lowercase letters to indicate its absence. In this example, the word RACE indicates the presence of racial diversity; the lowercase word race is used to indicate its absence. Similarly, the word CLASS is used to indicate the presence of class diversity; the lowercase class is used to indicate its absence. ELECTIONS is used to indicate the presence of open, competitive school board elections; elections is used to indicate the absence of this condition. UNIONS is used to indicate the presence of teachers' unions; unions is used to indicate the absence of this condition. Finally, TRACKING is used to indicate the presence of tracking, and tracking is used to indicate its absence.

Thus, row 13 can be represented as

$$TRACKING = RACE \cdot CLASS \cdot elections \cdot unions$$

Row 14 can be shown as

$$TRACKING = RACE \cdot CLASS \cdot elections \cdot UNIONS$$

where the multiplication symbol ($\cdot$) is used to indicate the combination of conditions. These two rows can be simplified through combination

| Table 6.3 | Truth Table for Data on Tracking in School Districts[*] |

Row	Racial Diversity	Class Diversity	Competitive Elections	Unionized Teachers	Ability Tracking	Number of Districts[†]
1	0	0	0	0	0	3
2	0	0	0	1	1	2
3	0	0	1	0	0	1
4	0	0	1	1	1	1
5	0	1	0	0	0	4
6	0	1	0	1	1	1
7	0	1	1	0	0	1
8	0	1	1	1	1	1
9	1	0	0	0	1	2
10	1	0	0	1	1	4
11	1	0	1	0	0	3
12	1	0	1	1	0	1
13	1	1	0	0	1	1
14	1	1	0	1	1	2
15	1	1	1	0	0	1
16	1	1	1	1	0	2

[*]In the columns with causal or outcome conditions, the number 1 indicates the presence of a condition, or "yes"; 0 indicates its absence, or "no."
[†]The number of districts is reported simply to remind the reader that each row of a truth table may represent more than one case.

because they have the same outcome and differ on only one causal condition: the presence or absence of teachers' unions. This simplification strategy follows the logic of an experiment. Only one condition at a time is allowed to vary (the "experimental" condition). If varying this condition has no discernible impact on the outcome, it can be eliminated as a factor. Thus, the comparison of rows 13 and 14 results in a simpler combination:

$$TRACKING = RACE \cdot CLASS \cdot elections$$

This rule for combining rows of the truth table as a way of simplifying them can be stated formally: If two rows of a truth table differ on only one causal condition yet result in the same outcome, then the causal condition that distinguishes the two rows can be considered irrelevant and can be removed to create a simpler combination of causal conditions (a simpler term).

The process of combining rows to create simpler terms can be carried on until no more simplification is possible. Table 6.4 shows all the simplifications that are possible for the truth table in Table 6.3, using presence of ability tracking as the outcome of interest. In Table 6.4, the truth table rows from Table 6.3 with outcomes of "1" (presence of tracking) have been translated into the upper- and lowercase names in the manner just described. Panel A of this table simply lists the eight kinds of districts that track students according to ability. Panel B shows the first round of simplification. Each of the terms from panel A can be combined with one or more other terms to create simpler terms. Whenever two terms with four conditions are combined, the new term has three conditions because one condition has been eliminated.

Panel C of Table 6.4 shows the second round of simplification. In this round, terms with three conditions (from panel B) are combined to form terms with two conditions. For example, the term labeled #17 in panel B (race·class·UNIONS) can be combined with the term labeled #21 (race·CLASS·UNIONS) to form a two-condition term (race·UNIONS). All the terms from panel B combine with one or more terms from the same panel to produce the 3 two-condition terms listed in panel C.

The three terms in panel C can be represented in a single statement describing the conditions under which tracking in these suburban school districts occurs:

$$TRACKING = race \cdot UNIONS + RACE \cdot elections + elections \cdot UNIONS$$

Tracking occurs when

1. Racial diversity is absent and teachers' unions are present;

2. Racial diversity is present and competitive school board elections are absent; or

3. Competitive school board elections are absent and teachers' unions are present.

Table 6.4	Simplification of Truth Table for Tracking (Table 6.3)

Panel A. Districts That Track Students

Rows	Causal Configurations
2	race·class·elections·UNIONS
4	race·class·ELECTIONS·UNIONS
6	race·CLASS·elections·UNIONS
8	race·CLASS·ELECTIONS·UNIONS
9	RACE·class·elections·unions
10	RACE·class·elections·UNIONS
13	RACE·CLASS·elections·unions
14	RACE·CLASS·elections·UNIONS

Panel B. First Round of Simplification

					Simplified Terms	Label for New Term
Rows	2	+	4	→	race·class·UNIONS	#17
Rows	2	+	6	→	race·elections·UNIONS	#18
Rows	2	+	10	→	class·elections·UNIONS	#19
Rows	4	+	8	→	race·ELECTIONS·UNIONS	#20
Rows	6	+	8	→	race·CLASS·UNIONS	#21
Rows	6	+	14	→	CLASS·elections·UNIONS	#22
Rows	9	+	10	→	RACE·class·elections	#23
Rows	9	+	13	→	RACE·elections·unions	#24
Rows	10	+	14	→	RACE·elections·UNIONS	#25
Rows	13	+	14	→	RACE·CLASS·elections	#26

(Continued)

Table 6.4   (Continued)

Panel C. Second Round of Simplification

				Simplified Terms
#17	+	#21	→	race·UNIONS
#18	+	#20	→	race·UNIONS
#18	+	#25	→	elections·UNIONS
#19	+	#22	→	elections·UNIONS
#23	+	#26	→	RACE·elections
#24	+	#25	→	RACE·elections

Before accepting these tentative results, it is important to determine if further simplification is possible, as is often the case. Sometimes the process of combining rows to produce simpler terms (presented in Table 6.4) generates "surplus" terms. A *surplus term* is redundant with other terms and is not needed in the statement describing the combinations of conditions linked to an outcome. In short, some of the terms that are left after the process of combining rows, just described, may be superfluous. Recall that the goal of comparative analysis is to describe diversity in a simple way. If the results can be further simplified by eliminating surplus terms, as is the case here, it is important to do so. The idea of surplus terms is best understood by examining the methods used to detect them.

The best way to check to see if there are surplus terms is to construct a chart showing which of the original terms in panel A of Table 6.4 are covered by which simplified terms in panel C of Table 6.4. A simplified term covers a truth table row if the row is a subset of the simplified term. For example, RACE·CLASS·elections·UNIONS (row 14 of the truth table) is a subset of the simplified term "elections·UNIONS."

The chart showing the coverage of the simplified terms is presented in Table 6.5. The simplified term "race·UNIONS" covers the first four terms from panel A of Table 6.4, while the term "RACE·elections" covers the other four. The third simplified term (elections·UNIONS) does not cover any of the rows uniquely; it covers two that are covered by the first simplified term and two that are covered by the second. Thus, the third simplified term is surplus; it is redundant with the other terms.

By eliminating the third simplified term, the results of the analysis of configurations can be reduced to

TRACKING = race·UNIONS + RACE·elections

This completes the procedure. The final statement says that tracking occurs

1. When racial diversity is absent and teachers' unions are present, or

2. When racial diversity is present and competitive school board elections are absent.

The first term (race·UNIONS) indicates that in school districts that are predominantly white, tracking is implemented if there are teachers' unions. This finding supports the researcher's belief that teachers' unions prefer tracking and specifies the conditions under which their interests are realized—in districts where there is an absence of racial diversity. It does not matter whether school board elections are open and competitive or whether the district contains a broad range of income groups. The second term (RACE·elections) indicates that in school districts where there is racial diversity, tracking occurs when school board elections are not competitive. They are routine matters that do not attract a lot of voter interest. In these districts, it does not matter whether teachers' unions are present or whether the district contains a broad range of income groups. The second term suggests that if voters become involved in school board elections, tracking would be eliminated in racially diverse districts.

The analysis of school districts presented here shows the major steps in using comparative techniques to unravel causal patterns:

1. Select causal and outcome conditions, using existing social science literature and substantive knowledge to guide the selection.

2. Construct a sorted data table showing the scores of cases on these causal and outcome conditions (Table 6.2).

3. Construct a truth table from the data table, making sure that cases with the same causal conditions actually have the same score on the outcome (Table 6.3).

4. Compare rows of the truth table and simplify them, eliminating one condition at a time from pairs of rows (Table 6.4).

5. Examine the coverage of the simplified terms to see if there are any surplus terms that can be eliminated (Table 6.5).

Table 6.5	Chart Showing Coverage of Simplified Terms

	Simplified Terms[†]		
Truth Table Rows[*]	race·UNIONS	RACE·elections	elections·UNIONS
race·class·elections·UNIONS	✓		✓
race·class·ELECTIONS·UNIONS	✓		
race·CLASS·elections·UNIONS	✓		✓
race·CLASS·ELECTIONS·UNIONS	✓		
RACE·class·elections·unions		✓	✓
RACE·class·elections·UNIONS		✓	
RACE·CLASS·elections·unions		✓	
RACE·CLASS·elections·UNIONS		✓	✓

*From panel A of Table 6.4.
† From panel C of Table 6.4.

The terms that remain after step 5 show the simplest way to represent the patterns of diversity in the data. In the comparative analysis presented in Tables 6.2 through 6.5, the goal was to explain why some school districts track elementary students. The results show which types of school district track elementary students and distinguish them from those that do not.

Conclusion

The brief overview of comparative methods presented in this chapter illustrates some of the key features of the comparative approach. The most important feature is its focus on diversity. Whenever a set of cases has different outcomes (cities with different reactions to Somali refugees, countries with different reactions to IMF-mandated austerity programs, bars with different ways of encouraging patrons to drink responsibly, and so on), comparative methods can be used to find simple ways of representing the patterns of diversity that exist among the cases. These methods identify similarities within subsets of cases that distinguish them from other subsets.

As in all forms of social research, analytic frames and images play an important part in comparative research. Analytic frames provide primary leads for the construction of truth tables, especially the selection of causal conditions. The construction of the truth table itself is an important part of the dialogue of ideas and evidence in comparative research because the truth table must be free of inconsistencies before it can be simplified. Evidence-based images emerge from the simplification of truth tables in the form of configurations of conditions that differentiate subsets of cases.

In many ways, the comparative approach lies halfway between the qualitative approach and the quantitative approach. The qualitative approach seeks in-depth knowledge of a relatively small number of cases. When the focus is on commonalities, it often narrows its scope to smaller sets of cases as it seeks to clarify their similarities. The comparative approach usually addresses more cases because of its emphasis on diversity, and it is applied to sets of cases that are clearly bounded in time and space. By contrast, as Chapter 7 will show, the quantitative study of covariation seeks broad familiarity with a large number of cases and often views them as generic, interchangeable observations.

7

Using Quantitative Methods to Study Covariation

Introduction

The starting point of quantitative analysis is the idea that the best route to understanding basic patterns and relationships is to examine phenomena across many cases. Focusing on any single case or on a small number of cases might give a very distorted picture. Looking across many cases makes it possible to average out the peculiarities of individual cases and to construct a picture of social life that is purified of phenomena that are specific to any case or to a small group of cases. Only the general pattern remains.

Quantitative researchers construct images by showing the covariation between two or more variables across many cases. Recall from Chapter 1 that a variable is a feature or attribute that differs from one case to the next. Suppose a researcher were to demonstrate in a study of the top 500 corporations that those offering better retirement benefits tend to pay lower wages. The two variables are retirement benefits and wages. The image that emerges is that corporations make trade-offs between retirement benefits and pay, with some corporations investing in long-term commitments to workers (retirement benefits) and some emphasizing short-term pay-offs (wages). Evidence-based images such as these are general because they describe patterns across many cases and they are *parsimonious*—that is, only a few attributes are involved.

Images that are constructed from broad patterns of covariation are considered general because they condense evidence on many cases—the greater the number of cases, the more general the pattern. A quantitative researcher might construct a general image of political radicalism, for example, that links degree of radicalism to some other individual-level attribute such as degree of insulation from popular culture, and he or she might use survey data on thousands of people (including people who are politically apathetic) to document the connection. Qualitative researchers studying this same question would go about the task very differently. The images they construct are detailed and specific, and they use methods that enhance rather than condense evidence. Using a qualitative approach, a researcher might construct an image of how political radicals nurture their radical commitments by studying the daily lives of 20 radicals in depth.

These two images of radicalism, one by a qualitative researcher and one by a quantitative researcher, might or might not contradict. Even if they did not contradict each other, the two images still would be very different in degree of detail and complexity. Quantitative researchers sacrifice in-depth knowledge of each individual case in order to achieve an understanding of broad patterns of covariation across many cases.

Quantitative researchers use the term **correlation** to describe a pattern of covariation between two measurable variables. In the previous example, degree of radicalism and degree of insulation from popular culture are correlated such that more radical people tend to be more insulated. Quantitative researchers also often describe a correlation between two variables as a **relationship,** which should not be confused with the more conventional use of the term to describe social bonds (for example, a parent–child relationship). Again using the previous example, there is a relationship between degree of radicalism and degree of insulation.

Usually, attributes of cases that can be linked in this way are understood as variables because they are phenomena that vary by level or degree. There are cases with high values of a variable (such as more than 18 years of education on the variable "educational attainment"), cases with moderate values (say, 12 years of education), and cases with low values (only a few years of education). Variables can also be presence–absence dichotomies where the variable takes on the value of either "yes" or "no" (e.g., the variable "received a 4-year college degree").

Some variables (called independent or causal variables) are defined as causes, and others (called dependent or outcome variables) are defined as effects in a given analysis. The **dependent variable** is the phenomenon the investigator wishes to explain; **independent variables** are the factors that are used to account for the variation in the dependent variable. A dependent variable in one analysis may appear as an independent variable in the next. For example, a study that seeks to explain why some countries are poor and others rich may use gross national product (GNP) per capita as the dependent variable (as the outcome being explained). Yet another study that seeks to explain why people in some countries have a higher life expectancy than people in other countries may use GNP as an independent variable (a causal factor). Quantitative researchers also include **control variables** in their models of social phenomena—features of the cases being studied (a type of independent variable) that the researcher believes may influence the outcome and so need to be taken into account, yet are not the focus of the study. Researchers include control variables to demonstrate that the pattern of covariation between the variables of interest remains in place, *all other things being equal.*

Quantitative researchers use advanced statistical techniques such as **multiple regression analysis** to disentangle correlations among independent variables and assess their separate effects on dependent variables (see Allison 1998 for an overview of regression). Advanced techniques, such as event history and survival models, enable researchers to look at relationships between variables over time (such as the relationship between liquidity and the survival or failure of small businesses). Other techniques model relationships within a hierarchy (see Luke 2004). For example, a policy researcher might want to examine the life expectancy of individuals with varying levels of income and wealth within countries. Exploratory data analysis (see Tukey 1977) is used to go beyond broad patterns of covariation to identify sets of cases that deviate from these patterns or to uncover very subtle ones.

The Goals of Quantitative Research

Because the quantitative approach favors general features across many cases, it is well suited for several of the basic goals of social research. These include the goals of identifying general patterns and relationships, testing theories, and making predictions. These three goals all dictate examination of many cases—the more, the better—and favor a dialogue of ideas and evidence that centers on how attributes of cases (variables) are linked to each other.

Identifying General Patterns and Relationships

One of the primary goals of social research is to identify general relationships. For a relationship to be general, it must be observed across many cases. In quantitative research, this is understood not as observing the same exact phenomenon in each and every case, but as observing an *association* between two or more phenomena across many cases. When a social researcher claims that poorer countries tend to have lower rates of literacy, he or she in essence is stating that there is a general correspondence between a country's wealth and its rate of literacy such that richer countries tend to have higher literacy rates and poorer countries tend to have lower rates. (There are striking exceptions to this general relationship, such as Sri Lanka and Saudi Arabia, described in Chapter 2.)

Identifying general patterns and relationships is important because they offer clues about causation. Obviously, if two variables are related across many cases, it doesn't necessarily mean that one caused the other. If we found that shoe size and income were related, we would not argue that big feet cause high incomes. However, when variables are systematically related, it is important to consider the *possibility* that one may cause the other. Alternatively, the two correlated variables both may be the effects of some third, unidentified variable.

Here is an example: In the United States throughout most of the 20th century, the more industrial states tended to offer stronger support for liberal Democratic candidates. This general pattern connects an independent variable (percentage of the state's adult population employed in industry) to a dependent variable (percentage of a state's electorate voting for liberal Democratic candidates). A causal relationship can be inferred from the correlation between these two variables: Conditions associated with having a lot of industry (such as urbanization, unionization, and so on) generate a preference for the liberal candidates among the people affected by these conditions. The explanation of liberal voting based on this evidence thus may emphasize the impact of industrial conditions on people's interests and the translation of these interests to a preference for liberal candidates. The causal images behind correlations are central to the representations of social life that quantitative researchers construct.

Generally, quantitative social researchers identify causation with explanation. Once the causes of a phenomenon have been identified, they consider it to be explained. The usual sequence is as follows:

1. A pattern of covariation is identified and the strength of the relationship is assessed.

2. Causation may be inferred from the correlation, and if so,

3. An explanation is built up from the inferred causal relationship.

Another way of understanding this is simply to say that quantitative social researchers construct images by examining patterns of covariation among variables and inferring causation from these broad patterns.

Testing Theories

While quantitative researchers often construct explanations and images from the broad patterns that they observe (like the rough correlation between income levels and education levels) and relate these evidence-based images to their ideas about social life, they also test ideas drawn directly from social theories. Recall from Part I of this book that all social researchers are involved in long-standing, abstract conversations about social life. Social researchers use this body of thought whenever they construct images, but they also seek to advance this body of thought and to construct formal tests of ideas drawn from it.

Testing an idea is different from using an idea to help make sense of some pattern in a set of data or body of evidence that already has been collected. When an idea is tested, it is first used to construct an image that is based on the ideas themselves, not the evidence. That is, the researcher constructs a theoretical image. Researchers use these theoretically based images to derive testable propositions (also called hypotheses) about evidence that has not yet been examined. Once examined, the evidence either supports or refutes the proposition.

This formal assessment of hypotheses helps social scientists determine which ideas are most useful for understanding social life. An idea that consistently fails to win support in these formal tests will eventually be dropped from the pool of ideas that social scientists use. Ideas that consistently receive support are retained.

For example, one theoretical image in the study of social inequality is the idea that advanced societies are *achievement* oriented (i.e., they reward performance), while less advanced societies are *ascription* oriented (i.e., they reward people for ascribed qualities—for who they are, such as for their family's social status, not for how well they have performed). Thus, in an achievement-oriented society, a person of great ability from a low-status, impoverished background should nevertheless be successful. By contrast, in an ascription-oriented society, people born into high-status families will be successful, regardless of their talents.

These are theoretical images. There is no society that is totally achievement oriented, nor is there any society that is totally ascription oriented. However, these theoretical images have implications for inequality in the United States, which is generally considered to be an advanced society. Has the United States become more achievement oriented over the last 60 years? Is it easier today for a talented person from a low-status, impoverished background to succeed than it was in the 1950s? The theoretical images just described link the ascendance of the achievement orientation to societal advancement, suggesting that over the last 60 years it should have become easier in the United States for a talented person from a low-status background to get ahead.

Thus, the testable proposition is that evidence on "social mobility" (the study of who gets ahead) should support the idea that achievement has become more important and ascription less important in U.S. society. The increased importance of achievement criteria, for example, might be discernible in the strength of the relationship between educational achievement and subsequent income. Is the correlation between these two variables stronger in 2010 than it was in 1950? The decreased importance of ascription might be visible in the strength of the inverse relationship between race and income. Is race a less significant factor in 2010 than it was in 1950? Of course, it is possible to examine the effects of a variety of achievement and ascription variables on income over the last 60 years (and at various points within this span of time) because there have been many surveys conducted over this period with data relevant to the proposition.

The quantitative approach is very useful for testing theoretical ideas and images such as these. Notice that these ideas are general—they are relevant to many cases, and they are parsimonious, meaning they concern the operation of only a few causal variables. When theoretical ideas are relevant to many cases, like ideas about ascription versus achievement, we have more confidence in a test when it includes a very large number and a wide range of cases.

Making Predictions

Another goal of social research that mandates examination of large numbers of cases is that of making predictions. In order to be able to make predictions, it is important to have as many cases as possible and to have a wide variety. When predictions are based on many cases, researchers have the largest possible data set at their disposal and are capable of making the most accurate predictions.

For example, to predict whether middle-aged, middle-class, white, Southern men will favor the Republican candidate in the next presidential election, it is necessary to know how people with this combination of characteristics generally vote in presidential elections. Do they always favor Republican candidates? Do they vote differently when the Democratic candidate is a Southerner? When issues related to national defense are important, are they more enthusiastic in their support for the Republican candidate? Clearly, the greater the volume of evidence on the political behavior of men in this category, the more precise the prediction for a future election will be.

Having a lot of evidence makes it easier to forecast future behavior. Knowledge of general patterns also helps. Suppose a researcher wants to predict the political behavior of middle-aged, middle-class, Southern white men in an election that pits a Democratic candidate from the South against a Republican candidate (from another region of the country) who favors greater military spending. Suppose further that this particular combination of candidate characteristics has never occurred before. How can social scientists extrapolate when one condition (Democratic candidate from the South) decreases this group's support for the Republican candidate, while the other (a pro-military spending posture) increases its support?

Accumulated knowledge of general patterns helps in these situations. If research shows that, in general, the personal characteristics of a candidate (for example, being a southerner) matter more to voters than the positions a candidate takes (for example, being in favor of military spending), then the prediction would be that the southern factor should outweigh the military factor.

Knowledge of general patterns helps social researchers sharpen their predictions by providing important clues about how to weight factors accurately, even in the face of many unknowns and great uncertainty. Because it is well suited for the production and accumulation of knowledge about general patterns, the variable-based approach offers a solid basis for making such predictions.

Contrasts With Other Research Strategies

When social researchers construct images from evidence, they may use any number of cases. Qualitative researchers typically use a small number of cases (from one to several handfuls), comparative researchers use a moderate number, and quantitative researchers use many (sometimes tens of thousands or even more). The images that qualitative researchers construct are based on general patterns of variation across many, many cases. These general images link variation in one attribute of cases to variation in other attributes. The patterns of covariation between two or more such variables across many cases provide the basic raw material for the images being constructed. These images tend to be less specific and in-depth than those based on fewer cases.

The quantitative strategy favors **generality**. For example, a quantitative researcher might show that there is a link between variation in income levels and variation in education levels in a large sample of U.S. adults. This pattern of covariation evokes a general image of how people in the United

States get ahead. If income levels covary more closely with educational levels than they do with other individual-level attributes (such as age, race, marital status, and so on), then it appears that success in the education system is the key to subsequent material well-being. This image of how income differences arise in U.S. society contrasts sharply with one that links differences in income levels to differences in other attributes such as physical attractiveness. A key issue in the application of the quantitative approach is the strength of the relationship of different causal variables, such as education level and physical attractiveness, to dependent variables, such as income.

The quantitative approach favors not only generality but also **parsimony**—using as few variables as possible to explain as much as possible. In a study of income levels, for example, the main concern of the quantitative researcher would be to identify the individual-level attributes with the strongest correlation with income levels. Is it education levels? Is it age? Is it household income? Is it skin color? Which variables have the strongest links with differences in income? By identifying the variables with the strongest correlations, quantitative researchers pinpoint key causal factors and use these to construct parsimonious images.

Parsimony and generality go together in quantitative research. Images that are general also tend to be parsimonious. It is clear that parsimony is not a key concern of the qualitative approach. Qualitative researchers believe that in order to represent subjects properly, they must be studied in depth—to uncover nuances and subtleties. Comparative researchers lie halfway between qualitative researchers and quantitative researchers on the issues of parsimony and generality. Rather than focus on patterns that are general across as many cases as possible—the primary concern of the quantitative approach, comparative researchers focus on diversity—on configurations of similarities and differences within a specific set of cases.

This difference between quantitative and comparative research is subtle but important. A parsimonious image that links attributes across many cases assumes that all cases are more or less the same in how they came to be the way they are. The person with low education and low income is, in this view, the reverse image of the person with high education and high income. They are two sides of a single coin.

The comparative approach, by contrast, focuses on diversity—how different causes combine in complex and sometimes contradictory ways to produce different outcomes. Thus, instead of focusing on attributes that covary with differences in income levels, such as education levels, the comparative researcher might focus on the diverse ways people achieve material success, with and without education, and contrast these with the diverse ways they fail to achieve success. From a comparative perspective, it is not a question of which attributes covary most closely with income levels, but of the different paths to achieving material success.

Research using comparative methods has largely been for the study of a moderate number of cases, not for the study of relationships across thousands of cases. Like the qualitative approach, the comparative approach values knowledge of individual cases. However, recent work has applied comparative methods to much larger sample sizes where in-depth knowledge of individual cases was not feasible (Amenta et al. 2009; Cooper 2005; Grant et al. 2009). The important point in this contrast between the quantitative approach and the comparative approach is the difference between looking for variables that seem to be systematically linked to each other across many cases (a central concern of the quantitative approach) and examining patterns of diversity (a major objective of the comparative approach).

The Process of Quantitative Research

The quantitative approach is the most structured of the three research strategies examined in this book. Its structured nature follows in part from the fact that it is well suited for testing theories. Whenever researchers test theories, they must exercise a great deal of caution in how they conduct their tests so that they do not rig their results in advance. Human beings are reactive creatures. There is a large body of research, for example, showing that when people are interviewed, their responses are shaped in part by the personal characteristics of the interviewer (such as whether the interviewer is male or female). If they know what a social scientist is trying to prove, they may try to undermine the study, or they may become overly compliant. Tests in any scientific field that are not conducted carefully cannot be trusted.

The more structured nature of quantitative research also follows from its emphasis on variables. Variables are the building blocks of the images that quantitative researchers construct. But before researchers have variables that they can connect through correlations, they must be able to specify their cases as members of a meaningful set, and they must be able to specify the aspects of their cases that are relevant to examine as variables. In short, much about the research tends to be fixed at the outset of the quantitative investigation.

This orientation contrasts sharply with those of the other two strategies. In qualitative research, investigators often do not decide what their case is a "case of" until they write up their results for publication (see Chapter 5). In the comparative approach, researchers assume that their cases are very diverse in how they came to be the way they are, and investigators often conclude their research by differentiating distinct types of cases (see Chapter 6). Of course, quantitative researchers are quite capable of differentiating types of cases, but their primary focus is on relating variables across all the cases on which they have data.

Cases and variables can be fixed at the outset of a study—as they tend to be in quantitative research—only if the study is well grounded in an analytic frame. Thus, analytic frames play a very important part in quantitative research.

Analytic Frames in Quantitative Research

Researchers use analytic frames to articulate theoretical ideas about social life (see Chapter 3). Frames specify the cases relevant to a theory and delineate their major features. The importance of frames to quantitative research can be seen most clearly in research that seeks to test theories. Once a theory has been translated into an analytic frame, specific propositions (or testable hypotheses) about how variables are thought to be related to each other can be stated. Researchers can then develop measures of the relevant variables, collect data, and use correlational techniques to assess the links among relevant variables. Relationships among variables either refute or support theoretically based images.

For example, a theory of job satisfaction may emphasize the match between a person's skills and the nature of the tasks he or she is required to perform. The basic theoretical idea is that people are happiest in their work when their jobs require them to do things they do well. Work that does not suit an employee makes the employee feel frustrated and dissatisfied, even useless. These theoretical ideas can be expressed in a frame that details employee and job characteristics relevant to job satisfaction.

To test the idea that job satisfaction is greatest when an employee's skills are well matched with his or her duties, it would be necessary to elaborate this frame in advance of data collection. The quantitative researcher does not sit down with the employees he or she is studying to discuss how a match or mismatch between skills and duties might be affecting the employee's level of satisfaction with his or her work. Of course, that does not mean that researchers should remain ignorant of their research subjects before testing a theory. They should learn all that they can. The point is simply that the data used to test a theory are not the same as the evidence the researcher uses in developing or refining the hypothesis to be tested.

The frame becomes more or less fixed once theory testing is initiated. The job satisfaction frame just described is fixed on employees as cases, job satisfaction as the dependent variable, and the match between employee and job characteristics as independent variables. When a frame is fixed, the images that can be constructed from evidence are constrained. When the goal is to test theory, the images that can be constructed are further constrained by the hypothesis. In the job satisfaction example, if the researcher finds that the employees who are well matched in terms of skills and duties are not the ones with the highest levels of job satisfaction, then the image constructed from the evidence rejects the theoretically based frame.

Even when quantitative researchers are not testing theories, the images they can construct from evidence are still constrained by their frames. In order to examine relationships among variables, it is necessary first to define relevant cases and variables. The examination of relationships among variables usually cannot begin until after all the evidence has been collected. Furthermore, the evidence collected must be in a form appropriate for quantitative analysis. There must be many cases, all more or less comparable to each other, and they must have data on all, or at least most, of the relevant variables. Thus, quantitative research implements frames directly, as guides to data collection, telling researchers which variables to measure.

From Analytic Frame to Data Matrix

In quantitative research, the collection of evidence is seen as a process of filling in the data matrix defined by the analytic frame. In the study of job satisfaction just described, the data on a single employee would fill one row of the data matrix, and there would be as many rows as employees. The columns of the data matrix would be the different employee and job characteristics relevant to the analysis. (Tables 6.1 and 7.1 are examples of data matrices.) Thus, in quantitative research, the data matrix mirrors the analytic frame.

The researcher would not fill in this matrix with data on just anyone. In a study of job satisfaction, for example, the researcher would probably want to collect data on all the employees of a particular factory or firm. (Of course, if the firm or factory were very large, the researcher would probably collect a systematic, random sample of its employees.) In order to construct a good test of the theory, the researcher would choose a work setting with many different kinds of jobs and with employees possessing many different kinds of skills. This combination would provide a good setting for testing the idea that matching skills with duties is important for job satisfaction. If the researcher chose a work setting where everyone did more or less the same thing and had more or less the same skills, then it would not be an appropriate setting for testing the idea that matching skills with duties matters.

Thus, quantitative researchers exercise considerable care when selecting the cases to be used for testing a particular theory. The cases must be relevant to the theory, and they must vary in ways that allow the theory to be tested. When a theory is relevant to very large numbers (for example, all adults in the United States), the quantitative researcher uses a random sample of such cases (for example, every 10,000th person listed in the census). When it is not possible to use a national sample, the researcher may sample the people in a single city or region—one that is representative of the population as a whole.

Of course, not all social theories are about variation among individuals. Sometimes they are about other basic units—families, classrooms, firms, factories, households, gangs, neighborhoods, cities, or even whole countries. In most quantitative research, cases are common, generic units like these. This preference for generic units follows from its emphasis on constructing broad, parsimonious images that reflect general patterns.

Measuring Variables

Quantitative researchers also exercise great care in developing measures of their variables. For example, in the study of job satisfaction, the measurement of the dependent variable is critically important to the study as a whole: How should it be measured? Is it enough simply to ask employees to rate their degree of satisfaction with their jobs? Can employees be trusted to give honest and accurate assessments, or will they worry that management is looking over their shoulders? Should the researcher also examine personnel files? Is this legal? Is it ethical? What about records on absenteeism? Is absenteeism a good measure of job dissatisfaction? What about asking supervisors to give their ratings of the people who work under them?

Not surprisingly, there is an immense literature on the problems of measuring job satisfaction, and comparably large literatures exist on the measurement of most of the many variables that interest social scientists. Even variables that seem straightforward are difficult to measure with precision, and controversies abound. For example, what do years of education measure? Knowledge? Job-relevant skills? Time spent in classrooms?

Consider another example: It is clear that nations differ in wealth. Gross national product in U.S. dollars per capita is a conventional measure of national wealth. However, GNP per capita has important liabilities, some of which are technical. In order to get all countries on the same yardstick, their currencies must be converted to U.S. dollars, but the relevant exchange rates for making these conversions fluctuate daily. Thus, the rankings of countries on GNP per capita fluctuate daily. However, wealth differences between countries are thought to be relatively long-standing, where differences induced by short-term exchange rate fluctuations are artificial.

A more serious problem is this: Some countries have great inequality, with a substantial class of very rich people, many poor people, and few in between. These countries may appear "statistically" to be much better off than they are because on the average—which is what GNP per capita represents—conditions seem acceptable. However, the reality may be one of widespread suffering in the face of extreme riches. For example, the GNP per capita of many oil-exporting countries skyrocketed from the mid-1970s to the mid-1980s, but living conditions for the majority remained on par with those of poorer, non–oil-exporting countries (such as Nigeria compared to Tanzania). Thus, it is possible to have a high GNP per capita and relatively poor living conditions, which contradicts the idea of GNP per capita as a measure of national wealth. A quantitative researcher relying solely on this measure as an indicator of the average citizen's circumstances would be presenting a misleading picture of living conditions in countries with high levels of inequality (such as Brazil, Haiti, and South Africa).

An alternative measure, the **Gini coefficient,** is commonly used to quantify the degree of inequality within a country. If all of the wealth of a country is concentrated in the hands of a single individual, the Gini coefficient will be 1.0. If wealth is evenly distributed across all of the country's residents, the Gini coefficient will be 0.0. In terms of understanding what it means to live in a particular country, considering both GNP per capita and the Gini coefficient is preferable to relying on either measure on its own. That said, two numbers alone are not going to provide a rich representation of what it means to live in one country compared to another.

The issue of using appropriate measures is known as the problem of validity (see also Chapter 1). Do data collection and measurement procedures work the way social researchers claim? One way to assess validity is to check the correlations among alternative measures that, according to the ideas that motivate the study, should covary. For example, a researcher may believe that years of education is a valid measure of general knowledge and could assess this by administering a test of general knowledge to a large group of people representative of the population to be surveyed. If their scores on this test correlate strongly with their years of education, then the researcher would be justified in treating years of education in the survey of the larger population as a measure of general knowledge.

Researchers are also concerned about the reliability of their measures. **Reliability** generally concerns how much randomness there is in a particular measure (what qualitative researchers refer to as *random error*). For example, day-to-day exchange rate fluctuations produce randomness in the

GNP per capita in U.S. dollars. The calculation of this statistic changes every time exchange rates change. Thus, GNP per capita calculated one day will not correlate perfectly with GNP per capita calculated the next, even if the estimates of the goods and services produced by each country's citizens are unchanged.

Returning to the earlier example, when employees are asked how satisfied they are with their jobs, their answers may reflect what happened that day or over the last few days. Ask them again in a month, and their answers may reflect what's happening then. Thus, when the measurements of job satisfaction taken one month apart are correlated, asking the same people the same question, the relationship may be weak because of the randomness induced by different surrounding events.

Researchers have developed a variety of ways to counteract unreliability. In research on job satisfaction, they might ask many questions that get at different aspects of job satisfaction and use these together to develop a broad measure (for example, by adding the responses to form a total score for each person). More than likely, employees' responses to most of the questions will not change over one month. Thus, by adding together the responses to many related questions on job satisfaction, the researcher might develop a measure that is more reliable.

In Chapter 1, we discussed how something that seems simple to measure can in fact be quite complicated. Results can differ vastly depending upon the way the variable is defined and measured. For example, determining the percentage of gay adult men in the United States has led to answers mostly within the range of 2% to 10%. When only those men who have been exclusively in same-sex relationships in the past year are counted as gay, the estimate is closer to 2.5%. When those men who have had at least one male partner since age 18 are counted, the estimate rises to 4.7% (Black et al. 2000). And there are numerous other ways to define who fits into the category of "gay adult man." Depending on a researcher's definition, one measure might be viewed as valid while another is invalid. A common approach is to let individuals identify themselves as homosexual, heterosexual, or bisexual. However, as research has demonstrated, self-reporting has a significant reliability issue because people may not report complete or accurate information. Using this example, people responding to a telephone survey are less likely to mention homosexual behaviors when the interviewer is a person rather than a computerized voice in a phone survey (Villarroel et al. 2006). This is a significant problem because valid and reliable estimates of the number of gay adult men by region would be useful to policymakers trying to effectively target HIV/AIDS prevention efforts. (Valid and reliable estimates of the number of men engaging in unprotected sex with other men would be even more useful to policymakers.) Decisions about how to measure something are part of the process of constructing a representation of social life and play a huge role in the final representation. This part of the process often reveals the complexities inherent in studying society and the attempt on the part of researchers to distill human practices into a few quantifiable attributes.

Measurement is one of the most difficult and important tasks facing the quantitative researcher because so much depends on its accuracy. If a relationship is weak, say between job satisfaction and a measure of the match between employees' skills and duties, is it because the theory is wrong or because the measures are bad? Is the measure of job satisfaction accurate? Is the measure of skills adequate? Is the measure of the match of employees' skills and duties properly conceived and executed? In the quantitative approach, there is no way to know for sure why a correlation that is expected to be strong comes out weak. Because researchers usually hold fast to their theories, they often blame their measures and the difficulty of measuring social phenomena with precision, rather than the theory itself.

Examining Correlations and Testing Theories

The examination of correlations among variables is the core of the quantitative approach, but quantitative researchers must travel a great distance before they can assess a single relationship. They must translate their theoretical ideas into analytic frames. They must choose appropriate cases. If there are many, many such cases, they must devise a sampling strategy. They must develop valid, reliable measures of all their variables. If the goal of the investigation is to test theory, they must also articulate the proposition to be tested and take great care in measuring the variables central to the proposition. In addition, they must fill in the data matrix defined by their analytic frames, the cases they have selected, and the measures they have devised.

After all this preparation, the technical computation involved in quantitative research may seem anticlimactic. In qualitative research, the investigator engages ideas in every stage of the research, refining and clarifying categories and concepts as new evidence is gathered (see Chapter 5). In comparative research, a similar process of linking ideas and evidence occurs during the process of examining the various configurations of cases (see Chapter 6). In quantitative research, investigators must learn as much as they can about the theories they want to test, about their cases, and about how to measure their variables before they collect the data that will be used to test their theories. Thus, the examination of relationships among variables (the technique quantitative researchers use to construct evidence-based images) occurs near the end of a very long journey.

When quantitative researchers test theories, the key question is whether or not the correlations follow patterns consistent with the theory. Sometimes this assessment involves the correlation between a single independent variable and a single dependent variable. In the study of job satisfaction just described, the question might be, how strong is the correlation between job satisfaction and the degree to which employees' skills and duties are matched? Sometimes testing a theory involves comparing the strength of a correlation in different times or settings. For example, is education level more strongly linked to income level in 2010 than it was in 1950? Sometimes testing involves comparing the correlations of several independent variables with one or more dependent variables: Is the effect of race on income stronger or weaker than the effect of education on income? Did the pattern change between 1950 and 2010?

What do researchers do when results do not support their theories? Sometimes they simply report that the evidence does not support their theory. In other words, they report that they attempted to construct an evidence-based image consistent with some theory, but were unable to do so, suggesting that the theory is wrong. In general, however, the audiences for social science expect social life to be represented in some way in a research report. They do not expect a report of a failed attempt to validate a representation. However, such reports should be more common than they are because the logic of theory testing (that is, the effort to figure out which ideas are best supported by evidence) indicates that negative findings (that is, failed representations) are very important to the social scientific community, as these reports allow researchers to discard incomplete or inaccurate theories.

More often, if the initial test of a hypothesis fails, researchers examine their evidence closely to see if there is support for their theory under specific conditions. For example, after finding a weak correlation between job satisfaction and the degree to which employees' skills and duties are matched, a researcher might consider the possibility that other factors need to be considered. Perhaps employees who have been with the firm the longest are more satisfied, regardless of how well their skills are matched to their duties. This factor would need to be taken into account when examining the relation between job satisfaction and the match of skills and duties. Generally, researchers try to use their general knowledge of the cases and their theoretical understanding to anticipate refinements like these before they collect the data. They may also specify additional hypotheses in advance as a way to anticipate such failures.

Using Quantitative Methods

An Introduction to Quantitative Methods

Quantitative methods focus directly on relationships among variables, especially the effects of causal or independent variables on outcome or dependent variables. Another way to think about the quantitative approach is to see the level of the dependent variable (for example, variation across countries in life expectancy) as something that depends on the level of other variables (for example, variation across countries in nutrition). Although statistical techniques have become very advanced, the foundation of these methods is the correlation between the independent and dependent variables. This introduction, therefore, focuses on this correlation. The strength of the correlation between the independent and the dependent variable provides evidence in favor of or against the idea that the two variables are causally connected or linked in some other way.

The exact degree to which two variables correlate can be determined by computing a **correlation coefficient.** The most common correlation coefficient is known as Pearson's r and is the main focus of this discussion. If the correlation is substantial and the implied cause-effect sequence makes sense, then the cause (the independent variable) is said to "explain variation" in the effect (the dependent variable).

For example, if cities in the United States with lower unemployment rates also tend to have lower crime rates, then these two features of cities go together—they correlate. Generally, social scientists would argue that the unemployment rate (the independent variable) explains variation across cities in the crime rate (the dependent variable). The general pattern of covariation in this hypothetical example is high unemployment rates with high crime rates, moderate unemployment rates with moderate crime rates, and low unemployment rates with low crime rates, as depicted with hypothetical data on cities in Figure 7.1. In this figure, there is a **positive correlation** because high unemployment rates go with high crime rates and low unemployment rates go with low crime rates.

Some general patterns of covariation display **negative correlations.** For example, if people who work in less bureaucratic settings display, on the average, more job satisfaction than people who work in more bureaucratic

Figure 7.1	Plot of Crime Rate With Rate of Unemployment Showing Positive Correlation

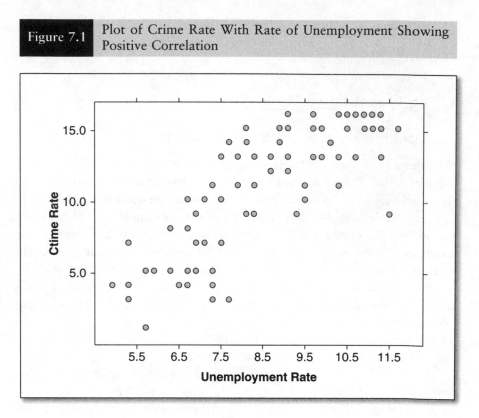

settings, then these two variables are negatively correlated. This pattern can be depicted in a plot of employee data, as in Figure 7.2, which presents hypothetical evidence conforming to the stated pattern. According to the diagram, bureaucratization explains variation in job satisfaction because job satisfaction is high when people work in settings that are less bureaucratized, and vice versa.

In both examples, features of cases, called variables, are observed not in the context of individual cases, but across many cases. It is the pattern across many cases that defines the relation between the two features, not how the two features fit together or relate in individual cases. In the example of the positive correlation just described, for instance, it may be that one of the cities combining high unemployment and high crime rates had a recent, dramatic increase in unemployment coupled with a decrease in its crime rate—the opposite of the general pattern across cities. (If this city's crime declined from a very high level to a merely high level, it would still appear in the high

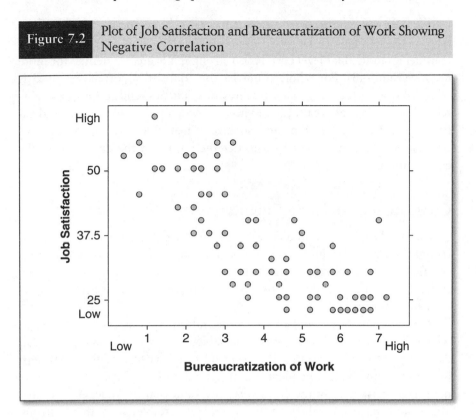

| Figure 7.2 | Plot of Job Satisfaction and Bureaucratization of Work Showing Negative Correlation |

unemployment/high crime rate portion of Figure 7.1.) What happened in one case over time cannot be addressed in the correlation across many cities at a single point in time. What matters is the general pattern: Do the cities with the highest unemployment rates also have the highest crime rates? In other words, the analysis of the relation between unemployment and crime in this example proceeds across cities, not within individual cities over time.

The correlation coefficient provides a way to make a direct, quantitative evaluation of the degree to which phenomena (e.g., unemployment rates and crime rates) covary across cases (such as cities in the United States). The Pearson correlation coefficient itself varies between −1.00 and +1.00. A value of −1.00 indicates a perfect negative correlation, a value of +1.00 indicates a perfect positive correlation, and a value of 0 indicates no correlation. Sometimes a finding of no correlation is important because social researchers may have strong reasons to believe that a correlation should exist. The finding of no correlation may challenge widely accepted ideas.

It is sometimes difficult to specify what value constitutes a "strong" correlation. People tend to be relatively unpredictable. Thus, some researchers consider an individual-level correlation strong if it is greater than .3 (or more negative than −.3). For whole countries, by contrast, a correlation of .3 is considered weak because many features of countries tend to be highly correlated (e.g., average wealth, life expectancy, literacy, level of industrialization, rate of car ownership, and so on). When assessing the strength of correlations, it is important to consider the nature of the data used in the computation.

Computing Correlation Coefficients

The hand calculation of a correlation coefficient is time consuming but straightforward. Usually, computers are used to compute correlation coefficients such as Pearson's r. However, the hand calculation is illustrated in the appendix of this book in order to show the underlying logic of the coefficient.

Remember that the goal of the computation is to assess the degree to which the values (or scores) of two variables covary across many cases, in either a positive or a negative direction. In other words, do the cases with high values on the independent variable tend to have high values on the dependent variable? Do the cases with low values on the independent variable tend to have low values on the dependent variable? If so, then a strong positive correlation exists. If high values on the independent variable tend to be associated with low values on the dependent variable, and low independent variable values are associated with high dependent variable values, then a strong negative correlation exists. If there is no pattern of covariation between two variables, then there is no correlation between them.

The key to calculating a correlation coefficient is to convert the scores on two variables to Z scores, as explained in the appendix. Z scores standardize variables so that they all have the same mean or average value (0) and the same degree of variation. Table 7.1 reports data on two variables for 40 countries: the average number of calories consumed per person each day (the independent variable) and life expectancy (the dependent variable). These two variables can be used to test the simple idea that in countries where nutrition is better (as reflected in more calories consumed per person), people tend to live longer (as indicated by a longer life expectancy). Table 7.1 also reports the Z scores for these two variables, for all 40 cases.

Notice that countries with high scores on life expectancy have positive scores on life expectancy Z scores, and countries with low scores on life expectancy have negative scores on life expectancy Z scores. The same is true for calorie consumption. When the Z scores for two variables are multiplied,

Table 7.1	Calculating the Correlation Between Calorie Consumption and Life Expectancy			

Country	Life Expectancy	Calorie Consumption	Life Expectancy Z Scores	Caloric Consumption Z Scores
Niger	45	2432	−2.04	−0.70
Ethiopia	47	1749	−1.85	−1.92
Mali	47	2074	−1.85	−1.34
Uganda	48	2344	−1.75	−0.86
Senegal	48	2350	−1.75	−0.85
Sudan	50	2208	−1.55	−1.10
Ghana	54	1759	−1.17	−1.90
Kenya	58	2060	−0.78	−1.37
Zimbabwe	58	2132	−0.78	−1.24
Botswana	59	2201	−0.68	−1.11
Indonesia	60	2579	−0.58	−0.44
Morocco	61	2915	−0.49	0.16
Peru	61	2246	−0.49	−1.03
Philippines	63	2372	−0.29	−0.81
Thailand	64	2331	−0.19	−0.88
Turkey	64	3229	−0.19	0.72
Syria	65	3260	−0.10	0.77
Brazil	65	2656	−0.10	−0.30
Colombia	66	2543	0.00	−0.50
Paraguay	67	2853	0.10	0.05
Mexico	69	3132	0.29	0.55
S. Korea	69	2907	0.29	0.15
Malaysia	70	2730	0.39	−0.17

(Continued)

| Table 7.1 | (Continued) |

Country	Life Expectancy	Calorie Consumption	Life Expectancy Z Scores	Calorie Consumption Z Scores
Hungary	70	3569	0.39	1.33
Poland	71	3336	0.49	0.91
Chile	72	2579	0.58	−0.44
Jamaica	74	2590	0.78	−0.42
Ireland	74	3632	0.78	1.44
United States	75	3645	0.87	1.46
Greece	76	3688	0.97	1.54
Australia	76	3326	0.97	0.89
Spain	77	3359	1.07	0.95
Italy	77	3523	1.07	1.24
Netherlands	77	3326	1.07	0.89
France	77	3336	1.07	0.91
Canada	77	3462	1.07	1.14
Sweden	77	3064	1.07	0.43
Norway	77	3223	1.07	0.71
Switzerland	77	3437	1.07	1.09
Japan	78	2864	1.17	0.07

the products tell much about the correlation. If high scores on one variable correspond to high scores on the other, and low scores on one correspond to low scores on the other, then the products of the Z scores will usually be positive, indicating a positive correlation. However, if low scores on one variable generally correspond to high scores on the other, and vice versa, then the products of the Z scores generally will be negative, indicating a negative correlation.

As the appendix illustrates, when the products of pairs of Z scores for two variables are averaged over all the cases, the number that results is Pearson's correlation coefficient. The correlation between life expectancy and calorie consumption for the 40 countries in Table 7.1 is 0.802, a strong positive correlation. The strong covariation between these two variables is clear from simply examining the table because the countries are sorted according to their values on life expectancy. The calculation of the correlation coefficient (see the appendix) provides a direct, quantitative assessment of the degree to which the two measures covary.

Using Correlation Coefficients

The most basic use of correlation coefficients is to assess the strength of the relation between two variables. The correlation between calorie consumption and life expectancy is strong ($r = 0.802$), suggesting that an important key to longer life expectancy is nutrition. But there are many other uses for correlations. Most of these involve the comparison of competing causes, as indicated in the strength of correlations.

Consider the correlations reported in Table 7.2. The table shows all the correlations among four variables: three independent variables (calorie consumption, GNP per capita, and doctors per capita) and one dependent variable (life expectancy). (Notice that a variable correlates perfectly with itself, as shown by the values of 1.000 in Table 7.2.) GNP per capita is a rough

| Table 7.2 | A Correlation Matrix With Three Independent Variables and a Dependent Variable |

	Dependent Variable	Independent Variables		
	Life Expectancy	Calorie Consumption	GNP per Capita (US$)	Doctors per Capita
Life Expectancy	1.000	0.802	0.651	0.721
Calorie Consumption	0.802	1.000	0.848	0.321
GNP per Capita (US$)	0.651	0.848	1.000	0.671
Doctors per Capita	0.721	0.321	0.671	1.000

measure of the wealth of a country. Doctors per capita is a rough measure of the availability of medical care.

The first column shows the correlations of the three independent variables with the dependent variable. Calorie consumption is the most strongly correlated with life expectancy ($r = 0.802$), followed by doctors per capita ($r = 0.721$), followed by GNP per capita ($r = 0.651$). Is it possible to conclude from this evidence that all that really matters for life expectancy is calorie consumption? In other words, if the goal is to understand the variation in life expectancy across countries, is knowing nutrition levels enough? Is it reasonable to ignore the correlations with GNP per capita and doctors per capita?

In order to answer a question like this, it is not enough simply to identify the independent variable with the strongest correlation with the dependent variable. It is also necessary to examine the correlations among the independent variables. Consider first the correlation between calorie consumption and GNP per capita. It is strong ($r = 0.848$), suggesting that countries with the best nutrition are also the richest. Given that (1) these two independent variables are strongly correlated and (2) calorie consumption has a stronger correlation with life expectancy than GNP per capita ($r = 0.802$ versus 0.651), it is reasonable to conclude that the link between calorie consumption and life expectancy is more fundamental than the link between GNP per capita and life expectancy. In short, richer countries have better nutrition, but it is good nutrition that causes greater life expectancy, not wealth per se.

What about doctors per capita? The correlation between doctors per capita and calorie consumption is positive, but not strong ($r = 0.321$), suggesting that in some countries the nutrition may not be good, but good health care is available, while in other countries, the opposite may be the case. In other words, doctors per capita and calorie consumption are not closely linked across countries in the same way that GNP per capita and calorie consumption are. Thus, the correlation between doctors per capita and life expectancy, the dependent variable, is relatively independent of and separate from the correlation between calorie consumption and life expectancy. Even though the correlation between doctors per capita and life expectancy ($r = 0.721$) is not as strong as the correlation between calorie consumption and life expectancy ($r = 0.802$), it is an important correlation. The pattern of correlations in Table 7.2 indicates that both doctors per capita and calorie consumption affect life expectancy.

A lot can be learned from looking at a correlation matrix like the one in Table 7.2. However, most quantitative studies examine many independent and dependent variables. As mentioned earlier, this section focuses on correlation because it is the basis of many advanced statistical techniques.

These complex, advanced statistical methods are very powerful, and they further the primary goals of quantitative research: assessing general patterns (including their limits), making projections about the future, and evaluating broad theories.

Conclusion

Quantitative methods are best suited for addressing differences across a large number of cases. These methods focus especially on the covariation between attributes that vary by level, usually across many cases. If two features of cases vary together in a systematic way, they are said to correlate. Correlation is important because it may suggest that a causal or some other kind of important relation exists between the two features that are linked. Quantitative methods provide a direct way to implement a researcher's interest in general patterns, and quantitative researchers believe that these patterns of covariation provide important clues about social life.

In many ways, the quantitative approach appears to be the most scientific of the three approaches presented in this book. It favors generality and parsimony. It uses generic units such as individuals, families, states, cities, and countries. It can be used to assess broad relationships across countless cases. It condenses evidence to simple coefficients, using mathematical procedures. It can be used to test broad theoretical arguments and to make projections about the future. In short, it imitates many of the features and practices of natural sciences such as physics and chemistry.

While the quantitative approach does have many of the features of a natural science, it would be a mistake to portray this approach as something radically different from the other two strategies. All social research engages theoretical ideas and analytic frames, at least indirectly. All social research involves constructing images from evidence, usually lots of it. And all social researchers construct images by connecting social phenomena.

Afterword

The Promise of Social Research

with Mary Driscoll

Social scientists study and represent social life in many different ways. Sometimes they try to see social life through the eyes of the people they study. Sometimes they reconstruct significant historical events and pinpoint the relevance to who we are and how we got here. Sometimes they uncover broad patterns linking social phenomena across many cases and assess the implications of these patterns. And sometimes they try to map the diverse ways that social life is organized and practiced.

Although social scientific representations vary, they are especially well suited to the task of generating useful knowledge about social life because they (1) address phenomena that are socially significant, (2) link these phenomena to social theory and other thinking about social life, (3) incorporate large amounts of purposefully collected evidence, and (4) are constructed from systematic analyses of such evidence. In general, social researchers believe that this basic "formula" results in representations of social life that offer the greatest insight into its fundamental character. The promise of social research rests on the strength of this formula for constructing representations.

The Unity and Diversity of Method

The three methods of linking ideas and evidence discussed in Part II of this book illustrate different ways of constructing representations following the general guidelines just described. While these research strategies are only three among the many strategies that social researchers use, they illustrate the wide range of possible approaches. What these strategies share is a concern with grounding representations in evidence and ideas; they differ in how this grounding is achieved. In each of the following studies, ideas and evidence are linked in different ways. The studies illustrate how strategies can be matched to goals to produce empirically grounded, theoretically informed representations.

The quantitative study of covariation looks across cases and attempts to show how features of cases vary together (see Chapter 7). For example, in *Village Republics,* Robert Wade (1988) studied agricultural villages in southern India and showed a systematic correspondence between water supply (the villages used the same irrigation canals) and the degree to which each village developed institutions to cope with villagewide issues. The pattern he found was straightforward: The more serious the problem of water scarcity, the greater the development of village institutions of self-government. Villages at the head of the irrigation canal had ample water supply and developed few institutions. Villages at the end of the canal faced serious water shortages and developed elaborate institutions of self-government. These institutions were important because the whole village could suffer if any single farmer took too much irrigation water. The self-government of villages situated near the middle of the irrigation canal was less elaborate than that of the villages at the end of the canal, but more elaborate than the villages at the head of the canal.

Representations of social life that are based on patterns of covariation, such as Wade's (1988), are grounded in evidence showing that there is a systematic relationship between variables. Two or more phenomena (such as water scarcity and institutions of self-government) parallel each other across many cases (villages). In Wade's study, the examination of covariation made it possible to show the ecological bases of village institutions.

Comparative studies of diversity, by contrast, pinpoint the differences among cases that separate them into distinct types (see Chapter 6). Generally, researchers who use this strategy attempt to identify *similarities* among the cases *within* a given type and *differences between* cases conforming to different types. Daniel Chirot (1993), for example, studied modern tyrants and showed that they fall into two major types—ideological and traditional. As it turns out, Chirot found ideological tyrants (such as Hitler and Stalin, who tried to use their social and political ideas and aims to create a specific type of society) caused much more human suffering than traditional tyrants. In fact, Chirot identified a number of factors, in addition to the amount of suffering, that separate ideological and traditional tyrants.

Representations that are based on the use of contrasts to elaborate different types, such as Chirot's (1993), are strongly grounded in evidence because the investigator identifies *clusters* of differences. By inspecting a range of different cases, investigators show that the differences separating cases into types are linked together empirically. For Chirot, this involved, among other things, showing the link between the content of the ideologies held by tyrants and the nature of the suffering they inflicted.

The qualitative study of commonalities reveals what the members of a group or category share (see Chapter 5). Mary Driscoll (1993), for example, studied women with food and body issues, including women who "shed" secondary sex characteristics by starving themselves and women who "take on size" by overeating. She also studied other groups, such as women who change their appearance through extreme covering with clothing and those who transform their apparent sex by dressing and passing as men. The commonality that unites these different groups is indirect—bodily resistance to gender prescriptions—detected by Driscoll through observation, in-depth interviews, and comparisons with studies of other groups.

Representations that are based on commonalities, such as Driscoll's (1993) representation of women with food and body issues, are strongly grounded in evidence because the investigator carefully pinpoints features that are consistent across cases. As explained in Chapter 5, this strategy achieves a solid grounding in evidence through in-depth study of many aspects of a relatively small number of cases. The search for commonalities continues until the researcher is confident that relevant commonalities have been identified and linked conceptually, and individual cases that deviate from the rest have been accounted for. In Driscoll's study, the search for commonalities made it possible for her to show that practices that appear to be very different on the surface (for example, starving, overeating, extreme cover, and cross-dressing) are body transformations that are common responses to gender limitations.

In a given investigation, most social researchers follow a single approach because the goals of the study usually dictate a particular strategy. For example, a researcher who wants to explain how crime rates vary across neighborhoods will use quantitative methods to examine the correlates of these rates. Some researchers, however, have goals that require the use of several analytic strategies in the same project. Arlie Hochschild, for example, used all three strategies described above in her study of working parents, *The Second Shift* (1989).

Hochschild based her book on interviews and observations of 50 working couples with children; their neighbors and friends; and their children's teachers, day care workers, and babysitters. Altogether, Hochschild and her research associates interviewed 145 people, hoping to answer a number of questions: What typically happens to housework and child care when both parents work? Who takes responsibility for which tasks? What different kinds of arrangements do couples negotiate? How do couples differ? In answering these questions, Hochschild identified *commonalities* across the 50 working couples, explored their *diversity,* and revealed important patterns of *covariation.*

One fundamental *commonality* that Hochschild identified across the 50 families is captured in the title of the book—*The Second Shift.* In the families she studied, she found it was almost universal that the wives, not the husbands, worked a "second shift" of housework and child care after completing a full day of work in the paid labor force. She calculated that, on average, this second shift added an extra month of 24-hour workdays each year to the work of women. In the relatively few families where the work of the second shift was shared equally by the husbands, it was still the case that the wives carried more of the emotional load and felt more responsible for the home front—worrying about the welfare of the children and the household and feeling torn between work responsibilities and the needs of family members.

Hochschild also explored the *diversity* of ways working couples cope with and adapt to the demands of two jobs, home, and family. Based on her examination of similarities and differences across the 50 families in her study, she specified a variety of common arrangements and accommodations. She used the orientations of the husbands and the wives (for example, traditional versus egalitarian) and their different ways of dividing labor in the home to sort the families into 10 different types. By specifying these different types and presenting representative cases, Hochschild was able to show the different strains and conflicts that accompany different adaptations to the pressures experienced by working parents.

Finally, Hochschild explored systematic patterns of covariation across the 50 families. In addition to documenting the inequality in the domestic workload of wives and husbands, especially the average number of hours they devote to specific tasks, she also examined more subtle relationships. For example, she examined the degree to which the ideologies of the husbands regarding helping out at home (that is, their expressed attitudes about sharing this work) actually corresponded with their behaviors. She found that husbands with a more traditional orientation helped out less than those with a more egalitarian orientation: A total of 22% of husbands with a traditional orientation shared child care and housework equally with their wives, while 70% of husbands with an egalitarian orientation shared these tasks equally. By examining patterns of correspondence, Hochschild was able to address general questions about differences among the 50 families.

Hochschild used several analytic strategies because her study of working couples addressed many different aspects of the phenomenon. By identifying commonalities, exploring diversity, and examining covariation, she constructed a rich portrait of working parents, the pressures they face, and their different ways of coping with these pressures.

Diverse ways of studying and representing social life exist because social researchers have many different goals. These goals range from broad objectives that are common to many types of scientific research, such as identifying general patterns and testing theories, to goals that are more specific to *social* research, such as interpreting historical events and giving voice to specific groups (see Chapter 2). While the goals of social research are diverse, there is unity in this diversity. All good social research contributes to knowledge of social life, which in turn provides important keys to understanding who we are, to comprehending social diversity, to addressing the root causes of social phenomena of general or public concern, and to anticipating future patterns and trends.

Social Research and Its Critics

While social scientific representations of social life derive strength from their grounding in strategically chosen ideas and evidence, they are necessarily partial and imperfect. Every representation is open to criticism, and it is thus important to address some common criticisms of social research.

Uniqueness

One common complaint about social research is based on the humanistic idea that every person and situation is unique and should be understood in its uniqueness. This thinking sees social scientific categories and variables as crude and cumbersome tools that can do more harm than good by lumping people together, generalizing about them, and ignoring their individuality.

While it is true that social research focuses on broad rather than particular understandings, social researchers do not reject the idea that everything should be appreciated in its uniqueness. However, the appreciation of uniqueness is simply not the task of social science. Social research is driven by a focus on understandings that extend beyond the singular, beyond our own selves and intimate others, and to the many—to groups, peoples, and societies. The individual case is woven into larger social patterns so that more general knowledge can be gained. Even studies of a single individual (e.g., Harper 1987) are driven by an interest in what one case can teach us about ourselves and others—something larger than that one person.

We have much to gain from connecting a particular case (i.e., data collected about a particular person, place, or event) with other accumulated data and with the general thinking and research on a topic. By interpreting the individual case as an elaboration of something more universal, social scientists can draw on a large body of ideas and previous research. This knowledge offers the discriminating researcher a valuable resource of accumulated wisdom as well as points of reference for comparison and analysis. The connection of individual cases to data sets and of data sets to abstract, long-standing debates about social life (e.g., about the causes and consequences of social inequality) anchors representations, tying them not only to the community of researchers but also to the concerns of the informed public.

What social research loses in not representing the unique person, place, or event, it strives to gain in representing social affairs in general. One of the main contributions of social research is the identification of social threads that run through individual problems, showing when they are in fact instances of massive trends. Consider the examples that follow.

Absenteeism, accidents on the job, and job turnover may increase among factory workers, even when factory jobs are scarce. Social researchers suspect there are important patterned responses in what may appear to be the unrelated, individual acts of workers. They may find that the increase in employee problems is in fact a reaction to work speedups and other changes caused by industry efforts to accelerate productivity in the face of international competition.

Here is another example: Many adults assume that differences in intelligence are the primary reason one child thrives in school while another does poorly. However, various studies addressing variation in academic performance pinpoint key social factors that influence concentration, learning, and test performance far more than IQ differences. This knowledge can be used to help children learn.

In still another example, some parents may be puzzled to find that their children seem especially prone to violence. Research on violence and the media can help them make informed decisions about the possible link between the upsurge in violent media images and their children's violent behavior.

And in a final example, parents and doctors struggle with a young girl who refuses to eat and who is literally starving to death. They may think that her problem lies solely within her individual psyche. It may benefit all concerned to learn that eating disorders, which reached startling levels among girls and young women in the 1980s and 1990s, mimic gendered illnesses from other historical periods (such as hysteria in the mid- to late 1800s and agoraphobia in the 1950s and 1960s). Scholars interpret epidemic levels of such disorders among females as constituting, in part, an unconscious protest against limiting gender roles. Knowledge of these trends may enlighten both caretakers and those who are stuck in self-defeating behaviors.

As these examples show, social scientists link the individual with society, and in doing so, extend the personal circumstances of everyday life into the realm of social issues. C. Wright Mills explained in his book *The Sociological Imagination* (1959) that it is the task of social scientists to take the "private troubles" that people experience, often in isolation from one another, and show their connection to "public issues." Researchers study and represent both the individual and the larger milieu in concert. The particular and the general inform each other, and good social scientific representations increase our understanding of both. In short, good social research helps us understand what is going on in the world and in ourselves.

Thus, as we consider what is lost when social and human characteristics are categorized, conceptualized, or correlated as data, we must also consider what is gained. The individual life is illuminated with general knowledge of social life. Social research lifts the individual into historical and cultural perspective.

The focus on the larger social order, versus the individual, has additional gains. In order to make predictions about the future, social scientists must rely on the broad, accumulated knowledge that links their cases with larger patterns. Knowledge of general patterns makes it possible to extrapolate future trends and possibilities. For example, what we know about crime, lifestyles and consumption, family patterns, job opportunities, and ethnic and racial conflict allows us to make useful predictions about them.

Another gain comes from the study of societies and settings that differ from our own. Research of this type may challenge conventional thinking because it often shows that what is normative and accepted as "the ways things are" is relative to time and place. Research on social milieus that differ from our own opens up new avenues of thinking and being. Alternative ways of addressing common social issues become possible. Differences between people are understood and accepted, and mutuality is increased. Thus, through an examination of similarities and differences, social research connects the individual to society, and societies to each other. Without the connecting of the particular and the general, the "social" would be missing from social research.

Multiplicity

The tension between representing social life in particular and representing it in general is inherent in the practice of social research. This tension is often the source of additional criticisms of social scientific representations.

Consider the problem of representing the differences that exist within any social category. The lives of homeless people, for example, are complex and diverse. The world of a homeless African American woman who lives with her children in the inner city is vastly different from that of a homeless white man who lives alone in a rural area. A researcher might try to study homelessness in an encompassing way, but it would be difficult to offer an understanding that embraces the worlds of these two people. Even the researcher who attempts to take race, age, gender, and other important defining factors into account will find innumerable other factors that differentiate the lives of homeless people. Thus, social scientific representations are sometimes criticized for failing to address important differences in an encompassing way.

On top of this, social scientific representations of a *single* situation, place, or event can diverge sharply. As a research subject, the same homeless person may be presented as a victim by one researcher and as a schemer by another. Another study might represent him as a mentally ill person. The fact that it is possible to represent the same subject of research in various ways casts doubts on the claim that social scientific representations derive strength from their grounding in evidence.

Yet a single, fixed picture of homelessness, or of any other topic that touches social life, would be a false one. A science that demands a clear, final portrait of phenomena could not be a *social* science. Human variation and the fluidity and open-endedness of social life require a science that is not static or fixed. These features of social life demand a science that can capture, with clarity, what is going on in the world and with people, while at the same time representing a good deal of its diversity, which is endless and ever changing. Of necessity, the social sciences must make room for imprecision and incompleteness in the study of human affairs.

Thus, the practice of social research tests researchers in many ways. How does a social scientist capture a meaningful picture of human ingenuity under oppression, the role of computers in the globalization of cultures, the collapse of Soviet-style communism in Eastern Europe, or the changing meaning of aging and dying across several generations in a small town? It is not enough for social scientists to bring their intellects to bear on the questions before them. They must bring their imaginations as well.

Many researchers talk about how they work back and forth between a rational research plan on the one hand, and hunches, intuitions, vague notions, gut reactions, brainstorming sessions, and other ways of stoking the imagination on the other. The toil of doing rigorous, grounded research is often aided by leaps of the imagination, which lead to breakthroughs and new discoveries. Some social researchers like to think of themselves not simply as scientists but also as artists or craftspersons. Their final products, the representations they construct, may embody both grounded scientific effort and creative flight.

Finally, depending on the nature of the investigator's questions and strategies, many a researcher's heart is deeply engaged in his or her research. In fact, a compassionate heart guides some researchers through their research projects as much as an engaged mind does. The idea that a researcher's deep emotional and political investments may offer guidance contradicts the natural science notion of doing objective, unbiased research. The study of human affairs is, by necessity, an artful science.

Social Research: A Collaborative Journey

The indefinite nature of studying human affairs and the impossibility of getting a "real take" on it lead some to conclude that social life cannot be represented in a valid way. In this view, everything, including life's problems, is a mere "social construction." It is true that our understandings of social life are based on somewhat subjective and variable interpretations of evidence that is laden with many meanings. However, these problems do not pose insurmountable challenges to social research.

First of all, the variability of social life does not change the fact that groups of people share large pools of common knowledge about the world. We have common, agreed-upon meanings for many things in life, from how to cross a busy street safely to how to interpret subtle cues in intimate relationships. Some of these understandings are informal and unconscious (e.g., many aspects of gender socialization), and others are explicitly learned (how to drive a car, how to groom oneself for job advancement, and so on). In order to get along in life, and even more, to prosper, we rely on myriad shared understandings of how the world works. Social research adds to our common "stock of knowledge" about life. It helps us understand the meaning of our world and larger historical processes and events.

The representations that convey these meanings are not perfectly precise or complete, but they embody the negotiated understandings of a community of scholars who review each other's work and who collectively, through time, determine which representations have the best basis in ideas and evidence. In essence, the multiplicity of the social world—the fact that the same evidence can be interpreted in many ways—is made manageable by the social scientific community, which decides which views of social life make the most sense. Just as the individual case becomes one within a chorus of cases, most social research represents a chorus of researchers. Social research is strengthened and clarified by scholars who contribute to one another's projects before and after they are published. The validity of social research lies in its contributions to common knowledge about the world, knowledge that is continuously revised and updated by the social scientific community.

It is reassuring to know that the representations that social scientists construct are accountable to a community of scholars, that they are grounded in carefully chosen ideas and evidence, and that they are informed by rigorous and well-tested theories and methods. Still, it should be clear that no study on a topic can be considered definitive. Different studies illuminate different aspects of a single topic. For example, images of the homeless person as victim, schemer, or "mentally ill" may be based on valid interpretations of different data collected on one person combined with different ideas about those data. Each representation may be valid social science, and each may add to our understanding of homelessness as a social phenomenon. We might think of each study of homelessness, or of any other social phenomenon, as a piece in a puzzle or as a patch in a quilt. Researchers who study homelessness each contribute a piece toward a fuller understanding of the problem, and each piece may contribute as well to solutions. Social research is a collaborative journey that brings together many people with different combinations of ideas and evidence and thus many different representations. These efforts, taken together as a whole, can far exceed their sum.

To conclude that we cannot understand social life because it is complex, shifting, and variously interpretable is tantamount to giving up on the idea that we can increase our understanding of human affairs and use this knowledge to improve it. This thinking may lead some to stop trying to understand others or feel concern for the common good. The fact that homelessness can be represented in a variety of ways, each imperfect and biased, does not mean homelessness is not a real problem, nor does it absolve our collective responsibility for it.

We live in an age of social scientific reasoning, in which the results of social research are filtered to the general public through bookstores, textbooks and school systems, governments and social agencies, and the media. The increasing importance of social scientific thinking for public audiences can be seen clearly in widespread public views and media treatment of social issues. Fifty years ago, most Americans would have flatly rejected the idea that many poor people are poor because there are not enough good jobs to go around. Instead, they would claim that poor people are poor because they are lazy. Today, most Americans would agree with the results of decades of social research showing that poverty has important *social* causes, not just individual ones.

In an age when information is quickly and easily disseminated, the representations of social life that social researchers construct take on a new significance. These representations often reach many people quickly, and contribute to their views on many topics. They affect social policy and may have a powerful impact on popular discussion of social issues, even when this impact is indirect. Thus, the results of social research are more accessible and perhaps more relevant than ever to people grappling with a complex, rapidly changing world.

This afterword has addressed several criticisms of social science. The problems of representing the diversity within social life and representing it adequately when there are so many ways to approach the same phenomenon are real. These and other issues that challenge our capacity to conduct good social research today are at the core of our current task. They also reflect the challenges that people face in today's world. The inherent tension between understanding the particular and the general in social life is as unresolved in us as a people as it is in the social sciences. Consider how we as a collectivity are confronted by questions about human uniqueness and how to respect essential rights. On the national level alone, we are immersed in issues of class, gender, race, and ethnicity; issues of democratic power and how much government we should have; conflicts over how to use versus how to protect the environment; and ethical issues centered on the body—abortion, euthanasia, reproduction technologies, cosmetic surgery, and the allocation of health care, to name only a few. These and other issues of freedom and responsibility abound.

How do we understand the great diversity within human affairs? How do people take into account a fast-changing world that connects societies and cultures more closely than ever before—through faster forms of travel and expanded migration, the media, new forms of technology and trade, international relations, and the globalization of markets?

Social research enters the new millennium with more than a hundred years of published research. Yet it is not enough to move into the 21st century with this stock of knowledge. Social scientists must address the specific concerns and questions of every age. It will take the collaborative powers of many to meet the questions of the 21st century and to construct useful representations of social life for all who are curious about people, concerned about social issues, and committed to the quality of human life.

Appendix

Computing Correlation Coefficients

The first step on the road to computing the correlation coefficient is the computation of the mean (or average) level of the independent and dependent variables. In this example, refer to Table A.1, which reports data on two variables for 40 countries: the average number of calories consumed per person each day (the independent variable) and life expectancy (the dependent variable). These two variables can be used to test the simple idea that in countries where nutrition is better (as reflected in more calories consumed per person), people tend to live longer (as indicated by a longer life expectancy).

It is first necessary to compute the mean level of calorie consumption per capita and life expectancy across the 40 countries so that it is possible to determine which values are high and which are low. Values that are well above the mean are considered high; values well below the mean are considered low.

The computation of the mean of a variable is straightforward. Simply sum the values for all the cases, and then divide by the number of cases. The formula for the mean is as follows:

$$\overline{X} = \frac{\sum x_i}{N}$$

where $\overline{X}$ is the symbol for the mean of the variable, $\sum$ indicates that the values are summed, x_i indicates the actual values of the variable to be summed (in our example, the 40 country scores), and N is the number of cases (40). The mean life expectancy for the 40 countries in Table A.1 is 66 (2640/40; see column 1); the mean calorie consumption is approximately 2825.52 (113,021/40; see column 3). (The tables in this appendix contain a good deal of rounding error because of limitations on the number of decimal places it is reasonable to report.)

The next step is to assess the degree to which cases are above or below the mean on the two variables. To do this, researchers use **deviation scores.** To compute a deviation score, subtract the mean value of a variable (computed according to the simple formula just described) from each case's score on that variable:

$$x_i \text{ deviation score} = x_i - \overline{X}.$$

A large positive result indicates that the case's score on the variable is well above the mean (a high value); a large negative result indicates that the case's score is well below the mean (a low value). Columns 2 and 4 of Table A.1 show the computation of deviation scores for all 40 cases on both variables. For example, Niger, the first country in the table, has a deviation score on life expectancy of −21 (a life expectancy score of 45 minus the mean life expectancy of 66).

Notice that the countries in Table A.1 are listed according to their scores on the dependent variable, life expectancy (column 1 of the table). The countries with the lowest scores on life expectancy are at the top of the table; the countries with the highest scores are at the bottom. Thus, the deviation scores on life expectancy (column 2) range from large negative numbers at the top to large positive numbers at the bottom. Because life expectancy and calorie consumption scores covary, the deviation scores for calorie consumption (column 4) also tend to range from negative at the top of the table to positive at the bottom. Of course, the computation of the correlation coefficient will provide an exact quantitative assessment of how closely these two variables covary.

One simple way to see if the scores of the two variables parallel each other in a positive or negative direction is to use their deviation scores (columns 2 and 4) to compute the **covariance** between the independent and the dependent variable. Covariance is the sum of the products of deviation scores and is computed as follows:

$$\frac{\sum(x_i - \overline{X})(y_i - \overline{Y})}{N}.$$

As the formula shows, for each case, the deviation score of the independent variable is multiplied by the deviation score of the dependent variable. After these products are calculated for each case, they are added together, and then this sum is divided by the number of cases. The result is the average product of the deviation scores (or covariance). The computation of the covariance between calorie consumption and life expectancy is shown in column 5 of Table A.1.

The computation of the covariance is very similar to the computation of the correlation coefficient, and it is useful to understand the strengths and weaknesses of the covariance before moving on to correlation. First, it should be noted that the sign of the covariance (positive or negative) is also the sign of the correlation. Notice that when the value of the independent variable is low, the sign of its deviation score is negative. The same is true for the dependent variable. When these low (that is, negative) deviation scores are multiplied, they result in a positive product. If low scores on one variable are generally matched with low scores on the other, and high scores are generally matched with high scores, then the sum of their products (as specified in the formula for covariance) will be a large positive number. A positive covariance indicates that the correlation between the two variables is also positive.

By contrast, if high scores on one variable are generally paired with low scores on the other, and vice versa, then their products will generally be negative. Adding these negative products together will result in a large negative number, indicating a negative correlation. Finally, if negative products and positive products balance each other out, then their sum (that is, their covariance) will be zero or close to zero, indicating that the two variables are not correlated.

Covariances tell us a lot, but they can be awkward to use. In Table A.1, the covariance between calorie consumption and life expectancy is a very large positive number, indicating these two variables are positively correlated (that is, in countries where there is better nutrition, people tend to live longer). But it is difficult to determine the *strength* of the correlation from this large positive number. If calorie consumption, for example, had been measured in calories consumed per person per year instead of per day, the covariance would be a much larger number (by a factor of 365, the number of days in a year), but the degree of actual correspondence between calorie consumption and life expectancy would be unchanged.

The problem is to find a way to standardize variables so that the multiplication of their deviation scores is not affected by the size of their units (e.g., calories per year versus calories per day). Ideally, this **standardization** should also produce a covariance that varies between −1.00 (indicating perfect negative correlation) and +1.00 (indicating perfect positive correlation). Fortunately, there is a way to standardize deviation scores so that the computation of the covariance results in just such a coefficient. Once variables are standardized, the computation of their covariance results in the Pearson correlation coefficient.

The best way to standardize a deviation score is to assess whether it is large or small relative to the size of the other deviation scores for a variable. Is a deviation score of 200 calories a large or a small positive deviation? This value must be compared to the typical deviation in order to make this assessment.

Table A.1 Calculating the Covariance of Calorie Consumption and Life Expectancy

	1	2	3	4	5	6
Country	Life Expectancy	Life Expectancy Deviations	Calorie Consumption	Calorie Consumption Deviations	Column 2 x Column 4	Column 2 squared
Niger	45	−21	2432	−393.52	8263.92	441.00
Ethiopia	47	−19	1749	−1076.52	20453.88	361.00
Mali	47	−19	2074	−751.52	14278.88	361.00
Uganda	48	−18	2344	−481.52	8667.36	324.00
Senegal	48	−18	2350	−475.52	8559.36	324.00
Sudan	50	−16	2208	−617.52	9880.32	256.00
Ghana	54	−12	1759	−1066.52	12798.24	144.00
Kenya	58	−8	2060	−765.52	6124.16	64.00
Zimbabwe	58	−8	2132	−693.52	5548.16	64.00
Botswana	59	−7	2201	−624.52	4371.64	49.00
Indonesia	60	−6	2579	−246.52	1479.12	36.00
Morocco	61	−5	2915	89.48	−447.40	25.00
Peru	61	−5	2246	−579.52	2897.60	25.00
Philippines	63	−3	2372	−453.52	1360.56	9.00
Thailand	64	−2	2331	−494.52	989.04	4.00
Turkey	64	−2	3229	403.48	−806.96	4.00
Syria	65	−1	3260	434.48	−434.48	1.00
Brazil	65	−1	2656	−169.52	169.52	1.00

204

Colombia	66	0	2543	−282.52	0.00	0.00
Paraguay	67	1	2853	27.48	27.48	1.00
Mexico	69	3	3132	306.48	919.44	9.00
S. Korea	69	3	2907	81.48	244.44	9.00
Malaysia	70	4	2730	−95.52	−382.08	16.00
Hungary	70	4	3569	743.48	2973.92	16.00
Poland	71	5	3336	510.48	2552.40	25.00
Chile	72	6	2579	−246.52	−1479.12	36.00
Jamaica	74	8	2590	−235.52	−1884.16	64.00
Ireland	74	8	3632	806.48	6451.84	64.00
United States	75	9	3645	819.48	7375.32	81.00
Greece	76	10	3688	862.48	8624.80	100.00
Australia	76	10	3326	500.48	5004.80	100.00
Spain	77	11	3359	533.48	5868.28	121.00
Italy	77	11	3523	697.48	7672.28	121.00
Netherlands	77	11	3326	500.48	5505.28	121.00
France	77	11	3336	510.48	5615.28	121.00
Canada	77	11	3462	636.48	7001.28	121.00
Sweden	77	11	3064	238.48	2623.28	121.00
Norway	77	11	3223	397.48	4372.28	121.00
Switzerland	77	11	3437	611.48	6726.28	121.00
Japan	78	12	2864	38.48	461.76	144.00
SUM	2,640	0.00	113,021.00	0.00	180,428.00	4,126.00
SUM/N	66	0.00	2,825.52	0.00	4,510.70	103.15

There are several ways to compute the typical deviation, the most useful of which is called the **standard deviation**, also indicated by the symbol σ. The standard deviation is computed as follows:

$$x \text{ standard deviation (or } \sigma_x) = \sqrt{\frac{\sum(x_i - \overline{X})^2}{N}}.$$

Deviations from the mean are first squared (making them all positive values), then they are summed and divided by N (producing the average squared deviation), and then the square root of the average squared deviation is computed. Because the deviations are squared and then averaged, and then the square root of this average is computed, the result is consistent with the original units of the variable, not the squared units (e.g., number of calories, not number of calories squared).

The computation of the standard deviation of life expectancy is shown in column 6 of Table A.1. This column shows what happens when life expectancy deviation scores (from column 2 of Table A.1) are squared. Notice that they are all positive values. These squared values are summed (shown at the bottom of column 6) and then divided by N (the number of cases, 40) to produce the average squared deviation, which for life expectancy is 103.15. Taking the square root of this number results in the standard deviation of life expectancy, 10.16. Parallel calculations on the deviation scores for calorie consumption result in a standard deviation of 560.7. (Again, these calculations reflect rounding error; spreadsheets or statistical packages give more exact figures.)

Once the standard deviation is computed, it is possible to correct deviation scores in a way that makes them uniform in their units. This is a very important step in the calculation of the correlation coefficient. Examine Table A.2. Columns 1 and 3 show the deviation scores for life expectancy and calorie consumption taken from columns 2 and 4 of Table A.1. To produce standardized deviation scores (also known as "standard scores" or Z scores), it is necessary simply to divide the deviation scores by the appropriate standard deviation. The formula is as follows:

$$x_i \text{ standardized score (or Z score)} = \frac{x_i - \overline{X}}{\sigma_x}.$$

Column 2 shows standardized scores for life expectancy (its deviation scores having been divided by 10.16); column 4 shows standardized scores for calorie consumption (its deviation scores having been divided by 560.7). Notice that both sets of scores now range more or less between the same values. The highest standardized score for life expectancy is 1.17; the lowest is −2.04. The highest standardized score for calorie consumption is 1.54; the lowest is −1.92.

The next step in the computation of the correlation coefficient is to compute the covariance of the standardized scores. As it turns out, the covariance of standardized scores is the Pearson correlation coefficient. The formula is as follows:

$$\text{correlation coefficient (or r)} = \frac{\sum\left[\left(\frac{x_i - \overline{X}}{\sigma_x}\right) \cdot \left(\frac{y_i - \overline{Y}}{\sigma_y}\right)\right]}{N}.$$

The Pearson correlation coefficient is a covariance that ranges from −1.00 to +1.00, and it equals 0 when there is no simple pattern of correspondence between two variables.

The computation of the correlation between life expectancy and calorie consumption is shown in column 5 of Table A.2. The values in column 2 are multiplied by the values in column 4 to produce the values in column 5. Notice that most of the products in column 5 of Table A.2 are positive. Thus, when this column is summed and the sum is divided by N, the result is a positive number. The last figure in column 5 is the correlation ($r = 0.80$), showing that there is a strong positive relationship between calorie consumption and life expectancy. This finding indicates that in countries where nutrition is better, people live longer.

	1	2	3	4	5
Country	Life Expectancy Deviations	Life Expectancy Z Scores	Calorie Consumption Deviations	Calorie Consumption Z Scores	Column 2 x Column 4
Niger	−21	−2.04	−393.52	−0.70	1.43
Ethiopia	−19	−1.85	−1076.52	−1.92	3.55
Mali	−19	−1.85	−751.52	−1.34	2.47
Uganda	−18	−1.75	−481.52	−0.86	1.50
Senegal	−18	−1.75	−475.52	−0.85	1.48
Sudan	−16	−1.55	−617.52	−1.10	1.71
Ghana	−12	−1.17	−1066.52	−1.90	2.22
Kenya	−8	−0.78	−765.52	−1.37	1.06
Zimbabwe	−8	−0.78	−693.52	−1.24	0.96
Botswana	−7	−0.68	−624.52	−1.11	0.76
Indonesia	−6	−0.58	−246.52	−0.44	0.26
Morocco	−5	−0.49	89.48	0.16	−0.08
Peru	−5	−0.49	−579.52	−1.03	0.50
Philippines	−3	−0.29	−453.52	−0.81	0.24
Thailand	−2	−0.19	−494.52	−0.88	0.17
Turkey	−2	−0.19	403.48	0.72	−0.14
Syria	−1	−0.10	434.48	0.77	−0.08
Brazil	−1	−0.10	−169.52	−0.30	0.03

Table A.2 Calculating the Correlation Between Life Expectancy and Calorie Consumption

Colombia	0	0.00	-282.52	-0.50	0.00
Paraguay	1	0.10	27.48	0.05	0.00
Mexico	3	0.29	306.48	0.55	0.16
S. Korea	3	0.29	81.48	0.15	0.04
Malaysia	4	0.39	-95.52	-0.17	-0.07
Hungary	4	0.39	743.48	1.33	0.52
Poland	5	0.49	510.48	0.91	0.44
Chile	6	0.58	-246.52	-0.44	-0.26
Jamaica	8	0.78	-235.52	-0.42	-0.33
Ireland	8	0.78	806.48	1.44	1.12
United States	9	0.87	819.48	1.46	1.28
Greece	10	0.97	862.48	1.54	1.49
Australia	10	0.97	500.48	0.89	0.87
Spain	11	1.07	533.48	0.95	1.02
Italy	11	1.07	697.48	1.24	1.33
Netherlands	11	1.07	500.48	0.89	0.95
France	11	1.07	510.48	0.91	0.97
Canada	11	1.07	636.48	1.14	1.21
Sweden	11	1.07	238.48	0.43	0.45
Norway	11	1.07	397.48	0.71	0.76
Switzerland	11	1.07	611.48	1.09	1.17
Japan	12	1.17	38.48	0.07	0.08
SUM					32.09
SUM/N					0.80

References

"Abu Ghraib Whistleblower Fears for Safety of His Family." 2007. [Press release]. *BBC.* August 7. London, UK: BBC Press Office.

Allison, Paul D. 1998. *Multiple Regression: A Primer.* Thousand Oaks, CA: Pine Forge Press.

Amenta, Edwin, Neal Caren, Sheera Joy Olasky, and James E. Stobaugh. 2009. "All the Movements Fit to Print: Who, What, When, Where, and Why SMO Families Appeared in the New York Times in the Twentieth Century." *American Sociological Review,* 74:636–656.

American Sociological Association (ASA). 1999. *Code of Ethics and Policies and Procedures of the ASA Committee on Professional Ethics.* Washington, DC: ASA.

Appelbaum, Lauren. 2001. "B-School and Prof. Sued by Restaurants." *Columbia Spectator.* November 2.

Babbie, Earl. 2008. *The Basics of Social Research.* 4th ed. Belmont, CA: Thomson Wadsworth.

Banks, Marcus. 2001. *Visual Methods in Social Research.* Thousand Oaks, CA: Sage.

Baran, Paul. 1957. *The Political Economy of Growth.* New York: Monthly Review Press.

Becker, Howard S. 1953. "Becoming a Marijuana User." *American Journal of Sociology,* 59:235–242.

———. 1963. *Outsiders: Studies in the Sociology of Deviance.* New York: Free Press.

———. 2007. *Telling About Society.* Chicago, IL: University of Chicago Press.

Beecher, Henry. 1966. "Ethics and Clinical Research." *New England Journal of Medicine,* 274:1354–1360.

Berheide, Catherine W., 1992. "Women Still 'Stuck' in Low-Level Jobs." *Women in Public Service* 3:1-4.

Black, Dan, Gary Gates, Seth Sanders, and Lowell Taylor. 2000. "Demographics of the Gay and Lesbian Population in the United States: Evidence From Available Systematic Data Sources." *Demography,* 37:139–154.

Blair-Loy, Mary. 2003. *Competing Devotions: Career and Family Among Women Executives.* Cambridge, MA: Harvard University Press.

Blanchard, Margaret A. 2002. "Should All Disciplines Be Subject to the Common Rule?" *Academe,* 88(3):62–69.

Bledsoe, Caroline H., Bruce Sherin, Adam G. Galinsky, Nathalia M. Headley, Carol A. Heimer, Erik Kjeldgaard, et al. 2007. "Regulating Creativity: Research and Survival in the IRB Iron Cage." *Northwestern University Law Review,* 101:593–642.

Blee, Kathleen M. 2003. *Inside Organized Racism: Women in the Hate Movement.* Berkeley, CA: University of California Press.

Burawoy, Michael. 1979. *Manufacturing Consent: Changes in the Labor Process Under Monopoly Capitalism.* Chicago: University of Chicago Press.

——. 2005. "For Public Sociology." *American Sociological Review,* 70:4–28.

Burger, Jerry M. 2009. "Replicating Milgram: Would People Still Obey Today?" *American Psychologist,* 64:1–11.

Burris, Scott, and Jen Walsh. 2007. "Regulatory Paradox: A Review of Enforcement Letters Issued by the Office for Human Research Protection." *Northwestern University Law Review,* 101:643–686.

Carpenter, Dale. 2007. "Institutional Review Boards, Regulatory Incentives, and Some Modest Proposals for Reform." *Northwestern University Law Review,* 101:687–706.

Chase, Alston. 2000. "Harvard and the Making of the Unabomber." *Atlantic Monthly,* 285:41–65.

Chirot, Daniel. 1993. *Modern Tyrants: The Power and Prevalence of Evil in Our Age.* New York: Free Press.

Clotfelter, Charles. 2004. *After Brown: The Rise and Retreat of School Desegregation.* Princeton, NJ: Princeton University Press.

Cooper, Barry. 2005. "Applying Ragin's Crisp and Fuzzy Set QCA to Large Datasets: Social Class and Educational Achievement in the National Child Development Study." *Sociological Research Online,* 10. Retrieved March 12, 2010 (http://www.socresonline.org.uk/10/2/cooper.html).

Cressey, Donald R. 1953. *Other People's Money.* New York: Free Press.

Dao, James, and Eric Lichtblau. 2004. "The Struggle for Iraq: The Images; Soldier's Family Set in Motion Chain of Events on Disclosure." *New York Times.* May 8.

Denzin, Norman K., 1989. *Interpretive Biography.* Beverly Hills, CA: Sage.

——. 2006. *Sociological Methods: A Sourcebook.* Piscataway, NJ: Transaction Publishers.

Denzin, Norman K., and Yvonna S. Lincoln. 2005. *Handbook of Qualitative Research.* 3rd ed. Thousand Oaks, CA: Sage.

Diesing, Paul. 1971. *Patterns of Discovery in the Social Sciences.* Chicago, IL: Aldine.

Doherty, Debbie S., and Michael W. Kramer. 2005. "Organizational Power and the Institutional Board." *Journal of Applied Communication Research,* 33:277–284.

Drass, Kriss, and Charles C. Ragin. 1989. *QCA: Qualitative Comparative Analysis.* Evanston, IL: Center for Urban Affairs and Policy Research, Northwestern University.

Driscoll, Mary. 1993. "Margin Work: Women and Nonconformity in the Gender Margins." Unpublished manuscript, Department of Sociology, Northwestern University.

Dumont, Louis. 1970. *Homo Hierarchicus: The Cast System and Its Implications.* Chicago, IL: University of Chicago Press.

Duneier, Mitchell. 1992. *Slim's Table: Race, Respectability, and Masculinity.* Chicago, IL: University of Chicago.

——. 2001. *Sidewalk.* 1st ed. New York: Farrar, Straus and Giroux.

Duneier, Mitchell, and Harvey Molotch. 1999. "Talking City Trouble: Interactional Vandalism, Social Inequality, and the 'Urban Interaction Problem.'" *American Journal of Sociology,* 104:1263–1295.

Durkheim, Émile. 1951. *Suicide: A Study in Sociology.* New York: Free Press.

Eckstein, Harry. 1992. *Regarding Politics: Essays on Political Theory, Stability, and Change*. Berkeley, CA: University of California Press.

Emerson, Robert M. 2001. *Contemporary Field Research: Perspectives and Formulations*. 2nd ed. Long Grove, IL: Waveland Press.

Emmison, Michael, and Philip Smith. 2000. *Researching the Visual: Images, Objects, Contexts and Interactions in Social and Cultural Inquiry*. Thousand Oaks, CA: Sage.

Esping-Andersen, Gosta. 1990. *The Three Worlds of Welfare Capitalism*. Princeton, NJ: Princeton University Press.

———. 1999. *Social Foundations of Postindustrial Economies*. New York: Oxford University Press.

Evans, Peter. 1995. *Embedded Autonomy: States and Industrial Transformation*. Princeton, NJ: Princeton University Press.

Falleti, Tulia G. 2005. "A Sequential Theory of Decentralization: Latin American Cases in Comparative Perspective." *American Political Science Review*, 99:327–346.

Feagin, Joe R., Anthony M. Orum, and Gideon Sjoberg. 1991. *A Case for the Case Study*. Chapel Hill, NC: University of North Carolina Press.

Fernandez-Mateo, Isabel. 2007. "Who Pays the Price of Brokerage? Transferring Constraint Through Price Setting in the Staffing Sector." *American Sociological Review*, 72:291–317.

Frank, Andre Gunder. 1967. *Capitalism and Underdevelopment in Latin America*. New York: Monthly Review Press.

———. 1969. *Latin America: Underdevelopment of Revolution*. New York: Monthly Review Press.

Glaser, Barney G., and Anselm L. Strauss. 1967. *The Discovery of Grounded Theory: Strategies for Qualitative Research*. London, UK: Weidenfeld & Nicholson.

Goffman, Erving. 1961. *Asylums: Essays on the Social Situation of Mental Patients and Other Inmates*. Garden City, NY: Anchor Books.

———. 1963. *Stigma: Notes on the Management of Spoiled Identity*. Englewood Cliffs, NJ: Prentice Hall.

Goliszek, Andrew. 2003. *In the Name of Sciences: A History of Secret Programs, Medical Research, and Human Experimentation*. New York: St. Martin's Press.

Grant, Don, Alfonso Morales, and Jeffrey J. Sallaz. 2009. "Pathways to Meaning: A New Approach to Studying Emotions at Work." *American Journal of Sociology*, 115:327–364.

Gregory, Paul R. 2009. *Terror by Quota: State Security From Lenin to Stalin*. New Haven, CT: Yale University Press.

Grimes v. Kennedy Krieger Institute, 366 Md. 29, 782 A.2d 807 (2001). Retrieved March 12, 2010 (http://www.law.uh.edu/healthlaw/law/StateMaterials/Maryland cases/grimesvkennedykrieger.pdf).

Hamburger, Philip. 2004. "The New Censorship: Institutional Review Boards." *2004 Supreme Court Review*, 271–354.

Haney, Craig, Curtis Banks, and Philip Zimbardo. 1973. "Interpersonal Dynamics in a Simulated Prison." *International Journal of Criminology & Penology*, 1:69–97.

Hanson, Norwood Russell. 1958. *Patterns of Discover: An Inquiry Into the Conceptual Foundations of Science*. Cambridge, UK: Cambridge University Press.

Harper, Douglas. 1987. *Working Knowledge: Skill and Community in a Small Shop*. Chicago, IL: University of Chicago Press.

———. 2001. *Changing Works: Visions of a Lost Agriculture*. Chicago, IL: University of Chicago Press.

———. 2002. "Talking About Pictures: A Case for Photo Elicitation." *Visual Studies*, 17:13–26.

Heath, Sue, and Elizabeth Cleaver. 2004. "Mapping the Spatial in Shared Household Life: A Missed Opportunity?" Pp. 65–78 in *Picturing the Social Landscape: Visual Methods in the Sociological Imagination*, edited by Caroline Knowles and Paul Sweetman. New York: Routledge.

Herron, Michael C., and Jasjeet S. Sekhon. 2003. "Overvoting and Representation: An Examination of Overvoted Presidential Ballots in Broward and Miami-Dade Counties." *Electoral Studies*, 22:21–47.

Hersh, Seymour M. 2004. *Chain of Command: The Road From 9/11 to Abu Ghraib*. New York: HarperCollins.

Hertz, Rosanna. 2006. *Single by Chance, Mothers by Choice: How Women Are Choosing Parenthood Without Marriage and Creating the New American Family*. New York: Oxford University Press.

Hochschild, Arlie. 1989. *The Second Shift*. New York: Viking.

Hodson, Randy. 2001. *Dignity at Work*. New York: Cambridge University Press.

Hoffman, Katherine E. 2008. *We Share Walls: Language, Land, and Gender in Berber Morocco*. Malden, MA: Blackwell.

Holliday, Ruth. 2004. "Filming 'The Closet': The Role of Video Diaries in Researching Sexualities." *American Behavioral Scientist*, 47:1597–1616.

Hondagneu-Sotelo, Pierrette. 2001. *Doméstica: Immigrant Workers Cleaning and Caring in the Shadows of Affluence*. Berkeley, CA: University of California Press.

Hull, Kathleen E. 2006. *Same-Sex Marriage: The Cultural Politics of Love and Law*. Cambridge, UK: Cambridge University Press.

Humphreys, Laud. [1970]1975. *Tearoom Trade: Impersonal Sex in Public Places*, 2nd ed. New York: Aldine Transaction.

Jenkins, J. Craig. 1994. "Resource Mobilization Theory and the Study of Social Movements." Pp. 527–553 in *American Society and Politics*, edited by T. Skocpol and J. Campbell. New York: McGraw-Hill.

Katz, Jack. 1984. *Poor People's Lawyers in Transition*. New Brunswick, NJ: Rutgers University Press.

Knowles, Caroline, and Paul Sweetman. 2004. *Picturing the Social Landscape: Visual Methods and the Sociological Imagination*. London, UK: Routledge.

Krauss, Lawrence M. 2003. "The Citizen-Scientist's Obligation to Stand Up for Standards." *New York Times*. April 22.

Krugman, Saul. 1986. "The Willowbrook Hepatitis Studies Revisited: Ethical Aspects." *Reviews of Infectious Diseases*, 8:157–162.

Kuhn, Thomas. 1962. *The Structure of Scientific Revolutions*. Chicago, IL: University of Chicago Press.

Lamont, Michèle. 2002. *The Dignity of Working Men: Morality and the Boundaries of Race, Class, and Immigration*. Cambridge, MA: Harvard University Press.

Lazarsfeld, Paul F., and Morris Rosenberg. 1955. *The Language of Social Research*. Glencoe, IL: Free Press.

Levitt, Peggy. 2001. *The Transnational Villagers*. Berkeley, CA: University of California Press.

Lieberson, Stanley. 1985. *Making It Count: The Improvement of Social Research and Theory*. Berkeley, CA: University of California Press.

Lindesmith, Alfred R. 1947. *Opiate Addiction.* Bloomington, IN: Principia Press.

Lipset, Seymour Martin. 1982. *Political Man: The Social Bases of Politics.* Baltimore, MD: Johns Hopkins University Press.

Lowell, B. Lindsay. 2001. *Developmental Effects of the International Migration of Highly Skilled Persons.* International Migration Papers 46. Geneva, Switzerland: International Labor Office.

Lucal, Betsy. 1999. "What It Means to Be Gendered Me: Life on the Boundaries of a Dichotomous Gender Society." *Gender and Society,* 13:781–797.

Luke, Douglas A. 2004. *Multilevel Modeling (Quantitative Applications in the Social Sciences).* Thousand Oaks, CA: Sage.

Luker, Kristin. 2008. *Salsa Dancing Into the Social Sciences: Research in the Age of Info-Glut.* Cambridge, MA: Harvard University Press.

Lyng, Stephen. 1990. "Edgework: A Social Psychological Analysis of Voluntary Risk Taking." *American Journal of Sociology,* 95:851–887.

———. 2005. "Sociology at the Edge: Social Theory and Voluntary Risk Taking." Pp. 17–50 in *Edgework: The Sociology of Risk-Taking,* edited by Stephen Lyng. New York: Routledge.

Mahoney, James, and Dietrich Rueschemeyer. 2003. *Comparative Historical Analysis in the Social Sciences.* New York: Cambridge University Press.

Marks, John. 1979. *The Search for the "Manchurian Candidate."* New York: Times Books.

Marwell, Nicole P. 2007. *Bargaining for Brooklyn: Community Organizations in the Entrepreneurial City.* Chicago, IL: University of Chicago Press.

Marx, Karl. 1976. *Capital: A Critique of Political Economy.* New York: Penguin and New Left Review. (Original work published 1867)

Massey, Douglas, and Nancy Denton. 1993. *American Apartheid: Segregation and the Making of the Underclass.* Cambridge, MA: Harvard University Press.

McDermott, Monica. 2006. *Working-Class White: The Makings and Unmaking of Race Relations.* Berkeley, CA: University of California Press.

McManus, Doyle. 2009. "Stop Handling Iran With Kid Gloves." *The Dallas Morning News.* November 2.

Meislin, Richard J. 1972. "Popkin Released From Jail; Steiner's Action 'Significant.'" *The Harvard Crimson.* November 29.

Merton, Robert K. 1973. *The Sociology of Science: Theoretical and Empirical Investigations.* Chicago: University of Chicago Press.

Michels, Robert. 1959. *Political Parties: A Sociological Study of the Oligarchical Tendencies of Modern Democracy.* New York: Dover.

Milgram, Stanley. 1974. *Obedience to Authority: An Experimental View.* New York: Harper & Row.

Mills, C. Wright. 1959. *The Sociological Imagination.* New York: Oxford University Press.

Morell, Carolyn M. 1994. *Unwomanly Conduct: The Challenges of Intentional Childlessness.* New York: Routledge.

National Commission for the Protection of Human Subjects of Biomedical and Behavioral Research. 1979. *The Belmont Report: Ethical Principles and Guidelines for the Protection of Human Subjects of Research* (DHEW Publication No. OS 78–0012). Washington, DC: Department of Health, Education, and Welfare.

Nuremberg Code. 1949. *Trials of War Criminals Before the Nuremberg Military Tribunals Under Control Council Law,* 2(10):181–182. Washington, DC: U.S. Government Printing Office.

Orne, Martin T. 1962. "On the Social Psychology of the Psychological Experiment: With Particular Reference to Demand Characteristics and Their Implications." *American Psychologist,* 17:776–783.

Page, Benjamin I., and Robert L. Shapiro. 1991. *The Rational Public.* Chicago, IL: University of Chicago Press.

Pattillo, Mary E. 2007. *Black on the Block: The Politics of Race and Class in the City.* Chicago, IL: University of Chicago Press.

Polya, George. 1968. *Patterns of Plausible Inference.* Princeton, NJ: Princeton University Press.

"Project MKULTRA, the CIA's Program of Research in Behavioral Modification." 1977. *Joint Hearing Before the Select Committee on Intelligence and the Subcommittee on Health and Scientific Research of the Committee on Human Resources, United States Senate,* 95th Cong., 1st Sess. Washington, DC: U.S. Government Printing Office. Retrieved March 12, 2010 (http://www.druglibrary.org/schaffer/history/e1950/mkultra/Hearing01.htm).

Ragin, Charles C. 1987. *The Comparative Method: Moving Beyond Qualitative and Quantitative Strategies.* Berkeley, CA: University of California Press.

——. 1991. "Introduction: The Problem of Balancing Discourse on Cases and Variables in Comparative Social Research." Pp. 1–8 in *Issues and Alternative in Comparative Social Research,* edited by Charles C. Ragin. Leiden, The Netherlands: E.J. Brill.

——. 2000. *Fuzzy-Set Social Science.* Chicago, IL: University of Chicago Press.

——. 2008. *Redesigning Social Inquiry.* Chicago, IL: University of Chicago Press.

Ragin, Charles C., and Howard S. Becker. 1992. *What Is a Case? Exploring the Foundations of Social Inquiry.* New York: Cambridge University Press.

Reicher, Stephen, and S. Alexander Haslam. 2006. "Rethinking the Psychology of Tyranny: The BBC Prison Study." *British Journal of Social Psychology,* 45:1–40.

Retherford, Robert D., Naohiro Ogawa, and Rikiya Matsukura. 2001. "Late Marriage and Less Marriage in Japan." *Population and Development Review,* 27:65–102.

Reverby, Susan M. 2000. *Tuskegee's Truths: Rethinking the Tuskegee Syphilis Study.* Chapel Hill, NC: University of North Carolina Press.

Robinson, W. S. 1951. "The Logical Structure of Analytic Induction." *American Sociological Review,* 16:812–818.

Ross, Lainie F. 2008. *Children in Medical Research.* New York: Oxford University Press.

Rossman, Gretchen B., and Sharon F. Rallis. 2003. *Learning in the Field: An Introduction to Qualitative Research.* 2nd ed. Thousand Oaks, CA: Sage.

Rueschemeyer, Dietrich, Evelyne Huber Stephens, and John D. Stephens. 1992. *Capitalist Development and Democracy.* Chicago, IL: University of Chicago Press.

Rupp, Leila J., and Verta Taylor. 2003. *Drag Queens at the 801 Cabaret.* Chicago, IL: University of Chicago Press.

Sargent, Joseph (Director). 1997. *Miss Evers' Boys.* [Motion picture]. Phoenix, AZ: Anasazi Productions and Home Box Office.

Scarce, Rik. 2005. *Contempt of Court: A Scholar's Battle for Free Speech From Behind Bars.* Lanham, MD: AltaMira Press.

Shaw, Clifford. 1930. *The Jackroller.* Chicago, IL: University of Chicago Press.

Shea, Christopher. 2000. "Don't Talk to the Humans: The Crackdown on Social Science Research." *Lingua Franca,* 10: 26–34.

Shulman, David. 2007. *From Hire to Liar: The Role of Deception in the Workplace.* New York: Cornell University Press.

Simmel, Georg. 1950. "Dyads and Triads." Pp. 122–169 in *The Sociology of Georg Simmel,* translated by Kurt Wolff. Glencoe, IL: Free Press.

Skocpol, Theda. 1979. *States and Social Revolutions: A Comparative Analysis of France, Russia, and China.* New York: Cambridge University Press.

——. 1984. "Emerging Agendas and Recurrent Strategies in Historical Sociology." Pp. 356–391 in *Vision and Method in Historical Sociology,* edited by Theda Skocpol. New York: Cambridge University Press.

Small, Mario. 2009. "How Many Cases Do I Need? On Science and the Logic of Case Selection in Field-Based Research." *Ethnography* 10:5–38.

Smith, Dorothy E. 1987. *The Everyday World as Problematic: A Feminist Sociology.* Boston, MA: Northeastern University.

Smith-Lahrman, Matthew. 1992. "Coffee House Cotillion: The Construction of Private Space in a Public Place." Unpublished manuscript, Department of Sociology, Northwestern University.

Snowdon, David A. 2001. *Aging With Grace: What the Nun Study Teaches Us About Leading Longer, Healthier, and More Meaningful Lives.* New York: Bantam.

Stark, Laura. 2007. "Victims in Our Own Minds? IRBs in Myth and Practice." *Law and Society Review,* 41:777–786.

Stephens, Evelyne Huber. 1989. "Capitalist Development and Democracy in South America." *Politics and Society,* 17:281–352.

Stephens, John D. 1979. *The Transition From Capitalism to Socialism.* Urbana, IL: University of Illinois Press.

Stinchcombe, Arthur L. 1968. *Constructing Social Theories.* New York: Harcourt Brace Jovanovich.

——. 1978. *Theoretical Methods in Social History.* New York: Academic Press.

Strauss, Anselm. 1987. *Qualitative Analysis for Social Scientists.* New York: Cambridge University Press.

"Symposium on Censorship and Institutional Review Boards." 2006. *Northwestern University Law Review,* 101(2).

ten Have, Paul. 2004. *Understanding Qualitative Research and Ethnomethodology.* Thousand Oaks, CA: Sage.

Tilly, Charles. 1984. *Big Structures, Large Processes, Huge Comparisons.* New York: Russell Sage Foundation.

Truzzi, Marcello. 1974. *Verstehen: Subjective Understanding in the Social Sciences.* Reading, MA: Addison-Wesley.

Tukey, John W. 1977. *Exploratory Data Analysis.* Reading, MA: Addison-Wesley.

Turner, Ralph. 1953. "The Quest for Universals in Sociological Research." *American Sociological Review,* 18:604–611.

Ui, Shiori. 1991. "'Unlikely Heroes': The Evolution of Female Leadership in a Cambodian Ethnic Enclave." Pp. 161–178 in *Ethnography Unbound: Power and Resistance in the Modern Metropolis,* by Michael Burawoy, Alice Burton, Ann Arnett Ferguson, Kathryn J. Fox, Joshua Gamson, Nadine Gartrell, et al. Berkeley, CA: University of California Press.

United Nations Educational Scientific and Cultural Organization (UNESCO). 2010. *Education for All Global Monitoring Report 2010: Reaching the Marginalized.* New York: Oxford University Press.

U.S. Department of Health and Human Services. 2009, January 15 (Rev ed.). *Public Welfare, Protection of Human Services Code of Federal Regulations* (Title 45 CFR 46.116(d)(1–4)).

Venkatesh, Sudhir. 2008. *Gang Leader for a Day: A Rogue Sociologist Takes to the Streets.* New York: Penguin.

Villarroel, Maria A., Charles F. Turner, Elizabeth Eggleston, Alia Al-Tayyib, Susan M. Rogers, Anthony M. Roman, et al. 2006. "Same-Gender Sex in the United States: Impact of T-ACASI on Prevalence Estimates." *Public Opinion Quarterly,* 70:166–196.

Wade, Robert. 1988. *Village Republics: Economic Conditions for Collective Action in South India.* New York: Cambridge University Press.

Walby, Sylvia. 2008. *Globalization and Inequalities: Complexity and Contested Modernities.* Thousand Oaks, CA: Sage.

Wallerstein, Immanuel. 1974. *The Modern World System: Capitalist Agriculture and the Origins of the European World Economy in the Sixteenth Century.* New York: Academic Press.

——. 1979. *The Capitalist World Economy.* New York: Cambridge University Press.

Walton, John. 1991. *Western Times and Water Wars: State, Culture, and Rebellion in California.* Berkeley, CA: University of California Press.

——. 1992. "Making the Theoretical Case." Pp. 121–138 in *What Is a Case? Exploring the Foundations of Social Inquiry,* edited by Charles C. Ragin and Howard S. Becker. New York: Cambridge University Press.

Walton, John, and Charles Ragin. 1990. "Global and National Sources of Political Protest: Third World Responses to the Debt Crisis." *American Sociological Review,* 55: 876–890.

Washington, Harriet A. 2008. *Medical Apartheid: The Dark History of Black Americans From Colonial Times to the Present.* New York: Harlem Moon.

Weber, Max. 1917/1949. "The Meaning of 'Ethical Neutrality' in Sociology and Economics," Pp. 1–47 in *The Methodology of the Social Sciences.* Glencoe, IL: Free Press.

——. [1922]1978. *Economy and Society* (edited by Guenther Roth and Claus Wittich). Berkeley, CA: University of California Press.

Wilkinson, Steven. 2004. *Votes and Violence: Electoral Competition and Ethnic Riots in India.* New York: Cambridge University Press.

Wilson, Robin. 2003. "Penn Anthropologist Fights Subpoenas for Field Notes Regarding Artificial Heart Surgery She Observed." *The Chronicle of Higher Education.* March 21.

Wilson, William J. 1980. *The Declining Significance of Race: Blacks and Changing American Institutions.* Chicago: University of Chicago Press.

——. 1987. *The Truly Disadvantaged: The Inner City, the Underclass, and Public Policy.* Chicago, IL: University of Chicago Press.

World Medical Association (WMA). 1964. *WMA Declaration of Helsinki.* Ferney-Voltaire, France: WMA. Retrieved March 12, 2010 (http://www.wma.net/en/30publications/10policies/b3/index.html).

Wright, Erik O. 1985. *Classes.* London: Verso.

Zablocki, Benjamin David. 1980. *The Joyful Community.* Chicago, IL: University of Chicago Press.

Ziller, R. C. 1990. *Photographing the Self: Observing Self, Social Environmental Orientations.* San Francisco: Sage.

Zimbardo, Philip. 2007. *The Lucifer Effect.* New York: Random House.

Glossary/Index

Abu Ghraib, 79–80, 107
Accomplished noninteraction, 64, 67
Accountability to research subjects,
    98–100, 104
Accumulated knowledge, 169, 194–95
    of general patterns, 40
    of history (past successes/failures), 40
Achievement orientation, 167
Activist research. *See* Advocacy research
Addams, Jane
    public sociology, 34
Advocacy research, 47–48
African Americans
    use as subjects in unethical research,
        82, 107
*After Brown: The Rise and Retreat of School
    Desegregation* (Clotfelter), 6
Allison, Paul D., 165
Al-Tayyib, Alia, 176
Amenta, Edwin, 171
American Anthropological Association
    Code of ethics, 103
    First Amendment rights, 103
*American Apartheid: Segregation and the
    Making of the Underclass* (Massey and
    Denton), 13
American Sociological Association Code of
    Ethics, 100
Analysis is the mental process of breaking a
    phenomenon into its constituent parts
    and viewing these parts in relationship to
    some whole. For example, an analysis of
    how people get ahead might focus on the
    relationship between years of education
    and subsequent income across a large
    sample of individuals. 16, 23, 57
Analytic frames are systematic, detailed
    sketches of ideas (or social theories) that
    a researcher develops in order to aid the
    examination of a specific phenomenon.
    In effect, an analytic frame articulates an
    idea in a way that makes it useful in

research. The process of analytic framing
    is primarily but not entirely deductive.
    as research guide, 3, 58–59
    concepts as key components of, 112
    data matrix defined by, 173–174
    described, 60–61, 63–68
    elaborated by qualitative research of, 121–122
    fixed, 77
    flexible, 77
    fluid, 77–78
    in comparative research, 144–145
    in qualitative research, 121–122
    in quantitative research, 172–173
    interaction with images, 74
    process of using, 63–65
    used by aspect, 65, 66–68, 74
    used by case, 65, 66, 74
    value of multiple, 77, 78
Analytic induction is a technique used
    primarily by qualitative researchers to
    assess commonalities across a number of
    cases and thereby clarify empirical
    categories and the concepts that are
    exemplified by the cases included in a
    category. It is a "double fitting" of ideas
    and evidence that focuses on similarities
    across a limited number of cases studied
    in depth.
    example of, 125–130
    used in comparative research, 145
    used in qualitative research, 124–125
Analytic methods
    deduction, 76
    induction, 76
    retroduction, 76
Appelbaum, Lauren, 90
Archival research is the term given to research
    that draws its evidence from collections
    of historical documents that were not
    originally gathered for specific research
    purposes. 101
Ascription orientation, 167

Case is a fundamental element of social research that is used most often to describe the members of a set of comparable phenomena, sometimes referred to as observations. Cases may be common units such as individuals and firms, but may also be singular events like the Civil War. What constitutes a case depends on the nature of the study and is part of the analytic framing of the study.
  analytic frame of, 121–122
  categorized by outcome, 139–140
  comparative research and selection of, 144
  configurations of, 145
  covariation between features across a set of, 13
  hypotheses formulated about, 15
  identifying clusters of differences among, 190–91
  pinpointing diversity among, 190
  qualitative research and selection of, 116–18
  representativeness of, 116
  "rich," 78, 134
  selection of new, 131
  study of a single, 14, 117, 133–134
  trade-off between number of features and number of, 109
Category is the term used by social researchers to refer to a set of empirical phenomena (or cases) that have been linked conceptually in some way. The members of a category typically share features that are relevant to an investigation.
  clarification of empirical, 113, 119–121
  evidence that can alter, 124–130
  of cases by outcome, 139–140
  used in scientific method, 15
  using historical context of, 141–142
Causal conditions, 150
Causal configurations
  producing, 149
  summarized by truth tables, 154–160
  See also Configurations
Causal explanations
  comparative research concerns with, 142–143
  described, 73
  linked to outcomes, 149–151
  quantitative research to identify, 166
  See also Configurations
Causal patterns, 159
Causal relationships, 23–24, 23–24
Causation, 166
Cause is used by social researchers to identify a particular kind of relationship, usually

between aspects of cases, where one aspect is seen as the source of change in another aspect. Cause is most often inferred from a connection that is made between aspects. 14
Central Intelligence Agency (CIA), 83
  destruction of research-related records, 83, 107
  MKULTRA Project, 83
Children
  diminished autonomy of, 89
  researcher's influence on, 101
  use as subjects in unethical research, 82, 90, 107
Chirot, Daniel, 77, 190
Class conflict, 118–119
Cleaver, Elizabeth, 47
Clotfelter, Charles, 6
Clusters of differences, 190–191
Commonalities
  qualitative methods to study, 51–53, 115–116
  social life representations based on, 192, 191–192
Comparative analysis, 160
  features of, 148
  goal of, 158
Comparative method
  example of, 148
  overview of, 146
  presence-absence dichotomies, 150–51
Comparative research is a basic strategy of social research that most often focuses on patterns of similarities and differences across a limited range of cases. Typically, the cases are empirically bounded in some way (for example, "Islamic fundamentalist movements since World War II").
  advancing theory through, 142–143
  compared to other strategies, 137–138, 169–171
  described, 36, 51
  flexible frames used in, 77
  goal of advancing theory, 48–50, 142–143
  goal of exploring diversity, 44–46, 139–140
  goal of interpreting culturally or historically significant phenomena, 42–44, 140–142
  goals of, 53–55, 138–143
  overview of methods of, 146–49
  selecting cases for, 144
  used to study diversity, 51–53, 135–137, 142–143
  using analytic frames for, 145
Comparative techniques
  causal patterns, 159
Comparison group, 130

About the Authors

Charles C. Ragin spent most of his youth in Texas and the southeastern United States. He attended the University of Texas at Austin as an undergraduate and received his BA degree in 1972 at the age of 19. That same year he began graduate work in sociology at the University of North Carolina at Chapel Hill and received his PhD in 1975. From 1975 until 2001, he lived in the Midwest, teaching first at Indiana University and then at Northwestern University. In 2001, he joined the faculty of the University of Arizona, Tucson, where he is currently a Professor of Sociology and Political Science. He has also taught at the University of Oslo. He is best known for his work on comparative methodology and for his research articles addressing broad issues in politics and society, with topics ranging from the causes of ethnic political mobilization to the shaping of the welfare state in advanced capitalist countries. He has written several books including *Redesigning Social Inquiry: Fuzzy Sets and Beyond* (2008) and *Fuzzy-Set Social Science* (2000). His book *The Comparative Method: Moving Beyond Qualitative and Quantitative Strategies* (1987) won the 1989 Stein Rokkan Prize of the International Social Science Council of UNESCO. He is married to Mary Driscoll, and they have two sons, Andrew and Daniel.

Lisa M. Amoroso spent her childhood in Pittsburgh and the suburbs of Chicago. She attended Northwestern University for her BA in economics and mathematical methods in the social sciences. After a number of years working in management consulting, she returned to Northwestern and the Kellogg School of Management to complete her PhD in a joint program in sociology and organization behavior in 2003. Since leading her first freshman seminar at Northwestern in 1997, she has been teaching in the Midwest—at Northwestern, Beloit College, Roosevelt University, and currently Dominican University in River Forest, Illinois. Research Methods and Quantitative Analysis are among her favorite courses to teach. She received Roosevelt's Excellence in Teaching Award in 2007. In 2010, she joined the faculty at Dominican's Brennan School of Business where she is an Associate Professor of Management. Her research focuses on managerial control, status, and diversity in organizations. She has published several journal articles including one on diversity education in the *Journal of Management Education*. She is married to Phil Tracy, and they have two children, Nate and Carmen.